The Sales Professional's Idea-a-Day Guide

250 Ways to Increase Your Top *and* Bottom Lines — Every Selling Day of the Year

Tony Alessandra, Ph.D.

Gregg Baron

Jim Cathcart

 DARTNELL

4660 N RAVENSWOOD AVE, CHICAGO, IL 60640-4595 PHONE: (800) 621-5463

DEDICATION

Collectively, we would like to dedicate this book to our late friend and colleague, Dr. Gary Couture. Individually, we dedicate this book:

To my maternal grandmother, Grace Imbriani.

— Tony

Paul Baron, a great dad and sales professional.

— Gregg

To C.E. Cathcart, my father and role model.

— Jim

Dartnell is a publisher serving the world of business with book manuals, newsletters and bulletins, and training materials for executives, managers, supervisors, salespeople, financial officials, personnel executives, and office employees. Dartnell also produces management and sales training videos and audiocassettes, publishes many useful business forms, and many of its materials and films are available in languages other than English. Dartnell, established in 1917, serves the world's business community. For details, catalogs, and product information, write:

THE DARTNELL CORPORATION

4660 N Ravenswood Ave
Chicago, IL 60640-4595, U.S.A.
or phone (800) 621-5463 in U.S. and Canada

ABOUT THE AUTHORS

DR. TONY ALESSANDRA

Tony Alessandra, Ph.D., is recognized by *Meeting & Conventions* magazine as "one of America's most electrifying speakers."

As a former graduate professor of marketing, Dr. Alessandra brings to the speaker's platform years of practical sales experience combined with a solid educational background. He grew up in New York City and worked his way through college learning sales the hard way — selling door-to-door for seven years. Dr. Alessandra earned his B.B.A., M.B.A. and Ph.D., all in Marketing, from the University of Notre Dame, University of Connecticut, and Georgia State University.

Since 1976, Tony Alessandra has delivered nearly 2,000 presentations, authored 12 books including *The Platinum Rule, Communicating at Work,* and *Collaborative Selling,* and has been featured in over 50 audio/video programs and films. He currently owns a sales force automation software company.

For more information, you can contact Tony Alessandra at (800) 222-4383; Fax: (619) 459-0435; Online: Dr Tony A@aol.com; Website: http://www.alessandra.com; http://www.platinumrule.com

GREGG BARON, CMC

Gregg Baron is a certified management consultant who has worked with companies around the world as a consultant, trainer, and speaker on customer service, team development, and collaborative selling.

As president of Success Sciences Inc., Gregg has forged an innovative organization that develops behavior change learning processes and utilizes the latest large-group technologies to assist clients in *Building Better Business Relationships*™ and creating lasting organizational change.

Success Sciences' clients include IBM Europe, Lucent Technologies, Household Credit Services, Continental Airlines, Novell, Royal Caribbean Cruise Lines, Intuit, and Motorola.

Gregg holds degrees in accounting and management from the University of South Florida, is a certified associate trainer in neurolinguistic programming, and a martial arts devotee.

For more information you can contact Gregg Baron at (813) 989-9900; (800) 767-5700; Fax: (813) 985-2617; Online: gmbaron@aol.com; Website: http://users.aol.com/ssciences/web/ssi.htm

JIM CATHCART

Jim Cathcart has sold everything from doughnuts to automobiles, securities, insurance, consulting services and banking. As the author of *Relationship Selling* and co-author of *Be Your Own Sales Manager,* he is known and published worldwide.

A leader among professional speakers, Jim is a powerful presenter with over 2,000 speeches to his credit. He is past president of the National Speakers Association and recipient of their highest awards.

For further information, please contact Jim Cathcart, CSP, CPAE at (800) 222-4883. Online: JECathcart@aol.com; Website: http://www.cathcart.com

TABLE OF CONTENTS

THE SALES PROFESSIONAL'S IDEA-A-DAY GUIDE

Section Five: Targeting **49**

Section Six: Preconditioning Your Prospects **65**

Section Seven: Contacting Prospects..93

Section Fourteen: Handling Customer Resistance.......................223

Section Fifteen: Confirming the Sale 241

Section Sixteen: Assuring Customer Satisfaction 257

HOW DO YOU DEFINE SERVICE?

INCREASING YOUR CUSTOMER AWARENESS

FOLLOWING UP AND STAYING IN TOUCH AFTER THE SALE

HANDLING CUSTOMER PROBLEMS

Section Seventeen: Be Your Own Sales Manager..299

SELLING BY THE NUMBERS

CONTROL YOUR TIME/BOOST YOUR PRODUCTIVITY

BOOST YOUR RESULTS

ELECTRONIC SALES SUPPORT

Section Eighteen: What Motivates You 329

GETTING MOTIVATED

VISUALIZING YOUR GOALS

GETTING MOTIVATED

SETTING YOUR STANDARDS

GETTING YOUR FINANCES IN SHAPE

INTRODUCTION

JIM CATHCART

In the early 1970s, I was a government clerk in a dead end job. With no particular vision for my future, I was going nowhere fast — until a few words spoken by motivational speaker Earl Nightingale changed my life.

"If you will spend one hour a day in study in your field of interest," he said during a radio broadcast, "you will be a national expert in that field within five years or less."

Five years or less! The prospect of becoming any kind of expert seemed unlikely to me. To become one in five years or less was incomprehensible. But his words opened my mind to possibilities I had never considered before.

After mulling over his words for some time, I decided I wanted to become an expert in the field of human development, especially as it relates to business success. I began to study books and tapes, and sought out examples of successful people. I attended seminars and had many discussions with people who seemed to know what they were doing. Over time, I developed my own ideas and indeed, five years later, I was a professional speaker and author who traveled the world sharing my expertise with others. After twenty years in this industry, my success has far exceeded my early expectations.

Earl Nightingale is right. If you spend an hour a day expanding your knowledge base and expertise in a particular field, your knowledge and skill will compound itself so much that you will truly rise to the absolute top of your profession.

The Sales Professional's Idea-a-Day Guide is a tool for accomplishing this in a very structured, yet flexible, fashion. In less than an hour a day, you can take the idea presented on any page in this book and use it to expand your own expertise or stimulate your own thinking in ways that will make you more effective.

Consider how far you've come already and project yourself five years ahead. Think of what would happen, and how things would evolve for you, if starting today you dedicated just 30 minutes a day to expanding your knowledge in your chosen field. Then turn to section one … and get going!

Tips on How Best to Use This Book

This is your book — not just because you purchased it, but because of the way it was made. *The Sales Professional's Idea-a-Day Guide* was conceived, designed, and developed with your needs — the working salesperson — in mind. It offers specific suggestions on how to sell more effectively, study your customers, present your product or service, and gain a commitment to buy. It also offers a great deal of material to help you manage yourself as a salesperson, including strategies for setting goals, finding prospects, and motivating yourself.

And it could be the most important book you'll ever use! Not just read—use. Because *The Sales Professional's Idea-a-Day Guide* is organized to meet your day-to-day success needs with 250 practical, ready-to-use sales ideas. It will help you build and increase your short- and long-term success the way other professionals do it: day after day, one day at a time, all year long.

This book has **three key components** you can use to unlock the door to success.

First is a self-diagnostic assessment located in Section 20. When completed, share the results with your supervisor, manager, a colleague, or a customer. Your answers will provide you with a thorough self-assessment and the beginning of an action plan for your future growth. You'll also get important feedback—to "see yourself as others see you"—that you will be able to incorporate into your self-assessment. The result will be a comprehensive, objective picture of your current professional development.

The second and third components—Ideas and Worksheets—work together as the main components of the book. Ideas are key facts, important insights, and sure-fire tips that will help you improve your productivity and effectiveness. The Worksheets help you organize your thoughts, test your ideas, and put them into action today, tomorrow, and all year long. Altogether, you get 250 fresh, new, money-making ideas—one for each working day of the year.

Your Choice

What makes *The Sales Professional's Idea-a-Day Guide* so important, so useful to your sales career is that you can **use it any way you want**. The Ideas and Worksheets are self-contained on a single page (the few exceptions, which give you more space for writing your own notes, are two pages). So you can:

1. **Scan it.** Flip through the book, read a single page, get an idea, close the book, and go out and take one more step down the road to success; or
2. **Select it.** Look over the detailed table of contents, pick out a particular section devoted to a particular set of skills, and read that entire section and get a whole grouping of ideas that meet your immediate needs in a particular skill; or
3. **Study it.** Read the entire book straight through, from page one to the end, and benefit that way.
4. **Skim it.** Focus on key areas only as needed and skip around from section to section based on today's needs.

The point is, you can use this book any way you want and still get its benefits. It is the most flexible and most usable sales book you will ever own.

10 Minutes a Day is All it Takes

There is more than one way you can use this book. Whether you've been in sales for 20 days or 20 years, you'll have an easy-to-use daily reference for getting a new idea or double-checking ones you haven't used for a while. Since the main components—the Self-Assessment, the Ideas, and the Worksheets—cover key points in selling success, you'll turn to *Idea-a-Day* for new insights and a mini refresher course in sales success.

And, you'll be able to use it every day of the year because it's organized on a page-by-page basis that takes only 10 minutes a day to use.

Get Started Now

There's one easy thing about success: The only time and place to start is here and now. So, right now, while the book is in your hands, turn to the table of contents and select a topic — all areas are represented from territory and time management to prospecting, responding to customer concerns, and ways to confirm the sale. Spend the minutes we mentioned above. We're sure you'll be impressed. More important, we're sure you'll be on your way to greater success in your sales career.

Tony Alessandra

Gregg Baron

Jim Cathcart

ACKNOWLEDGMENTS

The contributors to this collection of ideas range far and wide. First, we'd like to thank our thousands of clients and audiences for teaching us what they need and what they can use. We also thank the publishers of our many other works for bringing these concepts to the marketplace.

Specifically, we acknowledge our late friend and colleague Dr. Gary Couture, who refined many of these ideas in the Idea-a-Day format. Anne Basye did a wonderful job of converting our notes into useable tools and our thoughts into practical words.

We also thank Vera Derr of Dartnell for shepherding this project into reality.

SECTION ONE

THE RELATIONSHIP IS ALL THERE IS

WHAT'S IN IT FOR YOU?

- Build strong, lasting relationships with customers and prospects
- Learn how to design and manage relationships
- Discover the importance of the fifth "P" of marketing: people
- Examine your selling philosophy
- Increase your career "equity"

In the final analysis — after the sale is made, after the products or services are delivered — the only thing that truly matters is the relationship between the seller and the buyer.

What makes someone buy from a particular company or salesperson? In many cases, the reason is neither the product nor the price, but rather the relationship with the person with whom they're dealing. Products change, services change, prices change, economies and market places change — but if the relationship is strong, the account endures.

When you don't have an edge in product technology or price, then you need an edge in the way you connect with people. (In fact, you need that edge even if you do have a competitive product or price advantage.) This section suggests ways to strengthen your connection with prospects, customers, and colleagues — and to make selling easier as time goes on.

I D E A

- **Understand the benefit of improving skills**

MASTER THE SKILLS THAT MAKE SELLING EASIER

1.1 The Snowball Effect

Many years ago a veteran sales trainer told me, "The first five years you're in selling you will be underpaid for how hard you work. After that, if you've done it right, you'll be overpaid for how hard you work."

Notice that he didn't say overpaid or underpaid for *your value* as a salesperson. Simply overpaid or underpaid for *how hard* you work. During the early stage of a sales career, the salesperson is responsible for *building selling skills*. The tasks at hand are to

- become a greater expert in a chosen field
- establish a reputation
- develop maturity and a sense of self-awareness in order to roll with the punches and overcome problems easily
- study and understand the market place to determine where potential sales exist.

The process of becoming a sales professional is much like the process of becoming an adult. As a child, your primary job is to learn the fundamentals and to develop habits that will make you more successful later in life. If you do that effectively, then your adulthood will be under your control. If you don't, then your adult years will find you still under the control of others.

The quickest route to freedom is by acquiring the knowledge, habits, and skills that let you master your field and make your own choices. It's like a snowball rolling down a hill. As it rolls down the hill and gathers more snow, it increases in size until it's virtually unstoppable.

How hard are you working at becoming a sales professional? What skills and habits are you acquiring? On the continuum from rookie to sales master, where do you fall?

| Rookie | Developing | Expanding | Veteran | "Pro" | Sales Master |

←————————————————————————————————————→

I D E A

WHAT'S IN IT FOR YOU?

- **Discover the importance of connecting with your prospect**
- **Reconsider traditional marketing thinking**

MASTER THE SKILLS THAT MAKE SELLING EASIER

1.2 The Four P's of Marketing — Plus One

Almost every marketing class teaches the "four P's of marketing": product, price, place, and promotion. According to this philosophy, success comes from having the right product at the right price, in the right place, with the right promotion. Improving marketing and sales is a matter of tinkering with the four P's until the mix is right.

We propose a fifth P in the marketing mix: *people*. Product, price, place, or promotion may be effective, but the decision to buy often depends more on the salesperson than anything else.

But before we tell you why, let's take a moment to review the traditional four P's.

Product: If you have the right product for the market, you gain an edge over those who have a product that's only nearly the right product.

Price: If your price is the best in the market for the product or service you provide, you have a strong marketing edge.

Place: The more convenient you can make it for the buyer to buy, the more likely you are to get a sale.

Promotion: The best product in the world at a good price and in a convenient place will generate zero sales if it's not backed by adequate promotion. It's important to choose the type of promotion that will reach the people most likely to buy at the time when they are more likely to buy.

Even when product, price, place, and promotion are perfect, the decision to purchase is made by *people*. If you've ever found something you wanted at a decent price and then refused to buy it because you didn't like the way the person was selling it, then you've proved the importance of the people factor.

We believe that the people factor has more impact on a sale than the other four P's combined. The people factor determines whether you get a sale, what kind of sale you get, and how long you keep the account. If the people factor is strong enough, then the product, price, place, and promotion can change, and still you'll get the business.

Which of these five P's is your strongest area right now? How can you develop the others more effectively?

I D E A

WHAT'S IN IT FOR YOU?

- **Examine your philosophy of selling**
- **See how your philosophy affects everything you do**

MASTER THE SKILLS THAT MAKE SELLING EASIER

1.3 Your Sales Philosophy

Your success in sales is determined by your philosophy — your basic beliefs about the purpose, process, and goal of selling.

When we quiz our seminar audience about these three issues, they usually respond that the purpose of selling is to make a sale, the process of selling is to convince the customer to buy, and the goal of selling is to make a profit.

Don't you believe it! These extremely short-sighted beliefs may generate a few sales, but they will *not* build a lasting career.

In the final analysis, the *purpose* of selling is to make life better for the people who buy. Your persuasiveness may convince someone to buy once, but if your product or service doesn't enhance his or her life, that person will be unhappy with the purchase — and reluctant to purchase from you again.

The *process* of selling is to get someone to buy something he or she needs and then to make the person so happy that he or she converts from a customer (someone who has bought something from you) to a client (someone who considers you their primary provider). For example, if I buy a car from you, I am a customer; if I consider you my car salesperson and I buy all of my cars from you, then I have become your client.

The *goal* of selling is not just to generate an immediate profit from a transaction, but rather to establish a profitable business friendship that will produce revenue for a long time to come.

Compare the sales philosophy of other people you know with this sales philosophy, and then look at how they perform and how they feel about their career. You'll find a significant difference between those who see selling merely as a transaction-generating process and those who see selling as the beginning of an ongoing, mutually profitable relationship.

Take a moment to examine your assumptions about selling. What do you believe are the purpose, process, and goal of selling? How do you practice those beliefs in your approach?

I D E A

• Discover how your frame of mind influences your success

MASTER THE SKILLS THAT MAKE SELLING EASIER

1.4 The Sales Frame of Mind

In 1994, Jim Cathcart had the opportunity to tour the White House with a small group of professional speakers. At the end of the tour, the group had the good fortune of meeting the President, who spent about 10 minutes chatting with them. Someone mentioned that the president was a professional speaker, too. President Clinton's reply was, "Half my job is keeping people in the right frame of mind."

When you stop and think about it, keeping people in the right frame of mind is half of your job, too. If someone looks at you, your product, or your company unfavorably, you're unlikely to get the business no matter how great your price or product. But if you can keep a person looking at your ideas and the relationship with you and your company in a positive light, then everything else will be given full consideration and you will have an opportunity to make the sale.

Your frame of mind has a great deal to do with your customer's frame of mind. If you think your job is simply to make a sale, chances are your customer will know. But if you have a service-oriented frame of mind — if you see yourself as responsible for finding ways to make life better for your customer through your product or service — you will produce more sales, larger sales, and more pleasing sales experiences.

Do you ever find yourself getting tense and uneasy in a desperate effort to make a sale? When you do, shift your frame of mind from making a sale to asking yourself how, through your product or service, you can make life better for this client today.

W O R K S H E E T

WHAT'S IN IT FOR YOU?

• **Understand your impact on others**

MASTER THE SKILLS THAT MAKE SELLING EASIER

1.5 How Do You Make Life Better for People?

The purpose of business is to make life better for people. Any business that doesn't do this will soon be out of business. All it takes is one good competitor, for its accounts to be in jeopardy.

Consider the impact of what you do on those you know. In what ways does buying from you or doing business with you enhance someone else's life? Take time to write your answers below.

_____

_____

_____

_____

_____

_____

One day in the Atlanta Airport, Jim Cathcart encountered a bus boy cleaning tables in the food court. He was trudging through his work, avoiding eye contact, and looking bored. When Jim walked over and tapped him on the shoulder, he looked up as if expecting a problem or a complaint.

"Excuse me," Jim said, "but I just wanted you to know that cleaning these tables sure makes this a lot nicer place to be for those of us who eat here. Thank you for what you're doing." As Jim walked away, he looked back. Something special had happened to that bus boy. He was standing a little taller, had a more pleasant look on his face, and had begun to look directly at others.

Jim's remarks helped the bus boy see how his work made a difference — how it enhanced the experience of diners. He started taking more pride in his work, and the impact on his performance was noticeable immediately.

All of us need to remember how our actions impact others. Take a second look at your answer above. Rewrite it, if needed, to make it even more meaningful. Then read it everyday to remind yourself of how you make the world a better place.

I D E A

• **Discover the secrets of creating a successful sales relationship**

STRENGTHEN YOUR RELATIONSHIPS

1.6 Relationship Design and Management

Every sales relationship needs to be consciously designed and managed. When we take conscious responsibility for our relationships, we can create the types of relationships that we want, and we can manage our existing relationships so that they grow healthy and productive. The clearer you understand your role in the relationship, the better it will be.

Three categories need to be defined to design a successful, new sales relationship. First, define your role. Next, identify your areas of responsibility. Finally, clarify the expectations of both parties in the relationship. The more clearly you define these three categories, the better you will manage your relationships and design their future growth.

1. **Define your role.** Although many salespeople define their role as "making sales," the professional salesperson sees his or her role as building a profitable clientele. This entails much more than simply making sales. It involves establishing ongoing relationships that are continuously profitable to the company and generating continuous benefits to the customer.

2. **Define your areas of responsibility.** Practically every aspect of your company's operation could fall within the description, "build a profitable clientele." To do this, you'll need to specifically define your areas of responsibility, which might include identifying and contacting prospects, identifying needs, making sales, assuring delivery or installation, following through to guarantee that the customer is satisfied, and so forth.

3. **Clarify your expectations.** On a blank sheet of paper, write down expectations likely to arise in the relationship. On one side, list what you expect from your company. On the other side, list what your company can reasonably expect from you. Look for discrepancies in the two sets of expectations and discuss them with your sales manager. Repeat this exercise to clarify expectations likely to arise in a relationship between you and a customer.

W O R K S H E E T

WHAT'S IN IT FOR YOU?

- **Find out who is key to your career success**
- **Improve existing relationships**
- **Expand your capabilities**

STRENGTHEN YOUR RELATIONSHIPS

1.7 Defining Your Inner Circle

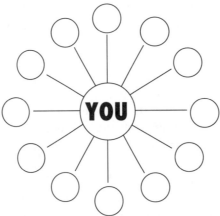

Each of us defines and expresses ourselves through our relationships. By paying attention to your relationships — and the types of people you deal with — you can upgrade your self-perception, and, in many cases, your performance. Improving existing relationships, adding new ones, or eliminating those that are unhealthy or unproductive can have a dramatic impact on your career.

At the heart of your sales career is a core or "inner circle" of people through whom you live your life as a sales professional. In the illustration above, write the names of your inner circle. Include people you see regularly who play a vital role in your sales career in a business or a social context.

The line between you and the name in each circle represents your relationship with that person. Spend a few minutes thinking about your relationship with each member of your inner circle. How can you enhance it? As each relationship is improved, the overall productivity of your sales career improves as well. The more people you know and the better your relationships, the better your productivity and the higher your potential will be.

W O R K S H E E T

WHAT'S IN IT FOR YOU?

• **Measure the quality of each of your relationships**
• **Pinpoint areas for improvement**

STRENGTHEN YOUR RELATIONSHIPS

1.8 The Three C's for Productive Relationships

A healthy and productive relationship requires three elements:

1. a mutual commitment to making the relationship work,
2. open frequent communication between the participants, and
3. clear expectations from each person.

For each relationship in your inner circle, ask yourself whether these three essential elements are in place. Are both parties mutually committed to make it work? Is there open, frequent communication where we clearly tell each other the truth? Are we clearly aware of what we expect from each other?

If a relationship has all three essentials, write "1, 2, 3" on the line that represents the relationship. If a relationship has strong commitment but lacks open communication, write in 1, but leave the 2 off. If a relationship has clear expectations, add a 3 to the line; if not, leave it off.

Once you've evaluated each relationship in your inner circle, these numbers will tell you where your strengths are and where you need to do your homework. Where numbers are present, you have strength. Where numbers are missing, you've got homework.

If the numbers indicate a relationship lacks mutual commitment, check your own commitment first. Are you committed to making this relationship productive and positive? If so, and you've done all you can, the balance of that commitment must come from the other person.

The quickest way to develop that commitment is to work on communication. The more honest and open your communication and the more frequently you are in touch with that person, the more likely they are to feel committed to the relationship.

Clear expectations also depend on communication. First, look at your own expectations. Do you expect the other person to give you access to useful information? Do you expect him or her to call you when a problem arises, or solve it alone? Write down your expectations, and then write what you think the other person expects from you. Then discuss your list with the other party and ask how he or she would change it. Encourage the person to write down any additions or deletions. The dialogue that will grow out of this exercise will be powerful. It can add tremendous potential to your sales career.

Reprinted with permission from *The Acorn Letter* by Jim Cathcart, © 1995.

W O R K S H E E T

WHAT'S IN IT FOR YOU?

- Discover the roles played by people in your life
- Pinpoint where you need to cultivate new relationships

STRENGTHEN YOUR RELATIONSHIPS

1.9 People To _____ With

We need different people to play different roles in our lives. We need people to celebrate our successes and accomplishments. We need people to commiserate with when we experience pain, confusion, or frustration. We need someone who can hear and understand our problems without trying to "fix us" or without encouraging us to dwell on those problems for too long. We need people to think with, and people to inspire us—people who lift our spirits and appeal to the nobler sides of our personalities. And, we need people to work with—people who make us roll up our sleeves, put in a full day's work, and get the job done no matter what.

Take a look now at the people in your inner circle and see how they fill these roles. You may find that some people are very good for certain functions but not others. Take note wherever you find a significant gap. If there's no one on your list to think with, celebrate with, be playful with, or help or be helped by, go shopping. Look for new relationships, or cultivate new qualities in the existing relationships so that your relationships become the major asset they can be to your life and to your career.

I D E A

STRENGTHEN YOUR RELATIONSHIPS

1.10 How Do You Want to Be Known?

If other people were talking about you in a favorable way, what would you want them to say? How would you like them to describe you?

Imagine for a moment that you could mold the way others think and talk about you. Using the following sentences as a prompt, describe yourself as you wish others would describe you.

He or she is a person who _____ . The way I feel toward him or her is _____ .

Here's an example: *She is a person who truly cares about her customer, who takes pride in her work, who is trustworthy and enjoyable. A person I admire and would like to learn from. I feel that she is someone I can trust to do a thorough job. Someone I look forward to meeting again. And someone who will continue to have a highly successful sales career.*

You actually can, and do, determine how others talk about you. You are in charge of how you are known by other people. No, you don't control it a 100 percent, but you clearly influence it every day with your choice of how you look, how you perform, how you follow through, how you relate to people, and how you manage yourself.

W O R K S H E E T

WHAT'S IN IT FOR YOU?

- **Pinpoint customers you can transform into "apostles" who will build your business**

STRENGTHEN YOUR RELATIONSHIPS

1.11 The Stairs of Satisfaction

Customers move through four predictable stages of satisfaction:

STAIRS OF CUSTOMER SATISFACTION

Apostle*

Customer

Sale

Prospect

* Apostles are "loyal fans" who preach the gospel according to your company.

An apostle is a loyal fan who "preaches the gospel (the good news)" about your company. Our task as salespeople is to move clients from prospect to apostle in the most efficient way possible. This four-step process will let you double the number of your customer apostles.

1. Identify your current apostles. How many excellent customers do you have today who spread the word about you?

_____

_____

_____

_____

_____

2. Next to each name, explain what you do that causes them to be such wonderful customers.

_____

_____

_____

_____

3. List other customers whom you would like to convert into apostles.

_____

_____

_____

_____

_____

4. Determine how you can apply the strategies and actions that created your current apostles to the customers you wish to convert into apostles. Then, next to each name, write in the strategy or action you will use.

_____

_____

_____

_____

_____

I D E A

• **Learn how to manage four issues that can make or break a sales relationship**

STRENGTHEN YOUR RELATIONSHIPS

1.12 Tension, Trust, Risk, Value: Four Critical Issues to Manage

To succeed, a sales professional must be a *relationship* professional—someone who can deftly manage a customer's expectations and perceptions. That's because customers make all of their incremental decisions on their perceptions in four areas:

- the quality of our products,
- the probability that our solutions will serve them best,
- our personal credibility, and
- the reputation of the company we represent.

To manage these expectations and perceptions, we need to focus on four issues that are critical to a business relationship: tension, trust, risk, and value. If mismanaged, they will likely cost you the relationship.

As trust in a relationship goes down, tension between the two parties tends to go up. As tension goes up, trust tends to decline. Can you think of *any* successful relationship in your life that was characterized by low trust and high tension? Of course not! This makes it highly unlikely that your customers and prospects who perceive low trust and high tension in working with you will want to do business with you.

Early in his career as a sales professional, a customer said to Gregg Baron, "Prospects are very responsive to their perceptions of financial and psychological risk." That has stuck with Gregg in every sale since then because the customer's perceptions about risk and value are directly linked to tension and trust. As the customer's perception of risk goes up, the tension the customer experiences goes up. As the perception of value goes down the customer's perception of risk rises.

When a customer perceives value to be low and risk to be high, a sale won't move forward. The salesperson encounters one objection after the other, and tension rises.

You can build trust by paying careful attention to the message you send to the customer and the message the customer sends you. Plan your messages to highlight value and minimize risk, and always be ready to adapt your approach when your customer's response suggests it.

You will systematically lower the natural tension in a sales situation by using genuine, active listening to meet your customer at his or her communication pace, and by focusing the conversation on important issues to the customer.

I D E A

BUILD YOUR PROFESSIONAL EQUITY

1.13 The Concept of Professional Equity

Equity is an important concept both in home ownership and in career development. Equity is ownership. When you own a home, equity is your property's value minus your mortgage. The more you pay off your debt, the more equity you have in the property.

The concept of professional equity also entails ownership — in this case, the number of assets you have built in your career. Professional assets include

- your reputation
- your credentials
- your relationships
- your education
- your product knowledge
- your professional experience
- your skill.

Each asset that you build eliminates a liability that could inhibit your career growth. Together, these assets build your professional equity.

W O R K S H E E T

WHAT'S IN IT FOR YOU?

- Discover your professional strengths
- Pinpoint areas that need work

BUILD YOUR PROFESSIONAL EQUITY

1.14 Evaluate Equity in Your Sales Career

Take a moment to assess how much equity you've built in your sales career. On a 1 to 10 scale, rate yourself in the following areas. Ten means you are at the optimal level of achievement in that category at this point in your sales career. One means you are at the bottom of that category *at this point* in your sales career.

For best results, do this exercise twice. Do it once alone to see how you perceive your level of equity and skill. Do it again with a partner to uncover how others perceive your strengths. Ask a trusted friend or sales manager to rate you in these areas and then discuss the results. Find out the implications of your score in each area, and see what you can do to advance your maturity and build more professional equity in each category. A small increase in each one of these areas will add up to a major advancement in your career.

Career Area	Ranking									
Professional credentials	1	2	3	4	5	6	7	8	9	10
Job experience	1	2	3	4	5	6	7	8	9	10
Professional maturity	1	2	3	4	5	6	7	8	9	10
Interpersonal skills	1	2	3	4	5	6	7	8	9	10
Self-management skills	1	2	3	4	5	6	7	8	9	10
Professional appearance	1	2	3	4	5	6	7	8	9	10
Professional demeanor	1	2	3	4	5	6	7	8	9	10
Social skills	1	2	3	4	5	6	7	8	9	10
Breadth of knowledge	1	2	3	4	5	6	7	8	9	10
Specific industry expertise	1	2	3	4	5	6	7	8	9	10

Career Area	Ranking									
Relationships with industry influentials	1	2	3	4	5	6	7	8	9	10
Vocabulary/ communication skills	1	2	3	4	5	6	7	8	9	10
Knowledge of business community trends	1	2	3	4	5	6	7	8	9	10

SECTION TWO

THE SALES PROCESS

WHAT'S IN IT FOR YOU?

- Sell more easily by understanding the selling process.
- Pinpoint the goal of each step in the selling process.
- Use your time effectively.
- Manage tension during the sales process.

In the decade or two just after World War II, salespeople perfected what we now call the "traditional" selling approach which relied heavily on a great opening pitch and a strong close. It was largely one-sided. The salesperson didn't take much time to understand the prospect and his or her needs. Instead, the prospect learned a great deal about the salesperson's product, and then decided whether it fit.

As Section One pointed out, selling today is all about relationships. Prospects are choosy. They don't want to waste a lot of time on unfocused pitches and old-fashioned glad handing. They want to develop a long-term relationship with salespeople and suppliers who can help them when problems and questions arise or needs change.

In relationship or collaborative selling, the salesperson takes time up front to build a sincere, committed relationship by investing time in learning about the customer's needs. Then, every step of the sales process that follows is conducted with the relationship in mind.

In this section, we examine each step of the sales process, identify its goal, and suggest strategies for achieving that goal. The following pages will help you understand where you are in the sale at any time and how to reach your ultimate goal: completing the sale and launching a successful business relationship.

I D E A

• **Understand and achieve the goals of each step in the sales process**

UNDERSTAND THE SALES PROCESS

2.1 The Six Steps in Selling

The sales process may seem overwhelming, but in reality it has just six steps:

1. planning and preparation, which we call targeting,
2. contacting the customer,
3. exploring the customer's situation and his or her needs,
4. collaborating with the customer to propose solutions to his or her problems,
5. confirming the sale and handling or eliminating any of the buyer's concerns, and
6. assuring satisfaction once the sale is completed.

At every step in the sales process, the accomplished sales professional focuses on the relationship with the customer. But each step has a different goal. Once you understand the goal of each step, you will be better able to choose the right behaviors and lead the prospect to a purchase.

The next time you encounter confusion or difficulty in a sales process, stop and determine which step you are in and what your goal should be. Until that goal is achieved, you're stuck in a loop—constantly cycling from one step to the one before it, back to the next step, and back to the one before it. But when that goal is achieved, you can progress naturally to the next step.

Targeting. The goal of this phase is preparation—being ready to do your job well. This means calling on the right people at the right time and in the right way—with the right information and the right materials on hand.

Contacting. In contacting, the goal is not simply to establish communication, but to establish *truthful* communication between you and the prospect. When both parties feel they can tell each other the real truth about their feelings, interests, and concerns, then the sale unfolds naturally and never degenerates into a simple game of words between seller and buyer.

Exploring. The goal of exploration is to discover. In this phase, you want to learn as much as you can about the client and his or her situation. Until you fully understand the client and his or her needs, a sale cannot progress effectively. In selling as in medicine, prescription without diagnosis is malpractice.

Collaborating. In the old style of selling, the emphasis was on talking to the prospective buyer, and the sales presentation was the main event. In relationship selling, the key is to collaborate *with* the client. Instead of relying on a memorized sales presentation, you tap into the client's interests and listen to his or her input. As partners in problem solving, you work together to identify ways to meet client needs and goals.

Confirming. The goal of confirming is to make the sale official. Using a signature, a handshake, an agreement, or some other kind of commitment, both parties signal that a sale has been consummated. It is at this point that traditional salespeople encounter "objections" from a client. In the collaborative sales process, customer concerns emerge and are resolved throughout your dialogue. There is no single point where concerns accumulate and tensions rise. That makes the confirming process simple, natural, and low in tension.

Assuring. In the assuring phase, your goal is to see that the customer is satisfied and happy with his or her decision. To do so, make your client aware of what he or she has bought, what will happen next, how questions can be answered, how to get support after the sale, and how best to enjoy the purchase.

I D E A

• **Use your selling time effectively**

UNDERSTAND THE SALES PROCESS

2.2 How to spend your time

The traditional sales method required salespeople to spend the majority of their selling time pitching, answering objections, and closing. Relationship or collaborative selling, as the chart below shows, places the emphasis on the first and last parts of the process: finding out as much as possible about the customer and his or her needs, and delivering post-sale customer service.

Traditional	**Collaborative**
This diagram illustrates the emphasis placed on each of the six phases in the traditional sales method.	This diagram illustrates the emphasis placed on each of the six phases in "Collaborative Selling."
Prospecting / Small Talk / Fact Finding / Pitching / Closing/Overcoming Objections / Reselling	Target / Contact / Explore / Collaborate / Confirm / Assure

Keep this chart in mind as you design your sales calls. Make sure you invest time in the interpersonal aspects of each sale. When you do, you'll win more sales in less time and build a strong base of lifetime customers who will act as references and sources of referrals.

I D E A

• **Understand the process that turns prospects into clients**

UNDERSTAND THE SALES PROCESS

2.3 The Sales Pipeline

A client moves through the sales process much the way that water moves through a pipeline. To ensure an uninterrupted flow of "water" or new sales, strive to always keep the pipeline full. Understanding all the elements will help you identify the best prospects to work with.

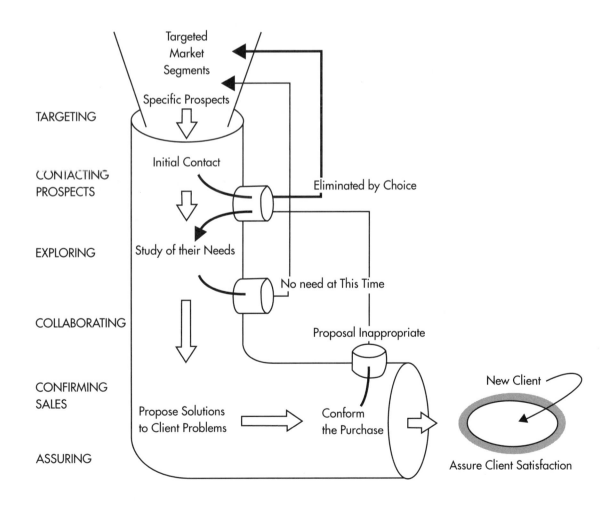

I D E A

• **Adapt your approach to fit the tension level of each step**

UNDERSTAND THE SALES PROCESS

2.4 Managing Tension in the Sales Process

During the sales process, tension rises and falls. In large part, the tension level depends on how you relate to your prospect or customer. It also depends on which phase of the sales process you are in.

The diagram below shows that both buyer and seller begin with high levels of tension, which subsides or rises depending on the phase. The buyer's tension is highest during and after the sale, whereas the seller's tension tends to diminish after confirming the sale. That's why it's so important to assure satisfaction and see to it that you eliminate the traditional "buyer's remorse" by specifying exactly how the customer will benefit from the purchase.

Tension During the Sales Process

Steps: Target — Contact — Explore — Collaborate — Confirm — Assure

Source: *Relationship Selling* by Jim Cathcart.

I D E A

- **Fully understand how the steps of the sales process make your job easier in the long run by optimizing your time**

UNDERSTANDING THE SALES PROCESS

2.5 The Sales Planning Process

It is one thing to plan for a sales call and quite another to plan your overall sales activities. This chart shows how these activities fit together.

Two-Stage Sales Planning Process

SITUATION ANALYSIS	Assessing Selling Opportunities within the Territory	
	Sales Problems Sales Opportunities	
OBJECTIVES	Establish Overall Territory and Account Objectives	
	Set Territory Strategy	
	Call Frequency Routing Prospecting Plans	
	Individual Account Analysis	
STRATEGIES	Plan/Prepare for the Sales Call	
	Contacting	
	Exploring	
	Collaborating	
	Confirming	
	Assuring	
CONTROLS	Recordkeeping and Control (Studying Yourself and Improving)	

STAGE ONE

STAGE TWO

SECTION THREE

PLANNING AND PREPARATION

WHAT'S IN IT FOR YOU?

- Be ready to do your job well.
- Get where you want to go faster — by knowing exactly how you'll get there.
- Set goals for improving your personal and professional performance.

The single most important step in the sales process takes place before the sales process even begins. If you don't have presence of mind, an optimistic attitude, or a genuine interest in helping your client—and if you lack the necessary information about your client—then even a thorough understanding of your product or service won't help you make the sale.

This section will show you how to prepare yourself to do the best job you can. First, it will help you clarify your goals and prepare yourself to be the person who can reach them. Then, it will aid you in reaching your target by setting sales goals that, with hard work and inspiration, can be achieved.

The beauty of professional selling is that *you* control the outcomes. You determine what goals you'll go after, what work you'll do, what strategies you'll apply, and what kind of results you'll get.

Goals come first. When you begin with a clear idea of what you want to achieve, you can be more specific about setting your sales goals. Far too many people set sales goals in a vacuum. They set arbitrary goals like "I'm going to make X number of sales for Y amount of money." And then they expect to be excited! That's a little like bowling with a curtain in front of the pins. When you roll the ball, you hear a noise—but you can't tell whether you've hit the target.

In this section, you'll learn how to increase your success by developing clear goals for

- the gross sales, number of sales, and percentage of sales coming from each product or service
- sales in each part of your territory
- how much time you'll devote to various sales activities.

W O R K S H E E T

WHAT'S IN IT FOR YOU?

• **Use your goals to motivate you to new achievements**

CLARIFY YOUR PERSONAL GOALS

3.1 What Is Your Ultimate Goal?

Most people do things because they want to — not just because they know how. That's why it's important to focus on the reasons behind your performance: to keep your eye on your goal. Know what you want to achieve and why you want to achieve it, and you'll find it easier to keep yourself motivated and focused as you sell.

How do you want your future to unfold? What would you like to happen this year? Using the space below or a separate sheet of paper, write down your thoughts about your future. Brainstorm about how you'd like to see things go over the next year. What would happen if all the lights turned green, so to speak? What would happen if you got all the breaks you needed and were actually able to do the things you would love to do?

Next, expand your thinking. How do you see yourself evolving in your sales career over the next five years?

Finally, think beyond those five years. How do you see the rest of your life going, if everything goes in a positive direction and unfolds in the ways that you want them to? Take as much time as you need, because this could be the most important self-motivation exercise you ever do. Once you've clarified your goals, look back over all your notes and find your primary goals. Whittle them down to a top 10 list, and then choose one or two that can help you accomplish all the rest. Sometimes you'll find that in achieving one goal, many of your other goals automatically become a byproduct of the process.

I D E A

• **Clarify what you need to be to reach your goals faster**

CLARIFY YOUR PERSONAL GOALS

3.2 Define the Qualities You Need

What kind of person do you need to be to reach your goals? Many people make the mistake of setting goals and then doing nothing, thinking that the goals themselves will be enough to keep them on their path to sales success.

We have found that it's much more helpful if you can focus clearly on the details of a goal. For example, if you decide that you'd like to be a sales leader in your industry, you'll need to ask yourself these questions (and answer them as specifically as possible):

- What kind of a person would be a sales leader in my industry, the kind that I would like to become?
- What sort of things would he or she know about?
- What skills would that salesperson possess?
- What organizations would he or she be active in?
- What kind of reputation would this person have?
- What sort of learning would this person do on a regular basis?
- What sort of daily habits, personal and professional, would this person cultivate?
- How would this person behave toward other people?
- How would this person react to problems and mistakes made by themselves or others?
- How would this person deal with the many challenges that I know I'll be dealing with in my own sales career?

As you ponder your answers, your mental image of the person you'd like to become will emerge. And, as it does, you will find it easy to find ways to cultivate those qualities.

The quickest, simplest path to achieving your sales goals is becoming the kind of person who would achieve those sales goals. When you do, you will achieve them almost automatically. Take time now to write your answers to these questions.

I D E A

CLARIFY YOUR PERSONAL GOALS

3.3 How Will the "Future You" Do Today's Tasks?

Many years ago, Tim Seward was in Jim Cathcart's audience. At the time, he was nineteen years old and the proud owner of a new business. Jim suggested that as a self-motivation exercise, Tim ask himself every day, "How would the person I'd like to become do the things I'm about to do?"

Tim used that question to motivate himself and guide his development so effectively that he built his auto detailing business, became its international sales leader, won awards, employed many other people to sell and work for him, and ultimately expanded his business into the automotive after-market. Today his business has four locations and earns over $6 million annually. He attributes it to constantly asking himself how the person he wanted to become would handle the things he needed to do.

It's a powerful question that works in all areas of your professional life. Now that you've defined the kind of person you would like to become...

- How would that person make the sales call you're about to make?
- How would that person keep his or her records?
- How would that person do the follow through on each contact?
- How would that person prepare for the day?
- How would that person dress?
- What kind of language would that person use?
- What kind of vocabulary would he or she cultivate?
- What would that person do with their spare time?

IDEA

WHAT'S IN IT FOR YOU?

• **Understand what it takes to market yourself and build a business**

SET SPECIFIC SALES GOALS

3.4 Four Rules of Dominos

Once you've set sales goals, your sales pipeline will start to fill. To see the results, however, you need to know what it takes to market and build a business. "Jim Cathcart's Four Rules of Dominos" may help you understand why.

Rule 1. **You must have dominos.** If you're going to build a business, you must have something to line up. In sales, it's prospects.

Rule 2. **You've got to line them up correctly.** If you line dominos up correctly, they'll all fall down nicely. Line them up incorrectly, and they won't fall against each other. Likewise, in sales, you have to do your marketing and prospecting in such a way that one sale naturally leads to another.

Rule 3. **You've got to push the first domino in the right direction.** Take each contact seriously. When you make your first call, do it in such a way that it leads you right into another call, and another. Be professional and service the client after the sale is confirmed. Most important, let each client know that you want to specialize in that particular market place, that you want to understand that industry so you can be of better service, and that you want to meet even more people in that field of business.

Rule 4. **When you knock over the first domino, be ready for the rest of them to fall.** They will fall, and if you're not ready for a lot of sales opportunities, you'll miss some—and possibly spoil the market place.

I D E A

• Discover why it takes marketing, sales, and service to create satisfied clients

SET SPECIFIC SALES GOALS

3.5 The Marketing, Sales and Service Mix

Marketing, selling, and service are not the same thing. *Marketing* is generating a desire for your product or service. *Selling* is converting that desire into transactions. *Service* converts those transactions into satisfied clients.

There are five ways to mix sales, service, and marketing...but only one guarantees success.

GREAT MARKETING + POOR SALES = POVERTY

Demand alone won't pay the bills. If you're not converting demand into transactions, you're not going to have much success.

GREAT SALES + POOR MARKETING = BURNOUT

Marketing can help you open doors by creating demand. Without marketing, everything is on your shoulders. Selling never gets any easier because nobody ever helps.

GREAT MARKETING + GREAT SALES + POOR SERVICE = SURPRISES

A dissatisfied client will come back to haunt you every time. This usually happens when you least expect it, are least prepared—and when it is most embarrassing.

GREAT SERVICE + POOR MARKETING + POOR SALES = LONELINESS

Great service can't overcome poor marketing and poor sales. If you provide great service but haven't generated marketing and sales, you'll suffer from the "Maytag Syndrome"—sitting around and wishing you had someone to serve!

GREAT MARKETING + GREAT SALES + GREAT SERVICE = SUCCESS

The dynamic mix of marketing (to generate demand), sales (to convert demand into purchases), and service (to assure that customers stay satisfied) is what it takes to generate outstanding results (success)!

W O R K S H E E T

WHAT'S IN IT FOR YOU?

- Develop a clear picture of where your company's current sales come from
- Gain insight into your company's promotional effectiveness, market saturation, and customer loyalty

WHAT PRODUCTS ARE SELLING AND WHICH CUSTOMERS ARE BUYING?

3.6 Breakdown of Current Year's Sales

For each product line and market segment, fill in the dollar amounts and percentages of current year's sales.

MARKET SEGMENT _____

Product Line	Existing Customers	New Customers	Total
1.	_____ $ _____ %	_____ $ _____ %	_____ $ 100 %
2.	_____ $ _____ %	_____ $ _____ %	_____ $ 100 %
3.	_____ $ _____ %	_____ $ _____ %	_____ $ 100 %
Total	_____ $ _____ %	_____ $ _____ %	_____ $ 100 %

W O R K S H E E T

WHAT PRODUCTS ARE SELLING AND WHICH CUSTOMERS ARE BUYING?

3.7 Projection of the Coming Year's Sales

Through research and/or discussions with your sales manager, find out where next year's sales are expected to come from in various market segments.

MARKET SEGMENT

Product Line	Existing Customers	New Customers	Total
1.	_____ $ _____ %	_____ $ _____ %	_____ $ 100 _____ %
2.	_____ $ _____ %	_____ $ _____ %	_____ $ 100 _____ %
3.	_____ $ _____ %	_____ $ _____ %	_____ $ 100 _____ %
Total	_____ $ _____ %	_____ $ _____ %	_____ $ 100 _____ %

WORKSHEET

WHAT'S IN IT FOR YOU?

- Understand your company's competitive posture in various market segments
- Determine the market segments that are most profitable to you
- Prioritize market segments in terms of profitability and company's strength of position

WHERE TO SPEND YOUR TIME AND ENERGY

3.8 Market Segment Categories

List the various market segments in your territory by the combination of profitability and your company's strength of position.

TERRITORY

	Very Low	STRENGTH OF POSITION	Very High

PROFITABILITY — Very High ... Very Low

I D E A

WHAT'S IN IT FOR YOU?

- **Grasp the true value of your customers**
- **Discover how much potential business lies in your market place**

WHERE TO SPEND YOUR TIME AND ENERGY

3.9 What Is A Customer Worth To You?

Some years ago, Jim Cathcart bought a set of tires from an automobile service company that specialized in tires. After they had been promptly and professionally installed, the technician called him over and pointed out a few things about his car that might need attention in the future. He told Jim that while he didn't have to do anything about them now, he should keep an eye on them and take action if they grew worse.

Jim was so impressed that his trust level soared, and he confided in the technician. "I have a list of 25 items that need to be fixed on this car, and I'd like your advice on where I can go to get these repaired," he said. Well, as it turned out about 23 of those items could be done right there.

What began as a $239 tire purchase ended up as a $1,600 renovation—on the same visit. Over the years, Jim spent $9,620.72 in parts and repairs on that automobile (yes, it was a lemon—but Jim liked it).

What made the difference that caused Jim to ultimately spend $9,600 instead of just $239? *Trust in the technician's expertise and his desire to be of service, whether or not he made an immediate profit from it.*

This technician knew that a customer is more than the revenue represented by one sale. A customer represents a lifetime of purchases. In *Customers For Life*, author and automobile salesperson extraordinaire Carl Sewel "guesstimated" that the typical automobile buyer spends something in the neighborhood of $344,000 in their lifetime on automobiles. When you're talking that kind of money, it doesn't make much sense to quibble over details when there's a problem or disagreement with a customer.

What's a customer worth to you? Take some time to evaluate your accounts, and see just how much business potentially exists in your current marketplace, and then think of creative ways to expand that value with the existing number of customers.

SECTION FOUR

PREPARING FOR THE SALES CONTACT

WHAT'S IN IT FOR YOU?

- Enhance your performance by understanding your company's goals.
- Increase your sales success by understanding your customer's goals.
- Increase your knowledge of your products and services.
- Increase your competitive knowledge.

What separates the confident, successful salesperson from the nervous, unsuccessful one is knowledge and preparation. The more you know about yourself, your company, industry, and prospect, the better you can connect and make the sale.

W O R K S H E E T

WHAT'S IN IT FOR YOU?

• Make your sales presentations more effective

PREPARE YOUR CUSTOMER KNOWLEDGE

4.1 Study Your Customer

In Sections Twelve and Thirteen, you'll master strategies for studying your customer and his or her situation. But first, you need to study your customer.

Use this page to list all the things you need to know to make an effective sales presentation to your prospect or customer. Beside them, list the sources where you can acquire that information.

Take a minute now to do this simple exercise. If you have difficulty determining what you need to know or how to find it, spend extra time on the following pages. They will help you clarify the customer information you need.

What I Need to Know for an Effective Sales Presentation   Where to Find It

_____

_____

_____

_____

_____

_____

_____

_____

_____

WORKSHEET

WHAT'S IN IT FOR YOU?

• Clearly define the role and responsibility of your sales position

PREPARE YOUR COMPANY KNOWLEDGE

4.2 Define Your Organizational Goals

Before you can approach customers and meet your sales goals, you need to understand what your company expects of you. Address the following questions to better understand your company's expectations. Use a blank sheet of paper if you need more room.

1. What is the current mission of the sales force in my firm (for example, to increase market share, increase profitability)?

   _____

2. What components of the product mix am I being asked to sell, and what is the relative importance of each?

   _____

3. What market segments are we going after, and what are their relative priorities?

   _____

4. How frequently and on what criteria will my performance be measured?

   _____

5. What constitutes good selling behavior in terms of these tasks and activities?

   _____

6. Are these organizational goals and priorities consistent with my personal goals?

   _____

W O R K S H E E T

WHAT'S IN IT FOR YOU?

- **Increase your company knowledge**
- **Give better, more credible presentations**
- **Boost your ability to market your product/service**

PREPARE YOUR COMPANY KNOWLEDGE

4.3 Know Your Company

Answer these critical questions about your company. If you don't know an answer off-hand, interview or research until you find the information you need.

1. List the key personnel of your company and their unique contributions to the firm.

_____

2. What unique capabilities or technical advantages does your company have?

_____

3. What is the company's image and reputation among
    a. present customers?
    b. prospects?
    c. the competition?

4. What are the company's relative strengths and weaknesses compared to the competition? How do these affect business?

_____

5. What is the marketing philosophy of your company?

_____

6. What are the present and future markets of your company?

_____

7. What has the company's sales history been during the last 3–5 years?

_____

8. What is your company's standard policy regarding

    a. pricing? _____

    b. discounts? _____

    c. guarantees?_____

    d. service? _____

    e. negotiating? _____

W O R K S H E E T

- **Increase your knowledge of your products/services**
- **Understand how your products/services compare to your competition**

PREPARE YOUR PRODUCT KNOWLEDGE

4.4 Know Your Products/Services

A solid grasp of your products/services—and how they compare to competitors'—will increase your credibility and help you sell the right product to the right customer.

1. What specific benefits do customers seek in your product/service?

_____

2. How does your product/service compare to the competition's in providing those benefits?

_____

3. Are there any features that make your product/service better than the competition's? If so, why?

_____

4. How does your product/service compare to the others in your territory in the following aspects:

    a. quality _____

    b. price _____

    c. delivery _____

    d. value-added _____

    e. reliability _____

    f. service _____

5. What factor(s) might prevent a customer from purchasing your product/service? What can you do about it?

_____

6. Is your company a leader (developer) or follower (imitator) in its field? Why?

_____

I D E A

WHAT'S IN IT FOR YOU?

- Learn what your competitors say about themselves and what others say about them
- Keeping up on the competition can enhance your reputation as a knowledgeable sales rep and help you compete more effectively in a crowded market place. Make the time to study your competitors, clipping and saving the most pertinent items you discover

PREPARE YOUR COMPETITIVE KNOWLEDGE

4.5 Sources of Competitive Information

WHERE TO FIND WHAT COMPETITORS SAY ABOUT THEMSELVES

Publications	Trade/Professional	Government Sources	Investors/Financial Services
Advertising	Manuals	SEC reports	Annual reports
Promotional materials	Technical papers	Court cases	Prospectuses
	Licenses/applications	Regulatory agencies	Annual meetings
Press releases	Patents	One-time studies	
Speeches	Courses/seminars	Government publications	
Books	Suppliers	Chambers of commerce	
Articles	Consultants		
Personnel changes			
Want ads			
In-house publications			
Catalogs/brochures			
Products/services			

WHERE TO FIND WHAT OTHERS SAY ABOUT YOUR COMPETITORS

Publications	Trade/Professional	Government Sources	Investors/Financial Services
Newspapers	Former employees	Court cases	Security analysts
Consumer groups	Customers	Federal/local agencies	Dun & Bradstreet
Unions	Competitors	Government programs	Standard & Poor's
Market research	Suppliers	Environmental filings & other permits	Commercial banks
Recruiting firms	Trade publications		
Specialized university libraries	Industry studies		
Industrial research centers			

I D E A

WHAT'S IN IT FOR YOU?

• **Increase your market share by "stealing" customers from your competitors**

PREPARE YOUR COMPETITIVE KNOWLEDGE

4.6 How to Win Competitors' Customers

"Stealing" customers from competitors is a fact of life for salespeople. Customers become dissatisfied and switch. Your market share will increase if they come to you. Here's how you entice prospects to switch.

1. **Think long term.** Don't give up when you hear, "I'm satisfied." Satisfaction may be temporary. Your prospect's needs may change, or you may provide a good reason for switching.

2. **Develop a relationship.** Once you've mastered the relationship strategies to be presented in Section Six, you will be able to determine quickly whether you can develop a rapport with a prospect, sale or no sale. By developing a friendship, you will be able to …

3. **Study needs.** Take your time, do research, and ask a lot of nonthreatening questions so you can find out your prospect's needs and how well they are being satisfied. The key is to find a need gap and offer a solution.

4. **Sell yourself.** Personal chemistry is important, but so is the knowledge that you are an enthusiastic, earnest, professional, ethical, caring expert who would be nothing but an asset to know and do business with. Come up with new ideas for your prospects. Show them that you are on their team, sale or no sale.

5. **Add value.** So many products and services are commodities that differentiation may be difficult. That is why you sell yourself. That is also why you have to differentiate your product with added value such as service and performance guarantees, superior services, better delivery schedules — whatever it takes to be better.

6. **Ask for a no-risk trial order.** Many customers are loyal to their suppliers, but will grant you a trial order if you ask for it. Make it a no-risk proposition. Ensure your prospect's satisfaction with some kind of guarantee, and bend over backward to make sure the trial order makes a very positive impression.

7. Ask for a portion of their business. "Stealing" a competitor's customer may not be an all-or-nothing deal. You may have to do it bit by bit, proving yourself slowly as you go along. Ask for a small percentage of the prospect's business and you may find that percentage will grow.

8. Be persistent. Nothing succeeds more than persistence. All things being equal, the persistent salesperson will win the account every time. Keep in touch with prospects, think long term, be a consultant and ally, and you will plant drought-resistant seeds.

W O R K S H E E T

WHAT'S IN IT FOR YOU?

• **Develop the frame of mind that enables sales success**

PREPARE YOUR ATTITUDE

4.7 Preparing Yourself Mentally

Have you ever tried to make a sales call when you were depressed, angry, or afraid? It probably didn't work very well. Use the sheet below to list the qualities it takes to be in the right mental frame of mind to make a successful sales call.

Recall a time when you were in the perfect frame of mind for a sales call. Write a narrative that describes the mood, attitude, and point of view you will need to be at your best. Once you're done, make some notes on how you can get yourself into that frame of mind. What are some tools, techniques, or strategies you can use?

_____

_____

_____

_____

_____

_____

_____

WORKSHEET

WHAT'S IN IT FOR YOU?

- Tell your customers what you do and why you're better than the competition — succinctly and with confidence

PREPARE YOUR ATTITUDE

4.8 Competitive Advantage Statement

For six years, Jim Cathcart worked with an insurance agency as a personal coach to individual agents. Many times, the individuals he coached were reluctant to make calls until they felt they had so much product knowledge that they could answer any question that came up. The fact was they were ready to make sales calls. They had enough product knowledge to do the job well, but their confidence level wasn't where it needed to be. One of the best confidence builders you can create is a competitive advantage statement. This document prepares you to tell your customers *what* you do and *why* you have an edge over others doing the same thing — so you'll never be tongue-tied again.

In 30 seconds or less, a competitive advantage statement tells your customers what differentiates *you* in the market place. It includes four elements:

1. Your name
2. Your company
3. A statement about a typical problem experienced by your target market
4. An intriguing statement about how you can help solve the problem.

Use the space below to develop a Competitive Advantage Statement for your primary market.

Primary Target Market

Your Name: _____

Your Company: _____

What is a typical problem experienced in this target market?

_____

_____

What's an intriguing statement about how you and your product solve this problem?

_____

_____

SECTION FIVE

TARGETING

WHAT'S IN IT FOR YOU?

- Identify the prospects who most need your product or service.
- Develop a profile of your current market.
- Gain a clear picture of the desirability of your current accounts.
- Build your business by securing referrals from current customers.

The first step in successful sales is accurate *targeting*. Targeting includes two phases. The first phase is identifying your best prospects. The second is using personal marketing techniques to generate leads.

This section helps you analyze your current customers and prospects to find your best prospects—the people who are most likely to need your product or service. Many of these people are business associates or acquaintances of your current customers. By mastering the secrets of prospecting presented here, you can build your business through networking and referrals.

IDEA

• **Identify particular markets and control their growth**

IDENTIFY YOUR BEST PROSPECTS

5.1 What Is a Market?

A market is a group of people with enough in common that you can establish a reputation among them. If you can build a reputation among a group of people, then each sales call becomes easier. The goal of marketing is to give you a large number of people who are willing to see you. The more you can create a demand for your product or service, the more you can build a reputation for yourself.

Markets fall into two categories: natural markets and chosen markets. A natural market is one that you've already begun to penetrate. You don't have to start at square one and build a lot of connections. These markets come out of existing relationships and leads that have grown out of previous contacts and experience.

A *chosen market* is one that you decide to go after. You see an opportunity, gather information, establish contacts, and develop and cultivate this chosen market. The natural market is an excellent source of potential clients. To define it, think of friends, neighbors, and family members who know your capabilities and would make good potential clients. Consider people you've met through your spouse or children, hobbies, church, social clubs, community activities, or past employment. What about people you do business with today? Any of these people might benefit from having your product or service.

IDEA

• **Sell your market segment more successfully by defining and understanding its characteristics**

IDENTIFY YOUR BEST PROSPECTS

5.2 The Market Profile

To fully reach your chosen market, you will need to develop a market profile. A market profile consists of

- A list of names of key people
- A demographic profile of the market place
- A list of associations and societies
- Publications read by key people
- Major events attended by key people
- Major categories within this market
- Psychographics (how key people think)
- Common fears, likes, dislikes, goals
- Challenges faced by key people
- Some of the catch words and jargon they use.

All of this will add to your understanding of your chosen or targeted market. The more fully you understand each market segment, the more likely you are to succeed in selling them.

I D E A

• **Discover sources of information on your competitors, your market place, your company, and your prospects**

IDENTIFY YOUR BUSINESS PROSPECTS

5.3 Where to Find the Market

Because managing your territory requires market or competitor research, you must know where to find information you need. In the following sources, you'll find answers to questions on the market place, your competition, your company, and your prospects.

Standard & Poor's industry surveys
Moody's Industrial Manual
Forbes annual report on business
S & P's corporate record
Dun & Bradstreet Reference Book of Corporate Management
Encyclopedia of Business Information Sources
Financial periodicals
Funk & Scott Index of Corporations and Industries

Government publications from:
U.S. Department of Commerce
Bureau of Economic Analysis
Local Chambers of Commerce
Internal Revenue Service
U.S. Treasury Department
Department of Labor
Bureau of Census

Newspapers, especially:
The Wall Street Journal
The New York Times
Barron's
Washington Post

Business magazines
Professional and trade journals
Annual reports, stock prospectuses, stock performance guides
Company sources, including marketing departments and ad agencies
Personal contacts
Trade associations
Trade shows

WORKSHEET

WHAT'S IN IT FOR YOU?

- **Identify current customers and prospects in each market segment you want to penetrate**

ANALYZE YOUR ACCOUNTS

5.4 Account and Prospect Identification

Break down each of your target markets into present and future customers. Complete the worksheet for each product/service you sell and market segment you are trying to penetrate. The order of your accounts is unimportant.

ACCOUNT IDENTIFICATION

Market Segment _____   Product Line _____

Existing Customers/Clients	*Prospects*

W O R K S H E E T

ANALYZE YOUR ACCOUNTS

5.5 Volume and Profit Matrix

List your accounts in the boxes that best correspond to the combinations of sales volume and profits. Your goal should be to work your accounts so they move up in profitability and sales volume.

SALES VOLUME

	Low	Medium	High
High			
Medium			
Low			

PROFITABILITY

W O R K S H E E T

WHAT'S IN IT FOR YOU?

- Classify your accounts in terms of profitability
- Prioritize your accounts
- Determine how and when to call on them

ANALYZE YOUR ACCOUNTS

5.6 Key Account Categories

Using data from your most recent sales year, rank your accounts by their profitability. Complete a separate sheet for each product/service you sell.

Product/Service _____

Date _____**through** _____

	Company	Contact	Phone
"A" ACCOUNTS Top 20% Very Profitable			
"B" ACCOUNTS Middle 30% Profitable			
"C" ACCOUNTS Bottom 50% Less Profitable			
PROSPECTS			

I D E A

WHAT'S IN IT FOR YOU?

• **Understand the importance of "panning" for new business**

REFERRAL PROSPECTING

5.7 Networking for Prospects

One of the primary elements in growing a sales business is building a network of productive relationships. The more people you know, the more people you're capable of knowing. The more people you know, the more possibilities you create.

Don't think of your sales career only in terms of your own limited energy, intellect, and resources. Think of it as something that can be multiplied by all of the possibilities in every person you meet, and all of the people to whom they are connected.

After all, your sales success depends on your customers. And prospecting for customers is very much like prospecting for gold. Just as an old-time prospector might pan a mountain's worth of rock, mud, and gravel to find a few valuable gold nuggets, today's salesperson must "mine" a potential area in hopes of finding individuals or companies that are truly worth digging for. These "nuggets" can be extremely valuable and can appreciate over time through repeat and referral business.

To find "nuggets," use your Rolodex. Keep records. Maintain a good database of the people you know, noting the needs they have that relate to your career.

I D E A

WHAT'S IN IT FOR YOU?

• Know the "tricks of the trade" when it comes to getting referrals

REFERRAL PROSPECTING

5.8 The 10 Steps of Referral Prospecting

These 10 steps from Tony Alessandra will help you remember the steps involved in securing referrals from your customers:

1. Ask for specific referrals to narrow the customer's focus.
2. Gather as much information about the referral as possible.
3. Ask your customer for permission to use his or her name.
4. Ask your customer for help in obtaining an appointment with the referral.
5. Contact the referral as soon as possible.
6. Inform your customer about the outcome of the contact.
7. Build referral alliances (this can be through sources such as tip clubs, centers of influence, key people in the industry).
8. Prospect for referrals just like you prospect for sales leads.
9. Rank your referrals as you do your customers:

    A for *hot* (you know a lot about the referral and the referrer introduces you)

    B for *warm* (you know little about the referral and you can use the referrer's name)

    C for *cold* (you know nothing about the referral, and you can't use the referrer's name).

10. Seek internal referrals (other departments, locations, divisions, branches, and subsidiaries).

W O R K S H E E T

REFERRAL PROSPECTING

5.9 Prospect Data Sheet

Use this form to make sure you gather pertinent data on each of your prospects.

PROSPECT DATA SHEET

Name of prospect _____

Address of prospect _____

Products purchased:

Product A _____   Product B _____   Product C _____

Product volume:

Product A $_____   Product B $ _____   Product C $ _____

Type of business: _____

SIC code: _____

Has prospect been qualified?   Yes   No

Actions required to:

1. Qualify the prospect:

   • _____

   • _____

   • _____

2. Follow-up:

   • _____

   • _____

   • _____

W O R K S H E E T

WHAT'S IN IT FOR YOU?

• Keep track of prospecting methods for future analysis

REFERRAL PROSPECTING

5.10 Methods of Prospecting

Periodically, you need to look back on your prospecting activities and evaluate which methods were most fruitful. This worksheet will help you. Start by keeping a record of the prospecting methods you have used with specific companies.

PROSPECTS (Company Name)	METHODS OF PROSPECTING					
	Company Leads	Direct Mail	Industrial Directories	Trade Shows	Trade Assns.	Other

W O R K S H E E T

WHAT'S IN IT FOR YOU?

- Identify the characteristics of your best and worst customers to help you find ideal prospects

REFERRAL PROSPECTING

5.11 Identifying Ideal Customers

This worksheet will help you identify your ideal customers. Once you have done so, you will be able to look for prospects or market segments that have similar profiles.

A. List five of your best customers.

1. _____
2. _____
3. _____
4. _____
5. _____

B. List the characteristics of your best customers.

_____
_____

C. List five of your worst customers.

1. _____
2. _____
3. _____
4. _____
5. _____

D. List the characteristics of your worst customers.

_____
_____

E. What prospecting methods can you employ to find more "best" customers?

_____
_____

WORKSHEET

WHAT'S IN IT FOR YOU?

- Identify your most productive sources of prospects
- Brainstorm more sources of prospects

REFERRAL PROSPECTING

5.12 Creative Prospect Source List

One of the most important aspects of prospecting is creatively generating a list of potential clients or sources for clients.

List the top 10 most fruitful sources of prospects you have used so far. Then brainstorm five less obvious sources.

Ten most-used sources of prospects:

1. _____
2. _____
3. _____
4. _____
5. _____
6. _____
7. _____
8. _____
9. _____
10. _____

Five less-used, more creative sources of prospects:

1. _____
2. _____
3. _____
4. _____
5. _____

W O R K S H E E T

WHAT'S IN IT FOR YOU?

- **Push yourself to find creative sources of prospects**

REFERRAL PROSPECTING

5.13 Prospecting Action Plan

Write five of your best prospect sources in the blank spaces below. Under each, brainstorm four ways to increase your exposure and generate more prospects.

1. _____

   a.

   b.

   c.

   d.

2. _____

   a.

   b.

   c.

   d.

3. _____

   a.

   b.

   c.

   d.

4. _____

   a.

   b.

   c.

   d.

5. _____

   a.

   b.

   c.

   d.

W O R K S H E E T

- **Brainstorm all the possible personal connections that may benefit you**

REFERRAL PROSPECTING

5.14 The Friendship Tree

Growing a friendship tree is simple. List all the people who know your capabilities and professionalism. Evaluate age, occupation, length of time known, how well known, how often seen, ability to provide referrals, and how easy they are to approach. When you make your first contact, ask for two more names. Do the same for each person you contact. You'll find the list of prospects growing and spreading like the branches of a tree.

Friendship Tree

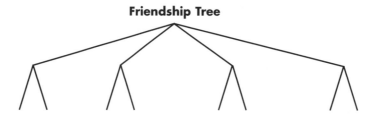

Type of Friend	List Two Names
School friends:	
Friends of family:	
Neighbors:	
Known through spouse:	
Known through children:	
Known through hobbies:	
Known through church:	
Known through social clubs:	
Known through community activities:	
Known through past employment:	
People you do business with:	
Other:	

SECTION SIX

PRECONDITIONING YOUR PROSPECTS

WHAT'S IN IT FOR YOU?

- Promote yourself as a salesperson.
- Learn the fine points of direct mail promotion.
- Create your own effective direct mail letter.

The toughest sale of all is selling to someone who is not expecting you and is not necessarily open to learning about your product or service. To overcome this situation, precondition your prospects so that they want to hear your message. In this section, you'll learn how to precondition prospects by promoting yourself and using direct mail wisely.

I D E A

- **Introduce yourself to prospects**
- **Stimulate off-season sales**
- **Develop long-term relationships with customers**
- **Expand your customer base**

PROMOTE YOURSELF

6.1 Blow Your Own Horn

Every company devises a marketing plan to promote its products or services. You, too, should promote yourself. Why bother? Most people think the company's advertising will bring in enough business to keep them busy. More often than not, this is not the case. A well-executed promotional program will accomplish many things for you:

- Introduce you, your company, and your product/service to prospects and smooth the way for followup calls
- Encourage more purchases by current customers
- Stimulate off-season business
- Keep abreast or ahead of your competition's promotional efforts
- Enlarge your customer base by spreading your sales to larger areas
- Keep in touch with customers and re-establish contact with former customers

There are four means of promoting a company or an individual: advertising, sales promotions, publicity, and public relations. The first two are designed to influence sales directly; the latter two increase sales by boosting a person's or company's image.

Advertising
Yellow Pages
Direct mail
Ads in trade and professional publications
Television, radio, billboards
Brochures and flyers
Online ads and Web sites

Sales Promotions
Special discounts and package deals, coupons, cross-promotions
Novelties such as pens, calendars, letter openers
Trade show exhibits
Special events, open houses

Public Relations and/or Publicity

Sending Christmas, birthday, and special-occasion cards
Membership and involvement in professional and trade groups
Speaking engagements, seminars, consulting, teaching classes
Press releases, feature articles, interviews

I D E A

PROMOTE YOURSELF

6.2 Advertising

Many salespeople advertise on their own, especially in real estate, insurance, professional services, and multi-level marketing. Answer the following questions to determine if advertising is suitable for you.

1. What message(s) do you want to convey? Should more emphasis be put on you or your product/service?
2. Who is your target market?
3. What is the most effective way to reach your target market?
4. How much can you afford to spend on advertising this year? Can you afford not to advertise? Will your company supplement your advertising budget, or contribute in any other way?
5. When is the best time to schedule your advertising? Is your product/service seasonal? Is your product/service tied in with an activity such as the purchase of a new car or home?

After you've answered these questions, you will have a better idea of your advertising capabilities. The most important issue is money. Repeated advertising is not cheap; one-time advertising is usually ineffective. You'll be better off concentrating a modest budget on direct mail than blowing it all on one TV commercial. Consider the following media carefully.

Brochures. Large or small, brochures should always be professionally designed, written, and printed on high-quality paper. Brochures increase credibility significantly.

Direct mail. Letters and brochures are effective for name recognition and general exposure. Direct mail's primary advantage is its ability to target your market with precision.

Novelties. Pens, calendars, and other novelties cheerfully remind customers of you. They are not inexpensive and, if possible, should be done with the financial help of your company.

Print ads. Magazine and newspaper ads are effective, yet expensive. In industries such as real estate, there is no substitute for a picture and description of a listing.

Billboards. Billboards come in all shapes and sizes. For the budgets of individual salespeople, the bus stop seat billboard is the most realistic.

Radio. One of the most effective media if used repeatedly, radio reaches the demographic group you desire, but at a price. Air time and production are expensive.

Television. The king of mass media, this high-priced advertising vehicle reaches the most people at the highest price. It would be absurd for a salesperson to advertise on national TV, but local cable channels offer less expensive opportunities for exposure.

Web site. For the millions of online users worldwide, the World Wide Web is the shopping center of the future. Create your own Web site or build a page on your company's site electronically.

W O R K S H E E T

WHAT'S IN IT FOR YOU?

- **Brainstorm the use of sales promotions for personal advancement**

PROMOTE YOURSELF

6.3 Sales Promotions

Advertising is an ongoing promotional activity. Sales promotions are one-time activities designed to stimulate sales for a special occasion. As a salesperson, you should think of ways to boost sales, especially if your company does not do this. Use this calendar to figure out when a product needs to be sold more heavily. Plan to begin your sales promotion well in advance, so that you gain the proper exposure. The time to run a Christmas special is not December 24.

What Can You Do? Brainstorm ways to use as many of the following sales promotions as possible.

1. Demonstrations of new products (either live or on video)

_____

2. Trade show exhibit booths — volunteer to work trade shows that your company is attending, or put together your own booth.

3. Promotional packages — seasonal sales, year-end specials, and our discount coupons. What are some specials you could suggest to your company?

_____

4. Specialty advertising items — ideas for novelties, knickknacks, and other things to be remembered by (be creative):

_____

5. Attractions — celebrity sports, raffles, etc. What would be appropriate for your business?

In addition to devising promotions you launch yourself or present to your company, take advantage of promotions your company sponsors. Volunteer for trade shows, distribute novelties or calendars (with your name, title, and telephone number stamped on them), and get involved to increase your exposure.

WORKSHEET

WHAT'S IN IT FOR YOU?

- **Find creative ways to benefit from free ink in newspapers and trade journals**

PROMOTE YOURSELF

6.4 Publicity

The best advertising is free advertising. Publicity, which can be positive or negative, is a form of free advertising. Let's just concern ourselves with positive publicity.

Exposure in the news media is a promotional tactic that must be orchestrated. Publicity requires a newsworthy event such as a promotion, grand opening, new business, scientific breakthrough, award, or large contract. The event should be described in a press release — a one- to two-page article that can be printed as is or followed up on for more details.

If the news is of greater significance — a scientific breakthrough, for example — a full-length, feature article may be in order. Articles and press releases must be written so that they do not sound like ads. That means no hype, no unsubstantiated claims, and no calls to action.

Sometimes a newspaper will accept an interesting or amusing photograph and caption. A photograph's first priority is journalistic merit; its second is publicizing you, your company, or your product/service.

Letters to the editor also serve as publicity. If you keep abreast of local issues, especially those in business, offer your opinion or insight in a letter. You'd be surprised how many people read the op-ed pages.

Publicity as a means to gain exposure and increase sales often succeeds where advertising fails due to three advantages:

- **Credibility.** People are much more likely to believe the facts in an article than in an advertisement. Most of us are skeptical of ads, but suspend that disbelief when we read an article, which is why the tabloids sell so well.
- **Subtlety.** Readers of press releases and feature articles do not resist the news as they resist other forms of contact.

- **Dramatization.** Advertising tends to make products, services, and companies seem larger than life. Publicity can do the same thing, but in a different way. Publicity can convey the message, "We are your neighbors, with the same concerns that you have. Let's all work together to make this a better community."

Think of three ways to capitalize on each of these forms of publicity.

Press releases:

1. _____
2. _____
3. _____

Feature articles:

1. _____
2. _____
3. _____

Photographs:

1. _____
2. _____
3. _____

Letters to the Editor:

1. _____
2. _____
3. _____

Publicity, unlike advertising, is an occasional promotional strategy. The results are long term, and may not even be measurable. With advertising, you can pick the location of an ad in a publication. With publicity, you are completely at the mercy of the editor, which is why public relations firms are necessary. Their strategic knowledge and working relationships with editors will give you and your company a better shot at getting exposure.

I D E A

WHAT'S IN IT FOR YOU?

- Determine ways to get involved in the community and gain favorable publicity
- Understand who your "publics" are

PROMOTE YOURSELF

6.5 Public Relations

Public relations and publicity are often confused. Public relations is simply the company's image — or your image — in relation to the community. Positive P.R. comes from the goodwill, altruism, and charity generated by acts as small as sponsoring a Little League team or as large as donating a building to a local university.

As an individual salesperson, you can gain excellent exposure for yourself by getting involved in your local community. Join the Chamber of Commerce, volunteer at the Lung Association, answer phones at the Cancer Society, register people to vote, or spend time at a children's hospital. Do whatever altruistic deeds interest you, but do something!

You want to convey that

- You care about your community and have a long-term interest in it
- You are an expert in your field
- You are open and accessible to help customers and noncustomers alike.

WHO ARE YOUR "PUBLICS"?

"Publics" are groups of people who perceive you as a businessperson. Some publics act on their perceptions to increase your sales; others just like you as a person. It is important to identify your publics and choose promotional strategies that will increase your profile with the most important ones. For example, if you sell real estate, your publics are bankers, loan officers, people in title and escrow companies, other brokers, attorneys, property managers, and real estate buyers and sellers in your community.

HOW DO YOU REACH YOUR PUBLICS?

In addition to community volunteer work, there are other ways to get involved.

- Contribute time or money to a worthy cause.
- Sponsor a team — bowling, Little League, volleyball.
- Give speeches or seminars free of charge. For example, an accountant might give a free lecture around tax time. A salesperson with an athletic shoe company might give a speech to high school students about getting

into shape before the summer. The possibilities are unlimited.

- Provide public service spots on local television or radio stations. National Public Radio's local affiliates are often looking for local people to provide two- to three-minute spots about topics of interest.
- Organize an event. You can help put together a celebration or an event to commemorate a city anniversary, honor a local hero, or start an annual charity gold tournament.
- Get involved in trade or professional associations. Show that you care about the industry by volunteering for committees.

Rub shoulders with the right people and doors begin to open.

W O R K S H E E T

WHAT'S IN IT FOR YOU?

• **Brainstorm ways to promote yourself using all the strategies discussed**

PROMOTE YOURSELF

6.6 Promotional Strategies Worksheet

List all the creative ways you can think of to promote yourself and your company, using each of the following methods.

Advertising:_____

_____

Publicity:_____

_____

Clubs/organizations: _____

_____

Brochures: _____

_____

Newsletters: _____

_____

Yellow Pages:_____

_____

Seminars/speaking: _____

_____

Publishing:_____

_____

Directories:_____

_____

Congratulation/welcome letters: _____

_____

Online communications: _____

_____

Other:_____

_____

IDEA

PROMOTE YOURSELF

6.7 Promote Yourself in Print

Publishing articles in local newspapers, magazines, trade journals, or company newsletters can help you gain clients, credibility, and recognition.

The best type of article for the beginning writer to tackle is the list article. It is easy to write, useful, and highly salable. In a list article, you discuss several points under a single theme, but its format gives you the freedom to jump from one topic to another. You do not have to worry about creating smooth transitions from one paragraph or section to the next. The beauty of the list article is that it is the perfect vehicle for you to show your expertise. You can address a specific problem or issue in a how-to style. There are several types of list articles.

THE PROBLEM-SOLVING LIST ARTICLE

This is the most common form of list article. It answers the primary question posed in the article's introduction by devoting one item in the list to each solution. For example, a financial planner could write an article on how to avoid real estate taxes. The article could list five ways and discuss each individually.

THE STEP-BY-STEP LIST ARTICLE

This type of article uses a cookbook approach to giving information. For example, a salesperson in your industry might write an article on negotiating. The order of the steps would be important, as they would be in a recipe.

THE GENERAL INFORMATION LIST

Some articles list information about people, places, companies, or products/services of interest. In this type of article, it is important to give the criteria on which your selection was made. For example, if you write an article on the five best ways to get leads in your business, tell your readers why these ways are the best.

The key to writing anything is organization and editing. Start out by organizing your article into an introduction, a list, and a conclusion. Outline as much as possible before sitting down to write. After you've written the article, let it sit for a few days. Then come back to it and read it again. Edit or rewrite spots that need work, and then give it to someone else for an objective opinion. Keep your ego out of the process, and remember that writing well takes patience and practice.

I D E A

• **Learn some valuable speech-making tips**

PROMOTE YOURSELF

6.8 Promote Yourself on the Podium

Whether you are selling yourself or your company, giving speeches will go along way toward increasing your exposure, your credibility, and your sales. Public speaking is many people's number one fear. Like everything else, however, it gets easier with practice. Keep these tips in mind as you prepare to mount the podium.

Give Yourself a Mental Edge. Realize that your audience will be with you, not against you. Think of the experience as a dialogue rather than a monologue.

Know Your Audience. What are their backgrounds, expectations, and business positions?

Define the Purpose of Your Speech. Is it to motivate, educate, persuade, or sell?

Use Visual Aids. Some speeches — especially brief ones — are fine without visual aids; others desperately need them.

Create a Catchy Title. A clever title not only describes your speech, it piques your audience's curiosity.

Do Your Homework. Company records, the library, magazines, and telephone interviews of industry experts are all sources of interesting information for your speech.

To put your speech together well, follow these steps.

Stay with an Outline. Think in terms of beginning, middle, and end of the speech. Edit your outline to include only relevant topics.

Concentrate on the Introduction and Conclusion. First, make a connection with your audience and answer the question, "Why should they listen to me?" Do it with impact. For your conclusion, do not simply restate your main points. Conclude by summarizing, but do it in a way that puts everything in a broader, more significant perspective. Your conclusion has to send people away changed (even slightly) for the better.

Use Statistics Wisely. Statistics can impress people, or put them to sleep. Consider the nature of your audience. If you are speaking to a group of engineers, use statistics. If you are talking to Socializers and Relaters, forget the statistics and use graphics instead. (See Section 8 for explanations of these types.)

Plan a Q&A Period. It is a good idea to rehearse the answers to probable questions. Put the Q&A session before your conclusion. This will allow you to tactfully cut off the questions and end your speech in control, with your ideas.

Use Index Cards. Know your material well enough to speak extemporaneously, with notes on index cards to jog your memory.

A speech is not unlike a sales presentation. The audience may be larger and the speech may be longer, but the following principles apply to both.

Rehearse Regularly. Practice your speech aloud in front of a mirror as often as necessary until it is smooth. Time your speech. Learn to pause. Record yourself and be ready for a surprise, but learn from it.

Make Sure All Systems Are Go. If you can, check out the room before your presentation. Make sure the P.A. system works, the slide projector is loaded and has a spare bulb, and the room temperature and lighting are comfortable.

Control Your Stage Fright. Everyone, yes, everyone, gets butterflies before going on stage. Expect stage fright but minimize it. Take some deep breaths. Tell yourself, "I am the expert; these people are going to like me; I don't have to be perfect (no one is) and I'm going to do a great job."

Vary Your Eye Contact During the Speech. You'll relax more if you realize you are talking to nice people. Look at a lot of different people. Keep your eyes moving around the room and make a connection with your audience. They'll appreciate it as well.

Move Around During Your Speech. Few great speakers stand behind a podium as if they were perfectly relaxed robots. They wander around, become animated, go out into the audience, and get people involved.

Persist. Comedians know this well. You cannot quit after you have died on stage. It happens to everyone. Come back for more. Practice. Improve yourself. The payoff could be tremendous.

IDEA

- **Discover an effective way to organize a direct mail campaign**
- **Generate 320 new prospects**
- **Avoid sales slumps**

PRECONDITION YOUR PROSPECTS WITH DIRECT MAIL

6.9 The Direct Mail Solution

Virtually every salesperson has experienced sales slumps, but few have mastered prospecting techniques that avoid them. The following direct mail system will eliminate or greatly reduce a sales slump by creating a steady stream of prospects. It will turn cold calling into warm calling, because it minimizes the chance that a prospect will ask "Who are you?" when you call. This unique system has several important elements.

1. You must work it for 90 days before modifying it to fit your personality, company, or industry.
2. It may take three to six months to smooth out your sales, depending on the normal cycle of your product or service.
3. It is more important for prospects to see your letter than it is to read it.
4. You are not trying to trigger a prospect's need — you are trying to establish name and company recognition. There is a big difference.

THE FOUR-LETTER-A-DAY SYSTEM

Your goal is to send one letter a week for four weeks to each prospect, then call for an appointment three to five days after sending the last letter. This is done by sending out four letters a day to your target market. Do not, however, send out more than four letters a day. After a couple of weeks, you will be sending out 12 to 16 letters a day. (First letters, second letters, third letters, etc.) If you become overly enthusiastic and contact more than four new prospects a day, you will be overwhelmed when it comes time to follow up.

If you have a computer, the system is quite easy. If you do not have a computer, farm out the work. Start by writing and entering the four letters (samples follow). Then enter the first month's 80 prospects (four a day for 20 days). Next, print out all 320 letters, but stagger the dates printed on the letters. This will take some calculating, so use a calculator and think in terms of groups of four every day, starting with letter one in the first week.

After you have printed and signed all 320 letters, put them in envelopes. Before you seal them, write the date on which each letter should be mailed in the upper right corner. On the appropriate day, you will cover that spot with a stamp. Finally, print out a list of your prospects and the date they should have received the fourth letter so you will know when to call them.

Adapted from *Direct Mail for Sales People* by Rick Barrera. Rick Barrera & Associates, P.O. Box 1466, Rancho Santa Fe, CA 92067.

IDEA

• Learn the key elements that make a direct mail letter effective

PRECONDITION YOUR PROSPECTS WITH DIRECT MAIL

6.10 Letters That Make Impressions

Although your letter may not be read from beginning to end, it must at least make an impression. To make an impression, it must be opened and read at least briefly. A letter that looks personal has the best chance of being opened.

How do you make a letter look personal?

- Address the envelope by hand or typewriter, not with a mailing label or personal computer. Also, write out the return address with your company name. A return address printed on the back of the envelope looks personal.
- Put a stamp on the envelope. Do not use a postage meter.
- To insure that the letter gets opened first, make it lumpy. Why lumpy? When lumpy mail arrives, the recipient thinks, "What could this be? It must be a gift!" The letter gets opened. Try enclosing a cassette, a novelty, a piece of candy . . . anything related to the message you are conveying.

FIVE KEYS TO EFFECTIVE LETTERS

1. Use a headline and a p.s. They should work together to convey your message succinctly, just in case the body of the letter is not read . . . and it usually isn't.
2. Write an upbeat, fun letter that focuses on problem solving. Write several letters and get feedback from people. Edit, rewrite, and perfect them before you mail them. Remember, you need to have four well-written letters.
3. Include a postage-paid reply card. This makes it easy for your prospect to respond.
4. Include a phone number, preferably a toll-free 800 number. This will encourage even more response than a reply card.
5. Follow the guidelines in worksheet 6.2, "Key Elements of Your Letters."

I D E A

PRECONDITION YOUR PROSPECTS WITH DIRECT MAIL

6.11 Two Sample Letters

These two sample letters illustrate catchy headlines, brief, easy-to-read text, and effective use of a p.s.

Are You Tired of Feeling Like Goldilocks?

Dear_____ :

First you look at one hotel and the meeting space is too big . . . then you look at another hotel and it is too small . . . but at the Hotel Barbera you will find the meeting space is just right!!

Because of our flexible design system, we can customize our space to fit your needs exactly. Try us. We are the sensible alternative.

Sincerely,

Rick Barbera

p.s. Because we are at the world's largest airport, you will also find flight schedules that fit just right.

sent by: Hotel Salesperson
target market: Corporate and Association Meeting Planners

Prescription Without Diagnosis Is Malpractice

Dear _____:

In business as in medicine we believe this is a truism. That is why I'd like to meet with you soon to learn more about your business and to help you find some creative ways to meet your goals.

I'll be calling you in a couple of days to set up an appointment for us to get together.

Sincerely,
Rick Barbera

p.s. I've enclosed a copy of our latest issue. The article on page 10 might be of particular interest to you.

sent by: Newspaper Advertising Salesperson
target market: Advertisers

W O R K S H E E T

WHAT'S IN IT FOR YOU?

• **Create an effective sales letter, step-by-step**

PRECONDITION YOUR PROSPECTS WITH DIRECT MAIL

6.12 Key Elements of Your Letters

Other time-tested elements also increase the chances of a letter's success. Not every letter will incorporate every element below. Pick and choose as you need them.

1. **Make it personal.** For immediate identification, your letterhead should appear at the top. And you should always use the prospect's name in the salutation. Form letters almost always end up in the garbage.

2. **Cover only one idea.** Sell one thing at a time. You can sell a product, service, your company, or yourself, but make it just one thing. Keep the letter focused and simple.
   The purpose of your letter is_____

3. **Sell benefits, not features.** Remember, you are a problem solver, not an educator. Don't try to overwhelm people. Just write about two or three of the most important benefits. The three benefits you will mention in your letter will be:
   a._____
   b._____
   c._____

4. **Write for readability.** Letters that are one page (maximum) in length and broken up into four or five paragraphs are easy to read. Consult an artist or direct mail specialist for ideas on how to make your letter attractive and inviting.

5. **Write with a logical flow.** Take the time to write out your answers to the questions that will naturally flow into your reader's minds:
   What is it? (Simple description) _____
   What does it do? _____
   How would I use it? _____
   Why do I need it? _____

How can I be sure this is a legitimate offer and a good value? _____

_____

What risks are involved for me? _____

Is it guaranteed? _____

How much does it cost?_____

How do I get one?_____

6. **Make a claim.** Tell your reader what is different and better about your product, service, company, or you. This claim goes beyond the simple description. Your claim is: _____

    _____

7. **Give examples.** Examples speak louder than descriptions and claims. Tell a brief success story. Use statistics and dollar amounts if you can. An example you can use is: _____

    _____

8. **Use testimonials.** Most prospects will read a direct mail letter with skepticism. Testimonials add credibility to your claims and examples, especially if they are from high-profile experts. List three people that would give you an impressive testimonial:

    a._____

    b._____

    c._____

9. **Guarantee your claim.** Money-back guarantees are powerful motivators. They take the risk out of buying. If you can, offer a guarantee and watch your response rate soar! Your guarantee will be: _____

    _____

10. **Include a call for action.** At the end of your letter, give your readers a nudge to get them to call or write. Your call for action will be: _____

    _____

11. **Make it easy to respond.** The easier, the better. Toll-free numbers make responding effortless. Self-addressed stamped envelopes are second best. If you promise to make a follow-up call (also desirable), be sure you call within two weeks. Your prospects will respond by:_____

    _____

(We highly recommend the book *Words That Sell* by Richard Bayan.)

W O R K S H E E T

WHAT'S IN IT FOR YOU?

• **Structure your next letter for maximum effect**

PRECONDITION YOUR PROSPECTS WITH DIRECT MAIL

6.13 Designing Your Own Direct Mail Letter

Use the sections below to guide you in designing your own direct mail letter:

• **Headline:**

_____

_____

_____

• **Key points for the body of your letter:**

_____

_____

_____

_____

_____

_____

_____

_____

_____

_____

• **P.S.:**

_____

_____

_____

• **Enclosure:**

_____

_____

W O R K S H E E T

WHAT'S IN IT FOR YOU?

• **Determine the specifications of your mailing list**
• **Determine the break-even return of your direct mail campaign**
• **Increase your understanding of some of the requirements of a direct mail campaign**

PRECONDITION YOUR PROSPECTS WITH DIRECT MAIL

6.14 Mailing List Checklist

Before you compile or buy a mailing list, you must know the "specifications" of your list. Fill in as many of the details as you can, and research what you don't know.

1. What are the characteristics of individuals and companies in your target market?
   Geographic location (s): _____
   Specific zip codes:_____
   Age range: _____
   Yearly income: _____
   Educational background:_____
   Occupations/industries: _____
   Interests:_____
   Targeted needs: _____

2. In what form will you need the mailing list?
   _____Computer disk (best for multiple use)
   _____Address labels (best for one-time use)

3. Will the list broker guarantee the list is current? What percentage can be guaranteed as "deliverable" or "clean"?_____

4. What is the total number of pieces to be mailed?_____

5. Will you need a disk so you can personalize letters through your computer's mail–merge function? _____

6. Will you enclose a brochure or other material that will need folding and stuffing? Who will do that work? _____

7. If you are sending over 500 pieces, you can use a bulk mail permit. Have you contacted the post office for details on doing so? _____

8. How many sales do you need to make this direct mail campaign break even?_____ To make a profit? _____How much of a profit would you like in order to consider this mailing worth the effort?_____

9. Based on your answers to the questions above, what response rate do you need to reach your goals (based on your sales/call average)? _____

10. Follow-up calls dramatically increase your response rate and overall success. Will phone number be supplied with the list and are calls possible within the target market? _____

11. Who will make the follow-up phone calls?_____

WORKSHEET

WHAT'S IN IT FOR YOU?

- An awareness of all expenses before you commit to the mailing so there will be no surprises later.

PRECONDITION YOUR PROSPECTS WITH DIRECT MAIL

6.15 Direct Mail Campaign Budget

You need to know the cost of a direct mail campaign to make it successful. Use this worksheet to estimate costs, and you'll be able to pinpoint the response you need to break even.

Name: _____

Mail Piece: _____

Objective: _____

Date: _____

Prepared by: _____

A. Direct Expenses

1. Planning/Administrative/Operating
   Salaries (Man Hours x Hourly Rate) $_____

2. Creative Costs/Preparations
   - a. Copy $ _____
   - b. Layout $ _____
   - c. Artwork $ _____
   - d. Photography/Retouching $ _____
   - e. Printing Preparation $ _____ $_____

3. Other enclosure $_____

4. Envelopes $_____

5. Mailing list rental/purchase $_____

6. Mailing list maintenance $_____

7. Mailing piece preparation $_____
   (folding, collating, inserting, labeling, addressing,
   metering, sorting, typing, etc.) $_____

8. Postage
   - a. Outgoing $_____
   - b. Return $_____ $_____

9. If Selling Merchandise
   a. Cost of merchandise $ _____
   b. Handling $ _____
   c. Postage/shipping $ _____
   d. Royalties $ _____
   e. Refunds/cancellations $ _____
   f. Refurbish returns $ _____
   g. Bad debts $ _____
   h. Storage $ _____ $ _____

10. Other $ _____

TOTAL DIRECT EXPENSES $ _____

I D E A

• An awareness of the many sources of mailing lists

PRECONDITION YOUR PROSPECTS WITH DIRECT MAIL

6.16 Sources of Direct Mail Lists

There are innumerable sources for prospects and information on companies in every industry. For ideas, pick the brain of a reference librarian at a large public or university library. The following categories of sources should not only get you started, but take you a long way:

Professional and trade associations

Clubs (golf, tennis, and other hobby and sport clubs)

Civic Groups (Kiwanis, Lions, Optimists)

Community business groups (Chambers of commerce, convention and tourism groups)

Magazines (lists of subscribers)

Women's organizations (NOW, League of Women Voters)

Special interest groups (Greenpeace, Cousteau Society, NAACP)

Business directories (Moody's, Poor's, Thomas Register)

The Yellow Pages

Religious groups (churches, businesses catering to religion)

List brokers (Dun & Bradstreet, TRW, local companies)

SECTION SEVEN

CONTACTING PROSPECTS

WHAT'S IN IT FOR YOU?

- Use the four basic contact methods effectively.
- Discover how to get the most out of telephone prospecting calls.
- Write effective business letters.
- Make the most of in-person calls.
- Tap the power of online contacts.

There are really only four ways to contact a prospect — by mail, by phone, by computer, and in person. Each makes a different impression and has its advantages and disadvantages. In this section, we'll show how to use the four methods most effectively.

I D E A

MAXIMIZE PROSPECT CONTACTS

7.1 Partner or Persuader?

Years ago, Jim Cathcart worked as a bill collector in the hills of northern Arkansas. His job was to repossess log trucks from past due customers — a very threatening job with severe challenges every day. While performing that job, Jim learned a principle that has applied to almost every business dealing he has been involved in: the principle of *partner versus persuader*. In any situation, the other person perceives you as a partner who will assist in getting where he or she wants to go, or an adversary who will inhibit progress.

Jim found that when he tried to collect bills treating people as a "misbehaving past due customer," he always met with resistance. But when he approached the customer as a partner in problem solving, he always got cooperation.

Likewise, the frame of mind in which you approach each contact will make a big difference in the way your customer responds to you. Before each sales call, set aside your concerns about making the sale, and focus on making life better for the customer. Ask yourself, in what ways can I help this customer? In what ways will this customer be better off by dealing with me? As you proceed, be a partner by helping the customer solve the problem of not yet enjoying the services or benefits that you can provide. In this way, you'll avoid being seen as the "persuader" who is there to talk the customer into buying. Since you're not trying to talk the customer into buying, he or she has no reason to resist, and will feel comfortable telling you the truth.

Partner or persuader. It makes all the difference in the world. Which one are you?

IDEA

MAXIMIZE PROSPECT CONTACTS

7.2 Only Four Ways to Make Contact

There are only four ways to contact a prospect: in person, by letter, by computer, or over the phone. Each has its advantages and disadvantages.

The quality of a contact depends on its effectiveness. Its effectiveness is determined by your ability to receive feedback from the prospect and your ability to reach some degree of resolution. The resolution doesn't have to be "the big close" — a commitment to the next step in the sales process will do. Using this criteria, personal contacts provide the best opportunity for feedback, both verbal and nonverbal. The computer and telephone are somewhat less effective means of contact, and direct mail is the least effective for generating feedback.

The number of contacts generated by a given contact method is inversely related to the degree of personal contact involved. Obviously, direct mail and online marketing let you reach more people than the telephone, and the telephone lets you reach more people than in-person calls.

Whatever your method of contact, it must be accomplished in ways that are

- Conducive to business
- Cost-effective
- Image-effective
- Tension reducing
- Trust-building

If you were to grade the four ways to contact people, they would receive report cards that look like this:

Type of Contact	Quantity Possible	Quality Possible
In-person	C	A
Telephone	B	B
Letter	A	C
Computer	A	B

There is no *best* way to contact a prospect. The most effective approach is to use all four in an organized, ongoing effort. The best results will be generated when you continually send letters, follow up with phone calls, and make appointments to meet prospects in person. Many people start by sending a letter to a large number of people. The leads that come from those letters are then called on the phone for appointments. Finally, at the face-to-face (high quality) meeting, the salesperson can really begin to build trust and establish the relationship. This is one of many possible combinations. Only you can determine the best strategy for your business.

To maximize your selling time, remember Pareto's 80–20 rule: 20 percent of your accounts will represent 80 percent of your sales volume. After you have categorized your accounts into A, B, C accounts, you will know which companies (the As) deserve the highest quality contact; that is, frequent personal visits. Your B accounts will receive fewer personal visits and more phone calls. The C accounts will be contacted primarily by letter, phone, computer, and occasionally in person.

I D E A

WHAT'S IN IT FOR YOU?

- • **Understand how you are perceived based on the way you contact prospects and customers**

MAXIMIZE PROSPECT CONTACTS

7.3 The Customer Perception Matrix

The way you contact a customer will determine the way or ways that he or she perceives you. These perceptions could be limited or unlimited depending on the method you choose. Being aware of the limitations will help you choose the most appropriate way to contact prospects and customers.

MODES OF PERCEPTION			
Ways to Contact	**Verbal**	**Vocal**	**Visual**
Letter	Words	Boldface	
		Italics	Quality
		Quotes	Type style
		Underline	Illustrations
		All caps	Brochures
Phone	Words	Enthusiasm	
		Accent	
		Volume	Mental pictures
		Pacing	
In person	Words	Enthusiasm	
		Accent	Image/looks
		Volume	Facial expressions
		Pacing	Body language
Computer	Words	Boldface	Resolution
		Italics	Quality
		Quotes	Type style
		Underline	Illustrations
		All caps	

W O R K S H E E T

WHAT'S IN IT FOR YOU?

- **Brainstorm the use of sales promotions for personal advancement**

MAXIMIZE PROSPECT CONTACTS

7.4 Common Brush-Offs

Occasionally you run into a prospect who tries to give you the brush-off before you've even had a chance to identify yourself. We've all heard the excuses: "I'm too busy," "I have everything I need," "I'm not interested," or "Not today."

In Section 10, we will discuss specific ways to handle these brush-offs. For now, it would be a valuable exercise to become aware of your five most common "early" prospect excuses.

1. Common Excuse: _____

    Your Response: _____

2. Common Excuse: _____

    Your Response: _____

3. Common Excuse: _____

    Your Response: _____

4. Common Excuse: _____

    Your Response: _____

5. Common Excuse: _____

    Your Response: _____

W O R K S H E E T

WHAT'S IN IT FOR YOU?

- Organize yourself before each call
- Save time by having concrete purposes for each sales call
- Have complete prospect information in front of you during each call

MAXIMIZE PROSPECT CONTACTS

7.5 Sales Planning Guide

Before you call on an account, you must have a purpose for the call. It can be as simple as calling to confirm that a delivery arrived on time, or as complex as a meeting face-to-face for an information-gathering session. No matter what the reason, the more organized you are, the greater your chances are of accomplishing your objective for the call. Answer the most relevant questions below before each call.

Company _____ Type of Business _____

Location_____ Phone _____ Date _____

Key Contact _____ Title_____

Who is the decision maker? _____

Current Situation? _____

_____

Goals and Objectives? _____

_____

Potential Problem(s)/Need(s)? _____

_____

What objectives should I seek to accomplish with this account?_____

_____

Next Call: _____

Overall:_____

If the key contact is not the decision maker, how can he/she influence the objective(s) I am trying to achieve? _____

_____

What questions can I ask to uncover, clarify, or amplify prospect problems, needs, and/or goals? _____

_____

What decision-making criteria are important to the prospect?_____

_____

_____

Possible Benefits Prospect Is Seeking _____

_____

_____

Service/Company Features That Provide Those Benefits _____

_____

_____

Proof Material (Letters, Brochures, Testimonials, To Be Used If Necessary) _____

_____

_____

How can I be of more benefit to this prospect than anyone else who has called on him/her?_____

_____

Possible Prospect Objections_____

_____

Potential Answers_____

_____

Based on my objective(s), what specific commitment will I ask this prospect to make?

_____

Why should the prospect want to make this commitment? _____

_____

By what criteria will the prospect judge whether or not my products/service/company was a satisfactory solution to his problem/need? _____

_____

_____

What methods, procedures, or forms can I use to measure whether or not the actual results did in fact meet the above criteria? _____

_____

_____

IDEA

- **Gain access to your prospect**
- **Get more appointments**

CONTACTING BY PHONE

7.6 Using the Phone as a Prospecting Tool

There are three key points to remember when using the phone as a prospecting tool. First, prepare beforehand. Research the company and the prospect and plan your strategy as well as some questions to ask. Second, remember that your objective is to get an appointment — *not* to make a sale. Finally, because prospects dislike receiving cold calls, a script is imperative. Ideas 7.7 through 7.13 show you how to write a smooth, effective script that will sound natural and put your prospect at ease.

The following guidelines are designed to increase your effectiveness on the phone. Keep these handy until the techniques become automatic.

For initial phone contacts:

- Ask the president's assistant for the name of the executive level person responsible for making decisions about your product
- Use the assistant's name in your introduction.

To gain access to the prospect:

- Ask for a direct-dial number.
- Leave a voice-mail message if the decision maker is not available. Repeat your name and number at the end of your message.
- Call before or after regular business hours, at lunch, or Saturday morning.
- Get the person who referred you to this prospect to make a call on your behalf.
- Ask for the prospect by his or her first name.
- Build a relationship with gatekeepers (that is, switchboard operators, secretaries, assistants, etc.).
- State your name/company clearly.
- Address the person by his/her name.
- Give the reason for your call; explain that you need just a minute to follow up on correspondence.

- Ask for your prospect to be paged, if necessary.
- Ask their advice if you're having difficulty getting through.
- Ask for names of others within the company who may be interested in your product or service.
- Limit your efforts to three calls, then a letter or fax, then three more calls.
- Use an original attention-getting approach if you aren't getting anywhere (one appropriate for you and the customer), such as signing a telegram, a letter of introduction from a mutual acquaintance, or sending a box of candy with a note saying you have a sweet idea to share with the customer if he'll meet with you in person.
- Keep a telephone log, and analyze it to determine good times to call and to identify which areas of your telephone skills most need improvement.

I D E A

- **Develop clear, concise openings for cold calls on the phone**
- **Put cold-call prospects at ease**
- **Get your cold-call phone presentations off to a good start**

CONTACTING BY PHONE

7.7 Introducing Yourself and Your Company

Most people don't like receiving cold calls. So remember, first impressions are important. Above all, be clear and concise when identifying yourself. Avoid lengthy explanations such as, "Hello, Mrs. Jones, this is Artimus Hercules Seidenspinner the Third with Goldstar Audio and Video Recording, which is a wholly-owned subsidiary of the United Electronics Consortium based in London." Forget it — your prospect will get lost in the maze of words. Just say, "Hello, Mrs. Jones, this is Art with Goldstar Recording, and this is what we do . . ."

Take some time to think about how you introduce yourself to a customer. Are you too talkative? Do you make it easy for the consumer?

I D E A

- **Put a phone prospect at ease**
- **Increase your chances of making the sale**

CONTACTING BY PHONE

7.8 Taking the Pressure Off the Call

Many prospects, especially consumers at home, immediately think to themselves, "Oh, brother, another sales call. What is this guy going to try to sell me now?" If you are calling a prospect at work, your call is an interruption. Make a statement that takes the rudeness out of the interruption, such as, "If you have a minute, I'd like to briefly introduce myself and tell you what we do. Would that be OK?" Or, "I'd like to take a moment to tell you who we are and what we do. Is this a good time for you?" If it's not a good time, ask when would be a better time. This way you don't waste your customer's (or your) time.

Think about making cold calls. Do you try to take the pressure off your prospect? Can you think of ways to sound more natural and put the consumer at ease?

I D E A

- **Establish rapport with your prospect by clarifying the reason for your call**
- **Increase your chances for moving the prospect toward confirmation**

CONTACTING BY PHONE

7.9 Explaining the Purpose of the Call

After you take the pressure off your prospect, you should follow with a brief, hard-hitting statement that explains why you have called. Do not, however, describe any of the benefits that you will present later. Some possible purposes for your call are:

- **To follow up to see if a direct mail piece was received**

   "Mr. Smith, this is Gene Kelly with Toes-A-Tappin'. I just wanted to see if you received the brochure I sent you last week on our dancing services?" If Mr. Smith says no, you can say, "May I take a minute or so now to tell you what it's all about?"

- **To mention a person who referred you to this prospect**

   "Mrs. Jones, a good friend of yours, Ernest Merritt, suggested I call you. He thought you would be interested in knowing about our personalized security service."

- **To tell your prospect about a product/service your company has designed that is of particular interest to people like the prospect**

   "Dr. Lee, if you have a minute or so, I'd like to quickly tell you about our health insurance billing software that we designed specifically for chiropractors."

- **To follow up on the prospect's response to your company's advertising**

   "Mrs. Ledyard, I'm calling in response to your inquiry about our financial planning services. Is this a good time for me to answer any questions you may have?"

Why are you calling your prospect? Think of other clear, concise ways to explain your purpose to your customer.

IDEA

- Draw the prospect into the conversation to identify benefits to the prospect
- Increase the likelihood of a sale

CONTACTING BY PHONE

7.10 Capturing Interest with a Powerful Statement

To answer two of the prospect's questions — "What's this all about?" and "What's in it for me?" — make a claim that includes a benefit, financial reward, or service. An example: "Mr. Schmidt, our software was designed to increase your staff's productivity by 25 percent while also decreasing overhead by 15 percent. And I'm aware of several companies in your industry that have achieved even better results. Are those numbers that you would like to achieve?"

Asking a question after your captivating statement will help keep your prospect's attention focused on you and your claim. What kind of captivating statement do you make about your products? Can you think of a strong follow-up question to that captivating claim?

I D E A

WHAT'S IN IT FOR YOU?

• **Increase prospect involvement**
• **Increase potential for a sale**

CONTACTING BY PHONE

7.11 Making a Request from your Prospect

If you don't ask, you don't get. So ask for an appointment, for an address where you can send more information, or for a sale — whatever is appropriate to your situation. If you are asking for an appointment, it's a good idea to tell your prospect how much time you are requesting. "I can show you everything in about 20 minutes. When might be a good time for us to get together?"

Avoid giving part of your presentation on the phone. That puts you at a significant disadvantage. Because selling is very much a people business, the opportunity to meet face-to-face can help create a rapport — and often close a sale.

Think about your current phone script. Do you ask for the appointment? the address? the sale? How might you improve your relationship with your existing customers? How might you establish a rapport with new prospects?

IDEA

- **Handle customer objections in a reasonable, positive way**
- **Increase the likelihood of a sale**

CONTACTING BY PHONE

7.12 Overcoming Resistance

Two immediate objections come up when you use the phone as a means to contact prospects; they object to taking the phone call, and they object to granting an appointment.

To deal with the first objection, be sensitive to their needs. "If I caught you at a bad time, Mrs. Smith, I can call back at another time." Handle the second objection by reassuring the prospect that an appointment will only take a short time and that your purpose is simply to introduce your product/service to see if there might be some basis for doing business together. "Mr. Green, there are some people that this service can help and others who do not need it. I don't know which you are, but after ten minutes with you, we'll both know. If it's not for you, I'll be the first to tell you."

How do you currently respond to customer objections? Can you think of ways to overcome them consistently?

I D E A

WHAT'S IN IT FOR YOU?

- **Move the sale forward**
- **Increase the likelihood of a sale**
- **Identify customer needs and concerns**

CONTACTING BY PHONE

7.13 Keeping it Brief

Taken together, the five or six elements that follow in your script should take up no more than three-quarters of a page, double-spaced. That's about 30–45 seconds. You should never talk that long before giving the prospect something to respond to. As a rule of thumb, ask the prospect a question every ten seconds or so.

Are you long-winded? Do you take too much of your prospect's time? Think about ways to cut your script to the bare essentials. You may lose customers if you don't.

W O R K S H E E T

WHAT'S IN IT FOR YOU?

- **Develop a plan that will increase your prospecting and sales success on the phone**
- **Identify the greatest possible number of issues for your script**

CONTACTING BY PHONE

7.14 Your Telephone Script

Using the following guidelines, write out several ideas that will help you write the first draft of your script. You can edit and change things later. Right now, brainstorm. (You may want to refer to Ideas 7.8 through 7.14.)

1. A two-sentence introduction of yourself and your company:

_____

_____

2. A short statement that takes the pressure off the call:

_____

_____

3. The purpose of your call (two sentences maximum):

_____

_____

4. A statement that will capture interest (no more than three sentences):

_____

_____

5. How you would like the prospect to respond (two sentences):

_____

_____

6. Two ways to answer your most common objections:

_____

_____

7. One additional way to keep it short, and keep the prospect actively involved in the conversation:

_____

_____

W O R K S H E E T

WHAT'S IN IT FOR YOU?

• **Organize and make the most of each sales call**

CONTACTING BY PHONE

7.15 The Telephone Planning Sheet

Fill in the following information before you call:

Industry segment: _____

Company: _____

Name: _____

Primary purpose of call: _____

Best time to call: _____

Opening statement: _____

Key points to cover: _____

Information to ask for: _____

Commitment to ask for: _____

Key phrases (if any): _____

W O R K S H E E T

WHAT'S IN IT FOR YOU?

• Keep track of your calls and remember their outcomes

CONTACTING BY PHONE

7.16 The Telephone Log

Activity Log						
Sales Professional_____ Date _____						
Company	**Contact**	**Type of Call**	**Rating (A, B, C)**	**Comments–Outcome**	**Time In**	**Time Out**

Type of Call   PA = Phone Appointment   P = Presentation   V = Appointment (Visit)
I = Incoming Call   S = Status/Follow-up   CC = Cold Call   L = Lunch

I D E A

WHAT'S IN IT FOR YOU?

• **Place your calls when prospects and customers are most receptive**

CONTACTING BY PHONE

7.17 The Best Times to Call

Type of People	Best Time to Call
Executives/Business owners	After 10:30 am
Physicians	11:00 am, 1:00–3:00 pm, 7:00–9:00 pm
CPAs	Anytime other than tax season
Publishers/Printers	After 3:00 pm
Engineers/Chemists	4:00–5:00 pm
Contractors/Builders	Before 9:00 am, after 5:00 pm
Clergy	Between Tuesday & Friday
Dentists	Before 9:30 am
Druggists	1:00–3:00 pm
Attorneys	11:00 am–2:00 pm, after 5:00 pm
Homemakers	11:00–noon; 2:00–4:30 pm
Professors/Teachers	At home, 7:00–9:00 pm
Butchers/Grocers	Before 9:00 am; 1:00–2:30 pm

IDEA

• Get a better picture of what you do well and what needs improvement

CONTACTING BY PHONE

7.18 Playing by the Numbers

Most salespeople dislike recordkeeping. It's just one more thing to do during the day. Recordkeeping is a necessary part of your job, however. Without it, you would be in the dark about your performance and ways to improve it. This is especially true for telephone work. You have to keep track of everything during the sales process, from the number of calls you make to the sales you confirm.

Calls (a.k.a. dials) per day shows the effort you are making.

Contacts (a.k.a. reaches) per day shows whether you are calling at the right time. Are you reaching your goal each day?

Appointments set per day shows how good your telephone skills are. You may have a goal set for this as well.

Meetings (actual appointments kept) show how many of your appointments are canceled versus kept.

Number of sales shows how good your presentation and sales skills are.

Referrals show you the number and quality of this source of prospects.

At the end of each month, do some simple math with the month's figures.

Number of reaches ÷ Number of dials. The closer this ratio is to one, the better you are at reaching your prospects in when you call.

Number of appointments set ÷ number of reaches. This ratio will show you how many calls you have to make to get an appointment.

Number of appointments ÷ number of actual meetings. If this ratio is low, you are getting a lot of cancellations. You may be manipulating your prospects into saying yes.

Number of sales ÷ number of meetings. If this ratio is low, you need to hone your presentation or sales skills.

These ratios will indicate two major things: 1) the areas in which you still need training or coaching, and 2) your sales ratios. For example, at your present skill level, you may need to make 20 calls to get five appointments to make one sale. That's a valuable ratio to know!

I D E A

• **Understand your impact on others**

CONTACTING BY PHONE

7.19 Key Telephone Skills

Work on these skills to make your phone contacts more productive.

1. Arrange a specific time each day to make calls.
2. Determine the number of calls to be made, and stick to that number.
3. Establish call objectives before picking up the phone.
4. Fine-tune your script until it is perfect.
5. Internalize your script so it sounds natural.
6. Develop a pleasing voice, which comes with a pleasing attitude.
7. Exude confidence and competence over the phone.
8. Match the vocal pace and task priorities of your prospect.
9. Be sure you know who the decision makers are.
10. Get useful information about decision makers from subordinates.
11. Be polite and you will turn the decision maker's assistant into an *ally*. Use humor if you can. Find out his or her name and use it.
12. If necessary, sell the decision maker's assistant on your product/service. He or she may be the one who makes appointments for the boss.
13. Find the right times to call to increase your chances of getting through.
14. Have your notes and objectives in order before making phone calls.
15. Don't let interruptions break up your phone-calling sessions.
16. Keep records. You can't improve without the insight they provide.
17. Keep yourself motivated. Aim for at least one small success every day.
18. Make phone calls during the time of day that you are most alert and energetic. Mornings work best for most people.
19. No matter where you are in your telephone session, follow up a success with another phone call. Success breeds success.
20. Be sure to pronounce people's names correctly. When in doubt, ask.
21. Be courteous, no matter what. Ask permission to launch into your script. Say thank you. Be sure you are not calling at a bad time.
22. Realize that any time you call you're interrupting, so make calls brief.

IDEA

• **Master the basics of good business writing**

CONTACTING BY LETTER

7.20 Guidelines for Business Letters

Business letters are written contacts with people outside your organization. They can introduce you, confirm appointments, present information and proposals, or capture the particulars of an agreement. They can also congratulate, cajole, admonish, placate, or thank. When they are written well, they enhance you, your reputation, and your business. But when they are poorly written, they will turn off your prospects.

Good business letters combine clear thinking, good organization, and effective presentation. Use proper grammar and spelling, and get to the point quickly. Be clear, courteous, and concise. Remember, your letter represents you and your company. Follow these guidelines and your readers will enjoy reading your letters.

- Hook your reader's interest in the first paragraph with a strong statement of your purpose. Don't beat around the bush. Clearly present your ideas. If you are presenting information or a proposal, emphasize its benefits to the reader.

- Write your letter from your customer's point of view. Take time to anticipate your reader's response, and address it.

- Use short words and phrases. Replace big, stuffy words with smaller words that get right to the point. Say *meet*, not *interact*. *Now*, not *at this point in time*. And never say *utilize* when *use* will do!

- Stick to short paragraphs that contain one idea.

- Consider using bullets and italics to highlight key points.

- Respect your reader's limited time and keep your letter to one page. Brief is always best, especially in the business environment.

- Use lots of white space to make your letter attractive and easy to read.

- Read your letter out loud to see if it sounds clear and pleasant, and if it accomplishes your purpose.

I D E A

• **Learn to write a good letter of introduction**

CONTACTING BY LETTER

7.21 How to Write a Personal Letter of Introduction

It's always awkward when a prospect asks, "Who are you?" when you call on the phone. Letters can help you avoid that.

Writing a letter is not unlike writing a telephone script. Keep it brief. Use a typewriter or computer printer and high quality stationery and break up the text so it reads easily. Follow these basic guidelines to ensure that your letter is effective.

1. Refer to your prospect by name. Look like you've done your homework, and personalize the letter.
2. Identify yourself and your company.
3. Mention who referred you, if possible.
4. State the purpose of the letter. Get to the point quickly.
5. Make your claim. Use benefits, service offers, guarantees.
6. Identify an area of probable interest. In your pre-call planning, you should have uncovered a possible need.
7. Sound like an insider. Use the jargon of your prospect's industry.
8. Give some reason why your customer should see you. Tie the benefits to your prospect's specific situation.
9. Include a brochure. Prospects, especially in technical fields, like to read impressive documents and see pictures of products.
10. Specify a follow-up time. Indicate when you will call or stop by, so your call will be accepted and received.

IDEA

WHAT'S IN IT FOR YOU?

• **Multiply your contacts with online marketing**

CONTACTING BY COMPUTER

7.22 Contacting Prospects Online

The online databases, news groups, forums, and Internet Web pages offer an exciting new way to seek out and contact new prospects.

- By participating in forums and newsgroups that discuss areas of interest to you or your company, you can cultivate a reputation as a knowledgeable source and generate new sales leads. Say, for example, you sell products that cater to children with special needs. By participating in a special needs forum, you can contact parents and teachers who want to educate these children.

- Use an online clipping service to track and save articles about your company or your industry. Send them to prospects or customers the same way you would send a hard copy — but send them by e-mail.

- Spend a few minutes a week browsing the Web for people or companies who match your profile.

- Search online databases for prospects who match your customer profile. Some databases let you dial up their computer, search for, and then download lists of contacts based on SIC code, location, number of employees, sales volume, product, and so forth. All in a matter of minutes!

- Set up a Web site that provides information about your product or service, or offers "extra value." Ragu Spaghetti Sauce offers coupons, promotional items, and recipes on its Web site. UPS and Federal Express let consumers track their packages online. For credibility, include testimonials and lists of clients. Be sure to include your Web site address in all of your printed promotional material.

- Exchange e-mail addresses with your prospects and customers, and you can advance a sale online by instantly responding to queries, transmitting quotes, and so on.

- Whenever you receive a lead online, *respond immediately!* There's no time to dawdle in the cyberspace. Check your e-mail and your newsgroup messages frequently so you can act promptly.

I D E A

WHAT'S IN IT FOR YOU?

• Ensure that your cold calls lead to productive relationships

CONTACTING IN PERSON

7.23 Making the Most of In-person Calls

The fourth method for contacting prospects is the in-person "cold" call. Many salespeople say they don't make cold calls. They respond only to company-supplied leads, advertising inquiries, or referrals. But these salespeople don't realize that every call they make on a new prospect is, in a sense, a cold call. When a salesperson contacts the prospect, that prospect is very likely preoccupied with something else. The salesperson must therefore help that prospect make a mental and physical transition from what they're doing now to what the salesperson would like them to be doing or thinking. In cold call selling, the salesperson may not only be competing with another company for that prospect's business, but more importantly, will very likely be competing for that prospect's time and attention.

Most of the techniques we discussed earlier for phone contacting are applicable to in-person contacts. Remember these key points in preparing for these contacts:

Preparing for the "In-Person" Call:

1. Research the prospect as much as possible beforehand.
2. Prepare some questions to ask (more on this in Section 8, Exploring).
3. Anticipate possible answers, problems, or opportunities.
4. Visualize your success.
5. Role play your cold call with your fellow salespeople or manager.
6. Go over your plan with your sales manager — get feedback.

On the "In-Person" Call:

1. Open with your competitive advantage statement in the first 30 seconds.
2. Don't say, "I was just in the neighborhood."
3. Acknowledge that you had planned to phone; then tie your drop-in to an appointment you just concluded in the same area.
4. Remind the prospect of the letter you already sent.
5. Follow up by sending a letter that summarizes your conversation, whether you get the appointment or not.

Keep in mind that it is the relationship that determines whether two people will want to do business together. The contacting phase, in turn, makes or breaks the relationship. The first minutes with a prospect can forge the nature of a relationship and determine your degree of success in the business.

W O R K S H E E T

WHAT'S IN IT FOR YOU?

• **Learn to convey to your prospects the benefits of meeting with you**

CONTACTING BY PHONE

7.24 Initial Benefit Statements

It is important to start a meeting off on the right foot. Nonmanipulative salespeople go into a meeting with the attitude, "I don't know if I can help you, so I'm here to find out. If my product/service is not what you need, I'll be the first to tell you. If it is what you need, we'll work together to make the sales process a mutually satisfying experience."

Although you don't want to state this attitude verbatim, you do want to convey your flexibility and nonmanipulative M.O. You also want to give your prospect a good idea of what's in it for him. An initial benefit statement tells your prospect what he or she might gain by taking the time to meet with you. For example, "Mr. Jones, I don't know yet if we have a fit between what you need and what I have to offer, but I can tell you that clients who have used my service saved over 50 percent on their photocopy and fax bills. Can we talk about your business for a couple of minutes to see what we might save for you?"

Think of three current customers or prospects with whom you have upcoming appointments. For each appointment, determine the purpose of the call and write an initial benefit statement.

Customer 1: _____

_____

Customer 2: _____

_____

Customer 3: _____

_____

I D E A

WHAT'S IN IT FOR YOU?

• **Gain an awareness of the subtle do's and don'ts of meeting with prospects**

CONTACTING IN PERSON

7.25 In-Person Do's and Don'ts

Do

Relax	Focus on fulfilling genuine needs
Be yourself	Be flexible in every way
Smile	Be patient with the sales process
Maintain eye contact	Maintain the initiative
Be confident	Gear benefits to client's needs
Be friendly and sincere	Be aware of client's time constraints
Be proud of your company	Be sincerely interested
Be sure you are dealing with the decision maker	Remember your call objective
Be sure you've asked for enough time for your presentation	Be enthusiastic and credible
	Be prepared for resistance

Don't

Be pushy	Exaggerate or lie
Be cocky	Rush the sales process
Be demanding	Try to close the sale in your opening statement
Be manipulative	Get drawn into an argument
Be rushed into cutting your presentation short	Recite a canned presentation
Focus on the sale to the exclusion of your prospect's needs	Get defensive
	Be too polished

I D E A

WHAT'S IN IT FOR YOU?

• **Understand the benefits of working a trade show**

TRADE SHOWS

7.26 Why Work a Trade Show?

A trade show is a microcosm of customers and competitors. You can learn a great deal and make many contacts in a very short time. If your company is picking up the tab for the booth, ask if you can help represent the company. If your company does not participate in trade shows, consider doing it yourself. The number of customers attending makes it a very wise use of your time.

1. Customers galore! You can't ask for a faster introduction to a large number of customers. Customers are there to do business. They want to see the latest. They want to be sold, by the right person, of course, but many intend to place orders. For the salesperson who can socialize and sell, there is a lot of money to be made.

2. Easy spying! Many of your competitors will be there. Of course, the secrets they reveal are the ones they want the public to see, but you will learn a lot. By talking to them — either openly or posing as a customer — you will find out about their features, benefits, delivery capabilities, services, guarantees, pricing, and so on.

3. Polish your presentations! Put an end to doubts about your product knowledge or presentation skills. Spending all day giving presentations to prospects will make you the consummate pro.

4. Sell from either side. You don't have to rent a booth to take advantage of a trade show. You can attend and sell to customers who have booths. There is no rule saying that sales must be conducted from a booth. Selling flows both ways. It is less expensive to sell to people at *their* booths.

5. For more information on trade shows, see *How to Participate Profitably in Trade Shows* by Robert B. Konikow, Dartnell Press, 4660 Ravenswood Ave., Chicago, IL 60640.

SECTION EIGHT

SELLING BY THE PLATINUM R

WHAT'S IN IT FOR YOU?

- **Greatly increase your understanding of human nature.**
- **Increase your insight into your own behavioral preferences.**
- **Minimize personality conflicts with people.**
- **Change your behavior in subtle ways to make your prospect more comfortable.**

The Golden Rule tells us to "Do unto others as we would have them do unto us." In other words, treat them as we would like to be treated. It is far more effective to treat others as they would like to be treated. Therefore, we offer you Tony Alessandra's "Platinum Rule": *Do unto others as they would like to be done unto.*

Part of treating others the way they want to be treated is recognizing personal behavioral styles, including your own. By recognizing these styles, you can adapt your behavior to fit others. The relationship strategies in this section will give you the insight needed to quickly get on the same wavelength with virtually anyone.

The first step in understanding behavior styles is to determine your style. Next, you will think about the styles of people with whom you work and live. Finally, you will learn how to specifically change your behaviors to conform to the different styles you meet while selling.

W O R K S H E E T

• Discover whether you are open or guarded

TYPES OF BEHAVIORAL STYLES

8.1 Behavioral Styles Self-Test (Part I)

Read the description on the left side of the page and circle the ones that fit you most of the time. Judging by the number of circled items, determine where you fall on a scale of one through four.

OPEN

OPEN
Relaxed and Warm
Opinion Oriented
Supportive
Flexible About Time
Relationship Oriented
Share Feelings Freely
Sensitive

4 VERY OPEN

3 SOMEWHAT OPEN

GUARDED
Formal and Proper
Fact Oriented
Controlling
Time Disciplined
Task Disciplined
Keeps feelings to Self
Thinking Oriented

2 SOMEWHAT GUARDED

1 VERY GUARDED

GUARDED

W O R K S H E E T

WHAT'S IN IT FOR YOU?

• Discover whether you are direct or indirect

TYPES OF BEHAVIORAL STYLES

8.2 Behavioral Styles Self-Test (Part II)

Read the following descriptions and circle the ones that fit you most of the time. Judging by the number of circled items, determine where you fall on a scale of A through D.

Indirect	Direct
Avoid Risks	Takes Risks
Slow Decision Maker	Swift Decisions
Passive	Aggressive
Easygoing	Impatient
Listens Well	Talkative
Reserved	Outgoing
Shy	Expresses Opinions Readily
Keeps Opinions to Self	

A	**B**	**C**	**D**
VERY INDIRECT	SOMEWHAT INDIRECT	SOMEWHAT DIRECT	VERY DIRECT

WORKSHEET

WHAT'S IN IT FOR YOU?

• See where you fall on the two behavioral scales

TYPES OF BEHAVIORAL STYLES

8.3 Combining the Scales

Now that you have a letter and number that represent where you stand on the two scales, circle the quadrant below that corresponds to your style.

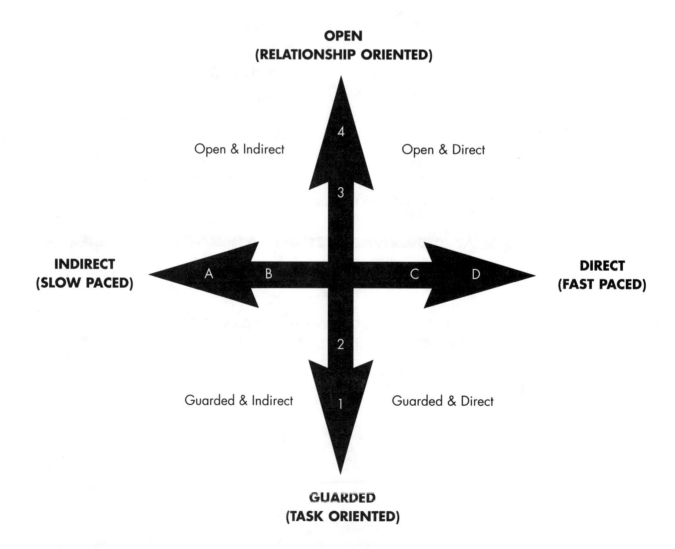

OPEN
(RELATIONSHIP ORIENTED)

Open & Indirect

Open & Direct

INDIRECT
(SLOW PACED)

A   B   C   D

DIRECT
(FAST PACED)

Guarded & Indirect

Guarded & Direct

GUARDED
(TASK ORIENTED)

I D E A

• **See which behavioral style describes you most of the time**

TYPES OF BEHAVIORAL STYLES

8.4 Meet the Styles

Now that you know the quadrant in which you fall, you can see whether you are a Relater, a Socializer, a Thinker, or a Director. It is important to realize that there are no "good" or "bad" personal styles. Each has its positive and negative aspects. In addition, we are all combinations of styles, but each of us has a dominant style that describes our behavior most of the time.

IDEA

• **Find out more about the characteristics of each behavioral style**

TYPES OF BEHAVIORAL STYLES

8.5 Summary of Behaviors (Part I)

The following generalizations will help you understand and appreciate the different behavioral styles. You will find some of them amusing. See if you can relate them to people you know.

	Relater	Thinker	Director	Socializer
BEHAVIOR PATTERN:	Open and indirect	Guarded and indirect	Guarded and direct	Open and direct
PACE:	Slow/relaxed	Slow/systematic	Fast/decisive	Fast/spontaneous
PRIORITY:	The relationship/ communication	The task or process	The task or results	The relationship and interaction
APPEARANCE:	Casual Conforming	Formal Functional	Business-like Powerful	Stylish, sometimes outrageous
WORKPLACE:	Personal Relaxed Friendly	Structured Functional Formal	Busy Efficient Structured	Stimulating Personal Cluttered
SOURCE OF SECURITY:	Friendship Cooperation	Preparation Thoroughness	Control Leadership	Playfulness Other's approval
FEARS:	Sudden change	Criticism of their work	Being taken advantage of	Loss of prestige
MEASURES PERSONAL WORTH BY:	Compatibility w/ others and depth of relationships	Precision Accuracy Activity	Results Track record Progress	Recognition Status, Number of friends
INTERNAL MOTIVATOR:	Involvement Being needed	The process Competence	Winning/ control	The chase Being included
CELEBRITIES:	Mary Tyler Moore Jane Pauley	Mr. Spock Sgt. Joe Friday	Lee Iacocca Margaret Thatcher	Carol Burnett Alan Alda

	Relater	**Thinker**	**Director**	**Socializer**
STRENGTHS:	Listening Teamwork Follow-through	Planning & organization Systematizing Numbers	Delegating Leadership Inspiring Others	Persuading Enthusiasm Entertaining
WEAKNESSES:	Oversensitive Slow to start Goal setting	Perfectionist Critical Slow decisions	Insensitive Impatient Dislikes details	Restless Ignores details No time discipline
TYPICAL JOBS:	Psychologist Social worker Teacher	Engineer Accountant Librarian	CEO/President Military leader High administrator	Sales Entertainer Bartender
ANIMAL:	Dove/koala	Owl	Bull/eagle	Chimp/peacock
IRRITATIONS:	Insensitivity Impatience	Disorganization Unpredictability	Inefficiency Indecision	Routine Perfectionism
UNDER STRESS:	Submissive Indecisive	Withdraws Headstrong	Dictatorial Critical	Sarcastic Superficial
DECISIONS ARE:	Made with others	Well thought-out	Decisive	Spontaneous
SEEKS:	Acceptance	Accuracy and information	Productivity/ bottom-line results	Recognition and fun

IDEA

TYPES OF BEHAVIORAL STYLES

8.6 Summary of Behaviors (Part II)

The Relater Style
Slow at taking action and making decisions
Likes close, personal relationships
Dislikes interpersonal conflict
Supports and actively listens to others
Weak at goal setting and self direction
Has excellent ability to gain support from others
Works slowly and cohesively with others
Seeks security and belongingness
Good counseling skills

The Socializer Style
Spontaneous actions and decisions
Likes involvement
Dislikes being alone
Exaggerates and generalizes
Tends to dream and gets others caught up in his dreams
Jumps from one activity to another
Works quickly and excitedly with others
Seeks esteem and acknowledgment
Good persuasive skills

The Thinker Style
Cautious actions and decisions
Likes organization and structure
Dislikes involvement
Asks many questions about specific details
Prefers objective, task-oriented, intellectual
    work environment
Wants to be right, so can be overly reliant
    on data collection
Works slowly and precisely alone
Good problem-solving skills

The Director Style
Decisive actions and decisions
Likes control, dislikes inaction
Prefers maximum freedom to manage himself and others
Cool, independent, and competitive
Low tolerance for feelings, attitudes, and advice of others
Works quickly and impressively alone
Good administrative skills

W O R K S H E E T

• **Increase your understanding of the people you know**

TYPES OF BEHAVIORAL STYLES

8.7 Identify Styles of the People You Know

With selected family members, people at work, and customers in mind, review the Open/Guarded and Direct/Indirect scales and the summary of behaviors. Determine the styles of people with whom you work, live, and play.

Family member _____   Style_____

Behavioral preferences _____   _____

Family member _____   Style_____

Behavioral preferences _____   _____

Someone at work _____   Style_____

Behavioral preferences _____   _____

Someone at work _____   Style_____

Behavioral preferences _____   _____

Someone at work _____   Style_____

Behavioral preferences _____   _____

A customer_____   Style_____

Behavioral preferences _____   _____

A customer_____   Style_____

Behavioral preferences _____   _____

A customer_____   Style_____

Behavioral preferences _____   _____

I D E A

• Learn about the verbal, vocal, and visual traits of the four behavioral styles

TYPES OF BEHAVIORAL STYLES

8.8 Observable Traits

	Verbal	**Vocal**	**Visual**
THE RELATER	Asks more than tells Listens more than talks Reserves opinions Less verbal communication	Steady, warm delivery Less forceful tone Lower volume Slower speech	Intermittent eye contact Gentle handshake Exhibits patience Slow moving
THE THINKER	Fact- and task-oriented Limited sharing of feelings Formal and proper Focused conversation	Little inflection Few pitch variations Less variety in vocal quality Steady, monotone delivery Low volume, slow speech	Few facial expressions Non-contact oriented Few gestures

THE DIRECTOR	Tells more than asks
	Talks more than listens
	Lots of verbal communication
	Makes emphatic statements
	Blunt and to the point
		Vocal variety
		Forceful tone
		Communicates readily
		High volume, faster speech
		Challenging voice
		   intonation
			Firm handshake
			Steady eye contact
			Gestures to emphasize
			   points
			Displays impatience
			Fast moving

THE SOCIALIZER	Tells stories, anecdotes
	Shares personal feelings
	Informal speech
	Expresses opinions readily
	Flexible time perspective
	Digresses from conversation
		Lots of inflection
		Pitch variation
		Variety in vocal quality
		Dramatic
		High volume
		Fast speech
			Animated facial
			   expressions
			Much hand/body
			   movement
			Contact-oriented
			Spontaneous actions

I D E A

WHAT'S IN IT FOR YOU?

• Discover the paces and priorities valued by each behavioral style

TYPES OF BEHAVIORAL STYLES

8.9 Pace and Priority Differences

Sometimes the most obvious differences between people are pace and priority preferences. Pace relates to how quickly you like to do things. Priority relates to your preference for getting down to work (task-oriented) versus socializing (relationship-oriented).

Tension develops when people of different styles fail to conform to each other's pace and/or priority. The diagram below suggests the types of adjustments that need to be made between different behavioral styles. For example, Relaters and Socializers have different paces, but the same priority. Relaters and Directors have pace *and* priority differences.

To adjust to another person's style, follow the guidelines given in Idea 8.10, "Prescriptions For Flexibility."

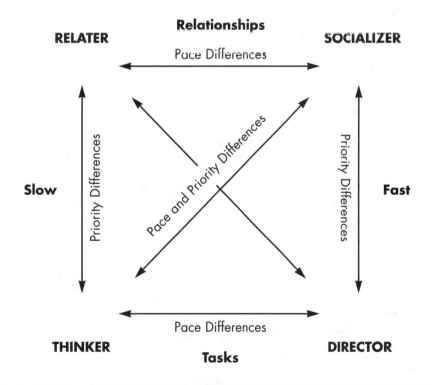

I D E A

ADJUSTING TO OTHER PEOPLE'S STYLES

8.10 Prescriptions for Flexibility

Use the following suggestions to help you adapt to other people's behavioral styles when you are dealing with customers.

	Relater	Thinker	Director	Socializer
NEEDS TO KNOW ABOUT:	How it will affect their personal circumstances	How they can justify it logically How it works	What it does/ By when/ What it costs	How it enhances their status and visibility
DO IT WITH:	Warmth	Accuracy	Conviction	Flair
SAVE THEM:	Conflict	Embarrassment	Time	Effort
TO FACILITATE DECISIONMAKING PROVIDE:	Personal service and assurances	Data and documentation	Options with supporting analysis	Testimonials and incentives
LIKES YOU TO BE:	Pleasant	Precise	To the Point	Stimulating
SUPPORT THEIR:	Feelings	Procedures	Goals	Ideas
CREATE THIS ENVIRONMENT:	Personal	Serious	Businesslike	Enthusiastic
MAINTAIN THIS PACE:	Slow/relaxed	Slow/systematic	Fast/decisive	Fast/spontaneous
FOCUS ON THIS PRIORITY:	The relationship/ Communication	The task/ The process	The task/ The results	The relationship/ Interaction
AT PLAY BE:	Casual and cooperative	Structured/play by the rules	Competitive and aggressive	Spontaneous and playful
USE TIME TO:	Develop the relationship	Ensure accuracy	Act efficiently	Enjoy the interaction
WRITE THIS WAY:	Warm and friendly	Detailed and precise	Short and to the point	Informal and dramatic
ON THE TELEPHONE BE:	Warm and pleasant	Businesslike and precise	Short and to the point	Conversational and playful

I D E A

• **Increase your knowledge of how to contact people of different behavior styles**

ADJUSTING TO OTHER PEOPLE'S STYLES

8.11 Contacting by Style

Each behavioral style is associated with a type of personality. Knowing the personality type of a potential customer can increase your chances for a sale because you will be able to approach that person in a way that best suits his or her personality.

Relater

Letters should be soft, pleasant, and specific. Mention person who referred you. Phone calls should also be anchored to a referral. Tell the Relater how your product or service benefited his/her friend. Strive to be polite and easily liked. In person, relax and talk warmly and informally. Ask questions about his/her family and coworkers. Focus on feelings, relationships, and building trust.

Socializer

Letters should have an upbeat, hip, friendly, and fast pace. Initial benefits statement should emphasize status, recognition, or being the first on the block to have a so and so. Phone calls should be upbeat and friendly as well. Flatter him/her and promise new greatness with your product or service.

In person, pretend he/she is running for office. Show great interest. Let him/her set pace and priority. Let him/her talk by asking, "How did you get into this business?" Socializers want to be friends first, so plan to have as many meetings as necessary to build the relationship.

In letters, give details and data to support your claims. On the phone, be considerate of his/her time constraints. Tell him/her what you'll cover in the meeting so he/she will know what to expect. In person, show logical proof, statistics, data, etc. that document your quality, track record, and value. Verify your credentials on paper. Speak slowly and succinctly. Get to the point. Don't bother to be sociable; be courteous and task-oriented.

When you write, call, or meet with a director, be formal, businesslike, and task-oriented. Don't socialize. Get right to the point by showing that you've done your homework and can deliver bottom line results. Always show a director what he/she has to gain by making an investment.

To get a meeting with a director, you have to provide sufficient information and incentive to deserve the meeting. That information and incentive will have to spell out what you propose and plant the seed that may grow interest. Directors take pride in being incredibly busy, so you will have to let them call the shots about a meeting time.

Thinker

Director

I D E A

WHAT'S IN IT FOR YOU?

• **Understand how to vary the needs study process to complement various personality types**

ADJUSTING TO OTHER PEOPLE'S STYLES

8.12 Exploring Needs by Style

Relater

When interviewing a Relater, talk warmly and informally. Ask gentle, open-ended questions and be sensitive about their feelings and privacy.

Relaters avoid saying negative things about people and situations. They also tend to tell you what they think you want to hear. It becomes a matter of diplomacy to extract from them accurate information about your competitors.

Socializer

Socializers love to talk about themselves. You must, therefore, give them sufficient time to do so before asking business-oriented questions. In the beginning, your business questions should be sprinkled throughout the personal/social questions. As you get to know them better, they will be willing to talk business more quickly.

Socializers can be very open and may tell you their life stories and fondest dreams. If you can demonstrate how your product or service ties in with their dreams, socializers will sell themselves. That's the slam-dunk we all love in sales.

Thinkers like to answer questions that reveal their expertise. Ask fact-oriented rather than feeling-oriented questions. Phrase your questions to elicit the right information — "How many ..." "How often ..." "What problems do you foresee ..." and that sort of thing. Let them show you how much they know.

When answering their questions, make your responses short and to the point. Leave your feelings out of it. Be left-brained, analytical, scientific, and factual. If you do not know the answer to a question, don't fake it. Tell them you will find the answer and get back to them by a specific time. Then do it.

Thinkers are very time-conscious, so be sensitive to their time constraints.

Thinker

Directors tend to be impatient, so you have to alternately ask interesting questions and give information. They want to know where your questions are leading. Aim your questions at the heart of the issue and only ask about those things that cannot be uncovered via other sources. In other words, don't waste a Director's time.

As mentioned before, you must appear to have done your homework. This will be reflected in the level of information that you pursue and the way you ask questions. "In the last four years, you have brought your company from number 15 to number 3 in the industry. What happens now?"

Director

I D E A

• **Learn how to gear your presentations to people of different behavioral styles**

ADJUSTING TO OTHER PEOPLE'S STYLES

8.13 Collaborating on Solutions by Style

Relater

Relaters are relationship-oriented, so you need to show them how your solution will support, enhance, or stabilize the people side of the business. They are also resistant to change, so present changes in a way that is nonthreatening. Assure them that daily operations will remain pretty much the same, with any changes implemented slowly and for the benefit of all.

Concentrate on security, relationships, harmony, steadiness, and concrete benefits. Involve Relaters in your presentation by asking for their opinions and feelings.

Socializer

Socializers are the group with whom you should sell the sizzle more than the steak. They are dramatic people who want to see how your product/service will increase their prestige, recognition, or image.

High entertainment value is essential when dealing with Socializers. Incorporate as many senses as possible in your presentation. Get your prospect involved. Back up your claims with testimonials and success stories about high profile people they know and respect.

Socializers like to jump on the bandwagon, so celebrity or executive endorsements work well. In fact, if you can find one person your prospect highly respects who uses your product/service, chances are good that your prospect will buy without hesitation.

The cornerstones of a presentation to a Thinker are logic, accurate information, perceived value, quality, and reliability. Honesty is important as well, which is why you should be upfront about any shortcomings. Thinkers are analytical people who look for bugs in the system, so point them out yourself and you will gain credibility.

Back up your claims with documentation, data, slides, computer printouts, etc. Always have copies of these support materials for them to keep. Testimonials from other technically minded people will carry a lot of weight, especially if your prospect knows and respects those people.

Your presentation should be as streamlined as possible and pack a lot of technological punch.

Thinker

A Director's priorities are usually making money, saving time, and becoming more efficient. Gear your presentation accordingly. Use quick benefit statements to show her how she can become more successful.

Due to their time crunch, directors want you to have done all the analyses. Simply present them with the results of your research and give them choices to make.

There will be times when you need to give a detailed presentation. Write the details and make a professional-looking proposal out of it. Give it to your prospect for future reference. Hit the main points in your presentation; if she asks about the details, provide them.

Directors, like Thinkers, are time-disciplined, so make your presentation short and to the point.

Director

IDEA

• **Adapt your confirming style to conform to your prospect's behaviorial style**

ADJUSTING TO OTHER PEOPLE'S STYLES

8.14 Confirming by Style

Relater

Relaters don't rush into decisions. They often solicit other people's opinions and then make up their minds. To help with the decision-making process, lay out a clear action plan and spell out the safest, most logical course of action that you are recommending. Relaters like guarantees because they minimize risk.

A Relater who says, "I have to think about it" may be avoiding the discomfort of saying no. Find out the truth and work with it. It is not wise to rush a Relater. You may, however, have to give a gentle nudge. This is done by acting as a consultant. You can say something like, "We both agree that this (solution) will solve your (problem), so why don't we go ahead and implement it now?"

Another gentle prod is, "Jean, I recommend you implement this plan. I wouldn't say that if I didn't really mean it."

Socializer

By the time you get to the confirming phase of the sale with a Socializer, he's your friend. So ask directly, "Where do we go from here?" or "What's our next step?"

Capitalize on the enthusiasm that Socializers exude, but don't throw cold water on the sale by getting very technical or insisting on filling out paperwork.

If you normally draw up a letter of commitment, have it prepared in advance and go over it quickly with your new customer. You can also send it as a follow-up to the confirmation. If there is someone other than your prospect who can work on the details, find that person and fill out the order forms with him. If your prospect must do it, make it quick. Socializers hate paperwork and details.

Like Directors, Thinkers like logical options that are backed up with proof. Unlike Directors and Socializers, Thinkers are not comfortable with snap decisions. In fact, if given the time, some will analyze a decision to death.

Thinkers are researchers and will compare your product/service to the competition. You can suggest features that your prospect should look for when making comparisons. Point out your company's strong points. You can even do a cost-benefit analysis for your prospect, but expect him to verify it before making a decision.

Thinkers, like Relaters, may need to be pushed gently. Do this the same way you would nudge a Relater.

Thinker

You can be direct with Directors. Ask, "Based on what we've just discussed, are you interested in ..." Often they will tell you yes or no. Some will put you off as if they have not yet decided, when, in fact, they aren't even thinking about your proposal. If a Director is not busy or does not have enough information, your proposal will not sink in and make an impression.

Give Directors options with probable outcomes. Include information on price versus quality. Include benefits that she cares about and leave out the irrelevant.

You must let a Director make her own decision. Remember, she has a need for power and that need cannot be ignored by a pushy salesperson.

Director

IDEA

WHAT'S IN IT FOR YOU?

- Learn how to follow up and maintain a close relationship with people of different behavioral styles

ADJUSTING TO OTHER PEOPLE'S STYLES

8.15 Assuring Satisfaction

Relater

The business relationship is important to a Relater, so provide consistent, regularly scheduled follow-up. Give lots of assurance that you are just a phone call away. In fact, you will score a lot of points if you give Relaters your home phone number. Send Christmas, birthday, and other cards. Stop by, if appropriate, to make sure all is running smoothly. Take him to lunch, dinner, or the ball game once in a while. In general, nurture this customer.

Thinker

Thinkers like to quantify their results, so work out a means for measuring the success of your product/service and a timetable for checking those measurements. Make yourself available to answer any question and assure him that you or someone in your company has the technical expertise to handle any situation.

Make it clear to your customer exactly when you will follow-up and then keep your promise. If you babysat a delivery or installation, report to your customer that you did so and that everything is in place as planned.

Through your business relationship with a Thinker, you have to continually prove your credibility, reliability, product/service quality, and value as a supplier.

Socializer

In business and love, Socializers are the ones who are most apt to buy before they are truly sold. They are also most apt to experience buyer's remorse, so it is your job to keep in touch, make sure everything is okay, and assure him that his purchase was wise. Make sure your customer is actually using your product/service. Socializers are easily frustrated by new technology and may shelve rather than learn your solution.

Socializers are usually disorganized. If necessary, you can help him become organized so that your product/service is properly implemented. After all, Socializers tend to talk about everything and anything. A purchase that was not implemented properly will get as bad a rap as a purchase that was defective.

Director

Follow-up with a Director is different than for other behavioral styles. A Director isn't concerned about the relationship; she just cares about the performance of your product or service. Assure your customer that you intend to follow-up to make sure everything is okay, but you will not take up much of her time.

Never simply stop by to see a Director—they're too busy for that. Call and quickly ask if all is well. If there are complaints, assure her that they will be resolved swiftly and then do so. After the resolution, report back to your customer to inform her that things are back to normal.

Unfortunately, selling to a Director does not necessarily give you an advantage for a future sale. You will have to earn the next sale the way you earned the last one—on the merits of your product/service and research.

I D E A

ADJUSTING TO OTHER PEOPLE'S STYLES

8.16 *Velocity*

Every person operates at a natural pace or velocity. *Velocity* is the intensity with which you live. Some people naturally operate at a highly intense pace and others at a slower pace. Our modern society tends to reward people of higher velocity — sales contests, sporting events, and games all acknowledge those who give it an all-out effort — but each velocity is valid. Plenty of people who operate at a slower pace contribute to the advancement of business or society.

Velocity is a combination of energy and drive. Each one of us has a natural range of energy that is enhanced or limited by nutrition, fitness, rest, stress management, and attitude. We also have a natural degree of drive or self-motivation. Our drive is affected by our self-esteem, clarity of purpose, awareness of possibilities, and the appeal of our goals. Energy and drive combine naturally to determine our velocity.

What is *your* velocity? What is your *prospect's* velocity?

High Velocity Self-motivated. Loves to work toward goals. Prefers long hours filled with varied activity. Uses leisure time to advance toward goals. Sets challenging goals. Has high aspirations. Enjoys competition. Finds inactivity frustrating. Expects a lot from self.

Moderate Velocity Somewhat self-motivated. Balances work and leisure. Prefers standard workdays with a moderate mix of activities. Uses leisure time to complete chores and socialize. Sets reachable goals. Has moderate aspirations. Accepts competition. Finds inactivity relaxing. Has mild expectations from self.

Low Velocity Motivated primarily by needs or by others. Finds work demotivating. Prefers to work as a team player rather than a leader. Uses leisure time to pursue personal or social interests casually. Takes things as they come, seldom sets goals. Has mild aspirations. Dislikes competition. Enjoys occasional inactivity. Doesn't expect much from self.

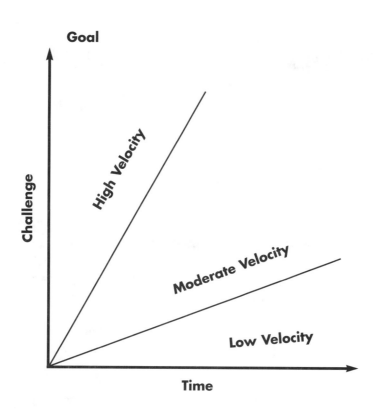

I D E A

ADJUST TO OTHER PEOPLE'S STYLES

8.17 Natural Values

Some values are learned; others are part of one's personality. Each of us shares seven "natural" values; however, each of us differs in the values we consider most important. Our values don't determine *whether* something will appeal to us, but rather *how* that thing will appeal to us. Understanding the value systems of your prospects can help you present proposals in a way that appeals most to a particular prospect.

People show their values all the time through what they say and don't say, do and don't do. Here are the seven categories as well as some indicators that will help you identify the values at the top of someone's priority list.

Sensuality. The relative importance of one's physical experiences. This is often betrayed by an interest in and affinity for physical experience: taste, touch, smell, fit, comfort, feelings, humidity, light, and so forth. A sensitivity to the physical aspects of an experience exists that stands out for this person. "Let's not go to that theater. The seats are uncomfortable and their soft drinks are watery."

Empathy. The relative importance of feeling connected to other people. People who value empathy need to be around others they care about. The helping impulse is very strong in these folks. They are drawn to the needs of others and are sensitive to their reactions and experiences. "I bought from them because I felt they really cared for me."

Wealth. The relative importance of ownership and value. These people note the market value of items. Quality is a major consideration. One cashmere jacket would be preferred over two wool-blend jackets. The sincerity of one's words is evaluated by what they do with money. "If he really meant that, he would put his money where his mouth is."

Power. The relative importance of control and recognition. Acknowledgment, praise, special privileges, honors, titles, and prestigious things are of prime consideration here. Position and control matter a lot. "His management ideas sounded good but he is not a manager, what could he know?" or "Sure I enjoyed the concert, but what I really liked was sitting in the VIP section."

Aesthetics. The relative importance of beauty, balance, and symmetry. Beautiful sunsets, organized systems, certain color combinations, paintings, landscapes, architecture, patterns, etc. appeal strongly. The look of a proposal may carry as much impact as the contents for them. "The meeting would have been much more productive if we weren't in such a dull looking room."

Commitment. The relative importance of a cause. Beliefs and affiliations get the center of attention. Working to advance a cause, crusading, and campaigning feel good. This person does things because it is what he or she feels is right. They like being part of an organization or group they believe in. "I trust her because she walks her talk. If she says it, you can take it to the bank."

Knowledge. The relative importance of learning and understanding. This person loves to learn. Knowledge is valued as an end in itself. Books, seminars, discussions, and problem solving are enjoyed. May tend to listen to learning tapes or public radio rather than music stations. Seems to have an endless curiosity. "I feel like I've really grown and yet I'm amazed at how little I know on this subject," or "So many books, so little time."

Reprinted with permission from *The Acorn Letter* by Jim Cathcart, © 1995.

IDEA

ADJUSTING TO OTHER PEOPLE'S STYLES

8.18 Multiple Smarts

Another important factor to discover about your customer or prospect is the variety of his or her intelligence. Recent research indicates at least seven "multiple intelligences" or ways of learning. Each one of us combines these intelligences into a unique package. Spend some time defining your own mix of intelligences, and make a point of discerning the same for your prospects and customers. Once you know someone's "smarts," you'll know how to reach them quickly and what will be easiest for them to understand.

Verbal intelligence. Good at explaining things. Likes writing and reading. Places importance on things that are written or verbal. Likes word pictures, puns, creative phrasing, new words. Enjoys expanding vocabulary. *Tip: Explain things in words or on paper.*

Visual intelligence. Uses charts and symbols to make a point. Sees things clearly in the mind. Can sense what something will look like. Likes pictures and demonstrations to help understand things. *Tip: Use charts, sketches, pictures.*

Physical intelligence. Learns best by doing. Wants to get hands-on contact with a subject. Feels a need to move while learning. Favorite pastimes involve activity or handiwork. *Tip: Involve this person in learning; give them a skill to practice.*

Musical intelligence. Remembers tunes and lyrics easily. Uses music as a frame of reference. Has a natural sense of timing or rhythm. Enjoys all types of sounds. Is easily distracted by sounds. Notices the cadence of things. *Tip: Present ideas poetically, put them to music, or use a rhyme to drive home a key point.*

Mathematical and logical intelligence. Likes to put things in order. Arranges things logically. Looks for patterns and relationships between things. Good at analysis, calculation, planning. Wants things to make sense. Speaks in sequences: "First … second … then third." *Tip: Outline and display your proposal in a logical, systematic way, and follow your outline.*

Introspective intelligence. Enjoys quiet time to be alone in thought. Understands his own motives and reasons for doing things. Likes to daydream about new ideas and explore his own feelings and thoughts. Reflective, thoughtful. *Tip: Give this person plenty of time to think things over.*

Interpersonal intelligence. People smart. Good with others. Can mediate arguments. Knows what to do to connect with someone else. Sensitive to others. Likes contact with people, teams, committees, social events. *Tip: Use group activities and team learning.*

Reprinted with permission from *The Acorn Letter* by Jim Cathcart, © 1995.

I D E A

• **Discover and complement your prospect's thinking level**

ADJUSTING TO OTHER PEOPLE'S STYLES

8.19 Thinking Levels

People think on three levels: conceptual, strategic, and operational. Everyone functions on all three levels of thought, but most people feel more comfortable with one type of thinking than another. If we are selling to a person whose level of thinking is different from ours, the conflict between the two types of thinking can create a roadblock that keeps us from completing the sale. Use this guide to discover your own level of thinking, and adapt it to other levels as necessary.

Conceptual thinkers. About two percent of the population rely on conceptual thinking most of the time. Conceptual thinkers tend to think in large terms and long time frames. They use metaphors and symbols and reflect on the future implications of decisions, or the concepts behind them. When you sell to a conceptual thinker, talk about concepts, ideas, and possibilities.

Strategic thinkers. About 18 percent of the population tends to think strategically. Strategic thinkers consider how to achieve their goals through various strategies, tactics, and moves. They look for combinations, angles, and alternative ways to accomplish things. Strategic thinkers translate concepts into reality, or the plans that eventually create the reality. Match their approach when you talk with them by discussing alternatives, plans, strategies, and tactics.

Operational thinkers. Eighty percent of us are operational thinkers. We think strictly in terms of function, or operation. When operational thinkers look at a door, they see a door—not a passageway, or the symbol of the dawn of a new era. Operational thinkers see black and white and deal with it as black and white. If they see gray, they deal with it as gray—not as a potential black or white. Operational thinkers accomplish most of the world's work. They prepare food, build buildings, drive cars, and deliver goods. When you meet with an operational thinker, talk about functions. Illustrate your products and show how things will operate. Be specific. Give examples.

SECTION NINE

COMMUNICATING FOR RESULTS

WHAT'S IN IT FOR YOU?

- Increase your understanding of communication in general.
- Gain insight into communication skills such as listening, feedback, body language, and vocal quality.
- Learn about behavioral styles — including your own — and discover how this knowledge will increase sales.

The information-gathering phase of the sales process is where you make or break the sale. Up to this point, you've done your homework, targeted and contacted the right prospects, and set up appointments. Now that you are meeting to find out what makes them tick, your all-important communication skills come into play.

Communication skills include questioning, active listening, feedback, the observation and use of body language and vocal qualities, and behavioral flexibility.

The cornerstone of good communication is sensitivity to the needs of the other person. All of the following skills will help you achieve this. If you have had success as a salesperson, you probably possess good communication skills. The Ideas and Worksheets that follow may seem simple to you, but study them anyway. They will strengthen the skills you use unconsciously and teach you new ones to use consciously.

I D E A

COMMUNICATE BETTER AND SELL MORE

9.1 The Communication Process

The following diagram shows the communication process for you as both a speaker and a listener. The key is to make yourself understood — verbally and nonverbally. The speaker (sender) wants (intends) to send a message to a listener (receiver). To succeed, the speaker must use the proper verbal and nonverbal cues to cut through "noise" (verbal and nonverbal distractions that might distort the receiver's perception).

The Communication Process

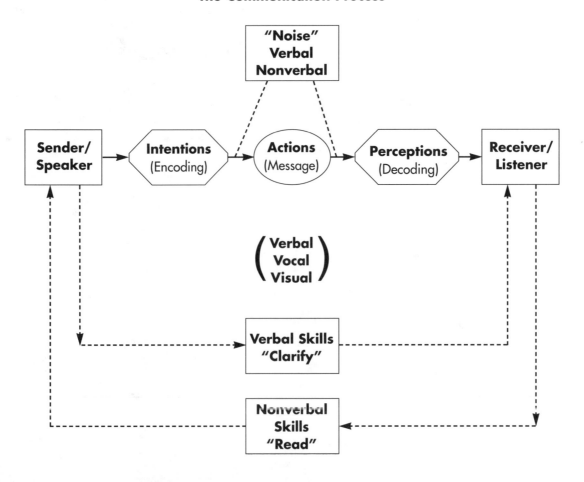

I D E A

• **Become a good listener**

LEARNING TO LISTEN

9.2 10 Keys to Active Listening

1. **Resist distractions.** Ignore external noises while you focus on what the other person is saying — verbally or nonverbally. Ignore the "internal" noise that we all have.

2. **Take notes.** Most people remember about 50 percent of what they hear, so take enough notes to help you recall the full content of the conversation.

3. **Let people tell their story.** When getting to know someone and his or her business — or when listening to the customer's problem — let that person tell the story the way he or she sees it. A great deal of valuable information is revealed in a person's narrative. Save your developmental and clarifying questions for later.

4. **Offer verbal feedback.** Let your prospect know you are paying close attention by giving verbal cues ("Uh-huh," "Yeah," "OK," "Sure," "I understand").

5. **Listen selectively.** Read between the lines. Look for the important messages that people convey in the *way* they say things. Sometimes what they mean to say is contained in what they leave out.

6. **Relax.** Create an environment in which your prospect will feel comfortable telling his story. Don't chime in with your two cents worth at every opportunity.

7. **Listen with your entire body.** Show you are listening by leaning forward in your chair. Keep your arms uncrossed, at your sides or on the table. Use good eye contact and nod in agreement when appropriate. Try not to react to negative comments.

8. **Be aware of "personal space."** If you are in the prospect's office, don't play with his trophies or fondle his paperweight. If you are standing next to someone, don't stand right in his or her face. Give people their space.

9. **Ask questions.** Gently ask the types of questions that will help you help your prospect, as we discussed previously.

10. **Care about your prospect.** If you do not sincerely care about people, you will have a hard time being a good listener. Remember, there is no such thing as an uninterested speaker, only uninterested listeners.

W O R K S H E E T

WHAT'S IN IT FOR YOU?

• **Identify positive and negative listening habits you observe in other people**

LEARNING TO LISTEN

9.3 Other People's Listening Habits

One of the easiest ways to change your behaviors is to see them in someone else. Below, list the five most important things you like to see another person do when listening to you:

1.

2.

3.

4.

5.

Now list five of the biggest turnoffs—things that people do that you dislike:

1.

2.

3.

4.

5.

Which of the above are you guilty of?

I D E A

• **Increase your awareness of other people's poor listening habits**

LEARNING TO LISTEN

9.4 Irritating Listening Habits

Listed below are 23 listening habits of superiors that have been distinctly irritating to one or more of their subordinates. Check the number of the habits listed that irritate you because they are practiced by your immediate supervisor or a coworker on your level. Then identify the five listening habits that to you are the worst.

_____ 1. He does all the talking; I go in with a problem and never get a chance to open my mouth.

_____ 2. She interrupts me when I talk.

_____ 3. He never looks at me when I talk. I'm not sure he's listening.

_____ 4. She continually toys with a pencil, paper, or some other item while I'm talking; I wonder if she's listening.

_____ 5. His poker face keeps me guessing whether he understands me or is even listening to me.

_____ 6. She never smiles — I'm afraid to talk to her.

_____ 7. He changes what I say by putting words into my mouth.

_____ 8. She puts me on the defensive when I ask a question.

_____ 9. Occasionally he asks a question about what I have just told him that shows he wasn't listening.

_____ 10. She argues with everything I say — even before I have a chance to finish my case.

_____ 11. Everything I say reminds him of an experience he's either had or heard of. I get frustrated when he interrupts, saying "That reminds me . . ."

_____ 12. When I am talking, she finishes sentences for me.

_____ 13. He acts as if he is just waiting for me to finish so he can interject something of his own.

_____ 14. All the time I'm talking, she's looking out the window.

_____ 15. He looks at me as if he is trying to stare me down.

_____ 16. She looks as if she's appraising me . . . I begin to wonder if I have a smudge on my face, a tear in my coat, etc.

_____ 17. He looks as if he is constantly thinking "No" or questioning the truthfulness or value of what I'm saying.

_____ 18. She overdoes showing she's following what I'm saying . . . too many nods of her head, or "mm-hm's" and "uh-huh's."

_____ 19. He sits too close to me.

_____ 20. She frequently looks at her watch or the clock while I'm talking.

_____ 21. He is completely withdrawn and distant when I'm talking.

_____ 22. She acts as if she is doing me a favor by seeing me.

_____ 23. He acts as if he knows it all, frequently relating incidents in which he was the hero.

W O R K S H E E T

WHAT'S IN IT FOR YOU?

- **Realize your weak points as a listener**
- **Specify ways to improve**

LEARNING TO LISTEN

9.5 Listening Action Plan

Answering the following questions will help you make a commitment to improving your listening skills.

1. I listen more effectively when _____
_____
_____

2. I tend not to listen effectively when _____
_____
_____

3. The three listening areas in which I am strongest are _____
_____
_____

4. My three areas of listening that need the most improvement are _____
_____
_____

5. I will practice good listening skills with the following people:
    a) _____
    b) _____
    c) _____

6. I will practice good listening skills in these situations:
    a) _____
    b) _____
    c) _____

7. I will know I have become a better listener when _____
_____
_____

IDEA

USING FEEDBACK

9.6 Verbal Feedback

Are you always sure you know what someone is saying? Of course not. Misunderstandings are common. In a sales situation, you cannot afford misunderstandings—they're amateurish. For this reason, you must use feedback to ensure clear communication. There are many reasons to use verbal feedback.

Confirming the Agenda. You may want to start gathering information when your prospect wants to socialize more; or you may want to confirm the sale when your prospect still has questions to ask. The only way to know if you are focusing on the right thing is to ask.

> "I'd like to ask you some questions about your business. Would that be ok?"

> "I'd like to write up an order. Did you have any more questions to ask me?"

Setting Pace and Priority. You will increase trust and build stronger relationships if you remain sensitive to your customers' needs and behavioral styles. Stop to ask, "Do you want me to slow down or go over anything I've already discussed?" or "Let me know if I should skip over these details and get right to the bottom line for you." You can test the priority waters by asking, "How would you like to start this meeting?"

Understanding Vague Statements. Language is an inexact form of communication. What does someone mean when he says, "It's too expensive"? The only way to know is to ask, "What exactly do you mean by … ?"

Increasing and Maintaining Interest. Few sales situations are ideal, so prospects may get distracted, bored, or lose interest. To keep them involved, ask questions such as, "How do you think this would solve your problem?"

Verbal feedback requests information. There are several phrases that can help you elicit feedback:

> "Let me be sure I understand your major concerns."

> "Let me summarize the key points we've discussed."

> "So what I hear you saying is …"

Be a stickler for accuracy and understanding while always being sensitive to the priority and pace needs of your customer.

W O R K S H E E T

WHAT'S IN IT FOR YOU?

• **Become aware of nonverbal feedback and learn to control it**

USING FEEDBACK

9.7 Nonverbal Feedback

Nonverbal feedback is basically comprised of body language and vocal quality. Both convey messages and should be used consciously to build the relationship. A skilled salesperson pays attention to others' feedback and uses nonverbal feedback to keep the lines of communication open and enthusiastic. Start by observing feedback from others, and become aware of your own. Later, you can strive to control it. How do you react in the following situations?

1. On the telephone, a secretary or receptionist refuses to put you through to a prospect. How does your vocal quality change?

2. In person, a prospect brushes you off by saying he's too busy to see you. What happens to your body language?

3. You walk into a prospect's office. How do you carry yourself and what does it say about you?

4. While you gather information, your prospect becomes bored or distracted. What does your facial expression reveal?

5. During a presentation, how does your body language reflect your enthusiasm and sincerity?

6. If, during a presentation, your prospect seems to be closed down, how does your body language or vocal tone change? How *should* it change?

7. When asking a doubtful prospect for the sale, what does your body language say about your disappointment?

SECTION TEN

STUDY THE CUSTOMER

WHAT'S IN IT FOR YOU?

- **Find out what you need to know about your customer.**
- **Use body language, neurolinguistic programming, and other techniques to understand your customer's behavior.**

You know all about your products—but often, you face prospects about whom you know nothing. Where do you start? What do you say to get the appointment? How do you know if you can help?

You are an expert on what *you* know. Your prospect is an expert on what he or she knows. If you don't learn from and about the prospect, you'll be forced to talk only about what you know and not about how your product or service can serve *this* prospect best.

W O R K S H E E T

WHAT'S IN IT FOR YOU?

- **Summarize the information you need about your prospect**

MAXIMIZING PROSPECT KNOWLEDGE

10.1 "Mackay's Sixty Six"

In his book, *Swim With The Sharks Without Being Eaten Alive*, Harvey Mackay explains how he profiles his customers and potential customers. He profiles them so thoroughly that he ends up knowing far more than any of his competitors take the time to find out! He calls his system "Mackay's Sixty Six"—66 questions he seeks to answer about each customer.

You may not need 66 separate pieces of information about your customer to get the edge on your competitors, but Mackay's thorough research is the right approach to build stronger, more familiar relationships with your prospects and customers. In the left column below, list the things you *need* to know about your customer. In the right column, list things you *would like* to know about your customer, such as a nickname, where he or she went to school, favorite hobbies and leisure activities, proudest accomplishments, etc. Use your list to guide you in your prospect and customer research.

**Things I Need to Know
about My Customer**

**Things I Want to Know
about My Customer**

_____ _____

_____ _____

_____ _____

_____ _____

_____ _____

_____ _____

_____ _____

I D E A

WHAT'S IN IT FOR YOU?

- **Gain in-depth knowledge of your prospect's company, behavioral style, and product/service needs**

MAXIMIZING PROSPECT KNOWLEDGE

10.2 Prospect Knowledge Checklist

Learn all you can about the decision maker at a prospective company. You should be able to answer most of the following questions, noting the particulars in the prospect's file.

1. What are the prospect's personal style, idiosyncrasies, and temperament?

2. What are his/her hobbies, sports, and other interests?

3. What are his/her family's interests?

4. Does he/she buy on opinion, fact, friendship, or reciprocity?

5. What is his/her present product usage?

6. Who is your current or potential competition for this account?

7. What are his/her specific needs for your product/service?

8. Why should he/she purchase from you rather than from a competitor?

9. What is his/her present volume of business and potential for expansion?

10. What type and quality of merchandise does he/she carry?

11. How is the merchandise marketed?

12. What is the company's credit rating?

13. Are there any industry trends that will affect the company's future purchasing pattern?

I D E A

• Brush up on your ability to read body language — one of the "master skills" in selling

BODY LANGUAGE

10.3 The Universal Language

Without speaking a word, people convey a tremendous amount of information about themselves and their attitude toward you. Body language is a universal language that goes beyond the intellect and the spoken word to reveal the depths of people's feelings. Once you have become a skilled body language observer, you can use your knowledge to 1) pick up people's nuances and gestures; 2) respond to them in ways that will put them at ease; and 3) use body language consciously to make your communication more effective.

WHAT TO LOOK FOR

The feelings conveyed in body language are fleeting. They go by like frames of a movie. Fortunately, they are easy to spot and are generally repeated often.

Observing body language is second nature to most people. But to use it to your advantage, you must make the observation conscious, which means concentrating on the person you're talking to. Of course, you do this anyway if you are practicing active listening, which you are, aren't you?

The areas to watch are the hands, arms, face, eyes, legs, and the combinations of movements between these areas. Facial expressions convey a lot, as do posture and eye contact.

CLUSTERS ARE THE KEY

Observing one gesture is almost *meaningless*. Someone rubbing his eyes can simply have itchy eyes. The key to interpreting body language is to observe clusters of gestures. If someone is rubbing his eyes, pulling an ear, tapping a foot, looking around the room, and shifting uneasily in his chair, there's a good chance he is bored, nervous, or frustrated. Careful observation will make the difference. When you do notice these clusters, it's time for you to do *something* different.

WHAT TO DO WITH WHAT YOU SEE

First, ask yourself how the observed clusters compare to this person's usual way of behaving. Some people always have poor eye contact. Some people always act aloof. Try not to jump to conclusions. You have to either observe people for a while or know them well before you can interpret their body language infallibly.

Second, get feedback on your hunches. If someone's behavior has changed, ask a non-threatening question to find out if you are the reason. You might say, "I hear you saying yes, but I get the impression that something else is on your mind. Would you mind sharing it with me?"

Last, remember what causes people to be comfortable. Some customers may get nervous until you reassure them that they are doing the right thing. Others react negatively to too much enthusiasm. You have to know when to tone it down and be more subtle.

I D E A

WHAT'S IN IT FOR YOU?

- **Increase your awareness of the body language associated with different attitudes**

BODY LANGUAGE

10.4 What Different Attitudes Look Like (Part I)

Openness	**Enthusiasm**
Open hands	Small upper or inward smile
Unbuttoned shirt collar	Erect body stance
Taking coat off	Hands open, arms extended
Moving closer	Eyes wide and alert
Leaning forward in chair	Lively and bouncy
Uncrossed legs and arms	

Nervousness	**Critical Evaluation**
Clearing throat	Body drawn back
Hand-to-mouth movements	One hand on cheek
Covering mouth when speaking	Chin in palm with index finger along side of nose or face and remaining fingers under mouth
Darting eyes or little eye contact	
Twitching lips or face	
Shifting weight while standing	
Tapping fingers	
Plucking at collar or ringing neck with finger inside shirt collar	
Incongruent laugh	
Pacing	
Jingling money in pockets	

Defensiveness	**Anger**
Rigid body	Body rigid
Arms or legs crossed tightly	Fists clenched
Minimal eye contact with occasional sideways or darting glances	Lips closed and held in a tight thin line
Pursed lips	Continued eye contact
Head down with chin against chest	Squinting of eyes (sometimes)
Fists clenched	Shallow breathing
Leaning back in chair	Flaring of nostrils

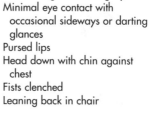

Readiness	**Evaluation**
Leaning forward in a chair in an open posture	Sitting in front of chair with upper torso projected forward
Hands possibly placed mid thigh	Slightly tilted head
Relaxed, but alive, facial expression	Hand to cheek gesture; head is often supported by the hand
Standing with hands on hips, feet slightly spread	Stroking the chin or pulling on beard

I D E A

WHAT'S IN IT FOR YOU?

• **Become aware of the body language associated with different attitudes**

BODY LANGUAGE

10.5 What Different Attitudes Look Like (Part II)

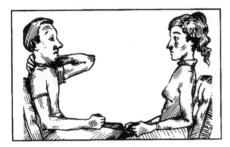

Frustration
Tightly clenched hands
Hand wringing
Rubbing back of neck
Controlled, short breathing
Blind staring
Running hands through hair
Tightly closed lips
Stamping a foot
Pacing

Self-Control
Wrists gripped behind the
  back
Crossed and locked angles
Fists clenched
Pupils contracted
Lips closed or pursed

Confidence and Authority
Steepling (the higher the
  hands, the greater the
  confidence)
Resting feet on the desk
Leaning back with hands
  together behind back with
  chin thrust forward
Proud, erect body stance
Continuing eye contact
Smiling inwardly
Tipping back in chair

Reassurance
Pinching the fleshy part of the
  hands
Gently rubbing or caressing
  some personal object such as
  a ring, watch or necklace

Boredom and Indifference
Head in hand
Drooping eyelids
Slouching
Tapping of foot or fingers
Feet swinging
Blank stares, little eye contact
Doodling
Slack lips
Posture aimed at exit

Acceptance
Spreading hands held to chest
  (for men)
Moving closer to the other person

Suspicion and Secrecy
Failing to make eye contact
  or resisting glances
Glancing sideways at you by
  turning the body slightly away
Rubbing or touching the nose
Squinting or peering over
  glasses

Rejection and Doubt
Touching and rubbing nose
Squinting or rubbing eyes
Arms and legs crossed
Body withdrawn
Clearing throat
Hand rubbing or ear tugging
Raising an eyebrow

I D E A

WHAT'S IN IT FOR YOU?

- **Understand how neurolinguistic programming can help you establish rapport with people**

NEUROLINGUISTIC PROGRAMMING (NLP)

10.6 Introduction to NLP

Another valuable tool for helping you quickly establish rapport with people is NLP. This study of human behavior was pioneered by linguist John Grinder and psychologist Richard Bandler. They studied ways in which therapists and clients developed an intuitive sense of each other and, thereby, produced outstanding results in psychotherapy. These observations led to a theory of how the human mind works.

According to NLP, everyone has a dominant mode of perceiving and understanding the world. The three modes are auditory, visual, and physical.

Auditory Some people are oriented to sounds and language. They learn more quickly by listening than by reading or seeing. They prefer to be *told* how much they are appreciated rather than *shown*. If you wanted to enhance your relationship with a client who is "auditory," you would be better off saying, "I really appreciate working with you" than sending a gift.

People who are auditory tend to say things such as, "I hear what you are saying," "That sounds good to me," and other hearing-oriented phrases.

Visual Some people perceive the world primarily through sight. To them, a picture is worth a thousand words. They learn more easily by seeing or visualizing rather than by hearing or feeling. Demonstrations work better than descriptions for people who are visual. Flowers and scenic restaurants are the way to a visual romantic's heart, not solely sweet words of endearment.

People who are visual reveal themselves by saying things such as, "I see what you mean," "I get the picture," or "I'll believe it when I see it."

Physical Some people are touchers. They like to be hugged and stroked. They experience the world through feeling, which often includes an acute sense of smell or taste. These are people who have to *do* something to learn it — a description or demonstration won't suffice. Physical individuals will respond to loving strokes or a home-cooked gourmet meal more than to a dozen roses or compliments on their appearance.

Phrases used by physical people include, "It just doesn't feel right to me," "If it feels good, do it," "How do you feel about that?" "This is heating up."

I D E A

WHAT'S IN IT FOR YOU?

• **Use eye cues to determine whether someone is auditory, visual, or physical**

NEUROLINGUISTIC PROGRAMMING

10.7 The Eyes Have It

Grinder and Bandler noted that the movement of one's eyes reveals whether a person is accessing information visually, auditorially, or physically. Eye movements in people are quite similar and the following generalizations are often true:

Visual perception	Looking up and left	Visualizing (remembering) from the past; picturing the past mentally
	Looking up and right	Visually constructing an image to see what it would eventually look like
Physical perception	Looking down and right	Remembering past feelings
Auditory perception	Looking sideways to left	Hearing sounds or voices from the past (remembering)
	Looking sideways to right	Constructing a future conversation; thinking of the right words to use
	Looking down to left	Holding an internal dialogue with oneself; trying out how something sounds

A few left-handed people reverse the normal right and left eye cues; therefore, eye cues can be used only as clues to be confirmed by further observation.

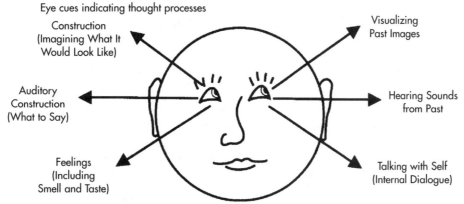

William G. Nickels, Robert F. Everett, and Ronald Klein, "Rapport Building for Salespeople: A Neuro-Linguistic Approach, "*Journal of Personal Selling & Sales Management* (November 1983), p.1.

I D E A

• Use action words (predicates) to learn more about a person's orientation

NEUROLINGUISTIC PROGRAMMING

10.8 Words That Tell

Among the clusters of behaviors you should observe are the words that people choose to express themselves. Along with eye movements, words speak volumes about our modes of perception. Individual words are less important than the general flavor of what a person is saying. Don't jump to conclusions based on one or two words. Take your time. Look for themes and style. The patterns below will give you a start in using NLP to create rapport.

Visual		Auditory		Physical	
analyze	look	announce	oral	active	lukewarm
angle	notice	articulate	proclaim	affected	motion
appear	obscure	audible	pronounce	bearable	muddled
clarity	observe	communicate	remark	charge	panicky
cognizant	obvious	converse	report	concrete	pressure
conspicuous	perception	discuss	roar	emotional	sensitive
demonstrate	perspective	dissonant	rumor	feel	set
dream	picture	divulge	say	firm	shallow
examine	scene	earshot	shrill	flow	softly
focus	see	enunciate	silence	foundation	solid
foresee	sight	gossip	sound	grasp	structured
glance	sketchy	hear	squeal	grip	support
hindsight	survey	hush	state	hanging	tension
horizon	vague	inquire	talk	hassle	tied
idea	view	interview	tell	heated	touch
illusion	vision	listen	tone	hold	unbearable
image	watch	mention	vocal	hustle	unsettled
inspect	witness	noise	voice	intuition	whipped

William G. Nickels, Robert F. Everett, and Robert Klein, "Rapport Building for Salespeople: A Neurolinguistic Approach," *Journal of Personal Selling & Sales Management* (November 1983), p. 2.

Note: This has been a very basic introduction to the power of NLP. For more detailed discussion, refer to *Beyond Selling: How to Maximize Your Personal Influence*, by Bagley and Reese.

I D E A

- **Learn various methods for establishing and maintaining rapport—regardless of the selling situation**
- **Learn how to quickly get in sync with your customer**

PACING

10.9 Types of Pacing

In sales, pacing means "being where the customer is." It is alignment on multiple levels. The proper pacing of your customer can be very helpful in truly building rapport with them. The following are the most common ways you can align or get in sync with the customer. Each method is a form of pacing.

1. **Emotional pacing.** Another term for emotional pacing is empathy, or understanding and appreciating the other person's feelings. We've all had our good and bad days. That goes for customers as well. If you can tune in to a customer's mood—to see things from his or her perspective—you will let that customer know you are on their wavelength. If a customer is very enthusiastic and energetic, align with that mood by pacing or acting as if you were in the same mood.

2. **Posture pacing.** Adopt the posture and general behavioral style of your customer. This does not mean mimicking the person you are speaking to. Rather, your body language and posture should subtly reflect the customer's body language and posture. For example, if your customer sits and talks with arms and legs crossed—a traditionally defensive posture—the worst thing you can do is lean forward and become more adamant—or enthusiastic—or charming. Your posture would be out of sync with that of your customer. Remember, you will be building rapport if you assume the same or similar posture and gestures of the person you are communicating with.

3. **Tone and tempo pacing.** Match the tone and tempo of your customer's speech as closely as possible without mimicking them. The best example can be seen in regional speech variations. People in some parts of the country are known for a rapid-fire, get-to-the-point style of speech. Others are more laid-back, slower, indirect, and use softer tones. Whichever it is, you will build rapport more quickly by using the general tone and tempo of your customer.

4. Language pacing. One form of language pacing is using the buzzwords your customer uses. Be certain to use these key words and phrases appropriately. Overusing or misusing these words will only get the opposite of the results you are seeking. Another form of language pacing is matching their patterns for processing information and expressing themselves. The three most common are visual (see), auditory (hear), and physical (feel). If a customer talks in one of these distinct patterns, you should phrase your comments in similar patterns. Most people are visually oriented. Using words that are visually oriented with visuals will assist in building rapport. Noting someone with an auditory or physical pattern will create an opportunity to align with that individual quickly and easily.

Other methods of pacing include values, beliefs, cultural, and content pacing.

W O R K S H E E T

WHAT'S IN IT FOR YOU?

- **Build higher levels of rapport with people**
- **Learn how to match and mirror the posture of clients**

PACING

10.10 Types of Pacing — Posture Pacing (Part I)

Practice matching and mirroring the physiology and posture of someone you are *not* communicating with. For example, in a restaurant or office, find someone sitting across the room and match the way they are sitting, moving, leaning, crossing arms, crossing legs, gesturing, etc. Try this over a period of time. The challenge is being subtle. Do not pace this person in a way that will draw conscious attention to what you are doing. Slowly and naturally shift into the way they are sitting, standing, walking, etc.

Below is a list that will help you learn how to pace an individual's posture. Use the list as a beginning point for matching the posture of someone you want to build rapport with.

Leans forward _____

Leans backward _____

Stands stiff and erect _____

Hunches _____

Rocking motion _____

Tilts head _____

Nods head _____

Crosses legs _____

Crosses arms _____

Holds pen _____

Points _____

Pounds fist _____

W O R K S H E E T

WHAT'S IN IT FOR YOU?

- **Build higher-level rapport with business associates**
- **Improve your posture pacing with people you communicate with regularly**

PACING

10.11 Types of Pacing — Posture Pacing (Part II)

Apply your posture pacing skills in meetings and with people you communicate with regularly. Pick one person and match his/her general posture and physical movements and gestures. Notice what happens over time to your level of rapport and influence as you add this dimension to your communication. Write down some of the key posture patterns of this individual.

Leans forward _____

Leans backward _____

Stands stiff and erect _____

Hunches_____

Rocking motion _____

Tilts head _____

Nods head _____

Crosses legs _____

Crosses arms _____

Holds pen _____

Points _____

Pounds fist_____

W O R K S H E E T

WHAT'S IN IT FOR YOU?

• **Build higher levels of rapport with business associates**
• **Develop your ability to adjust the tempo of your verbal communication**

PACING

10.12 Types of Pacing — Voice Tempo

Practice adjusting your rate of speech to the speed of the person you are communicating with. This form of pacing can be powerful but difficult to do without practice. It's important to practice in a "safe" environment. Try this initially with friends or family or, maybe, with a waiter or waitress before attempting to use this powerful tool in your business dealings.

The list below will help you identify and categorize important aspects of the tempo of the person you are communicating with. Check the appropriate items.

Very slow _____

Slow _____

Moderate _____

Fast _____

Very fast _____

Rhythmic _____

Arrhythmic _____

W O R K S H E E T

- **Build higher levels of rapport with business associates**
- **Develop the tone of your communication to that of the person you are communicating with**

PACING

10.13 Types of Pacing — Voice Tone Pacing

Practice adjusting the tone of your speech to that of the person you are communicating with. This kind of pacing can be very powerful but subtle. Before using it in a business environment, practice it in a safe environment, such as with family or friends.

The list below will help you identify important aspects of the tone of the person you are communicating with. Check the appropriate items.

Pitch

Low _____

Medium _____

High _____

Apologetic _____

Confidential_____

Monotone_____

Condescending _____

Demanding _____

W O R K S H E E T

WHAT'S IN IT FOR YOU?

- **Practice identifying the verbal patterns used by different people**
- **Practice responding in similar verbal patterns**

VERBAL PATTERNS

10.14 Language Patterns

Individuals organize and express their experiences in three primary categories: visual (picture images), auditory (listening images), and physical (feeling images) patterns. Listen to the radio or television or practice with an interested group of people.

Write the sensory-specific words you hear in the appropriate column below. Next to or below the term you list, write a word that would be an appropriate response to the speaker's verbal pattern.

Language Patterns

Visual	Auditory	Physical
see	hear	touch
look	listen	handle
focus	tell	grasp
show	talk to me	rough
scan	speak	smooth
stare	ask	excited
preview	rings true	impact
short-sighted	sounds like/good	hit on
clarify	rattle	move
graphic	tune in	grab
color	sing	stroke
dress up	voice	get the point
frame	harmonize	sad
visualize	harmony	scared
appearance	amplify	angry
cloud	tempo	cold
dark	volume	tough
fantasize	all ears	solid
	say nothing	irritate

W O R K S H E E T

WHAT'S IN IT FOR YOU?

- **Get practice at identifying the verbal patterns used by different people**
- **Get practice responding in similar verbal patterns**

VERBAL PATTERNS

10.15 Verbal Pattern Identification

Individuals organize and express their experiences in three primary categories: visual (picture images), auditory (listening images), and physical (feeling images) patterns. Listen to the radio or television or practice with an interested group of people.

Put a check in the appropriate column when an individual uses words in that pattern.

Exercise: Verbal Pattern Identification

Person A:

Visual	Auditory	Physical	Unspecified

Person B:

Visual	Auditory	Physical	Unspecified

I D E A

WHAT'S IN IT FOR YOU?

• Understand what vocal quality can reveal about prospects and customers

VOCAL QUALITY

10.16 How People Say What They Feel

Vocal quality is the flip side of body language. Although it deals with the spoken word — which is a product of the intellect — vocal quality is determined by emotions. How people say things reveals as much about how people feel as it does about what they think.

Vocal qualities come in three flavors: rhythm, pitch, volume. Like body language, the key is to first note the person's normal way of speaking. We all speak with our own blend of rhythm, pitch, and volume. After observing the norm, look for changes in these patterns. The changes are what give you clues about the person's feelings.

Rhythm Rhythm refers to speed and inflection. How quickly a person speaks is a part of his or her personal style. You can expect Socializers and Directors to speak quickly. Thinkers and Relaters tend to speak at a slower pace. Voice inflection — the natural expressiveness of the voice — also varies. Directors and Thinkers tend to have less drama in their voices than Relaters and Socializers.

Pitch This refers to the high or low tonal quality of the voice. Again, it is not where the pitch starts, but how it changes that tells you something

Volume Some people naturally speak louder than others. Directors and Socializers are more likely to speak louder than Relaters and Thinkers.

WHAT THE CHANGES MEAN

Always verify your hunches about changes in vocal quality by asking questions or observing more closely. There are, however, some generalizations to remember.

Upward changes in volume and rhythm usually indicate excitement or enthusiasm. Anger is also accompanied by these changes, but we'll assume that you would never do anything to get a customer this mad.

Downward changes in volume and rhythm indicate boredom, fatigue, frustration, and sadness. Sometimes these changes, if accompanied by an increase in pitch, can mean the person is content. So be careful and check it out.

Increases in pitch indicate that the person is impatient or annoyed. Anger usually reveals itself with an increase in rhythm and volume as well.

IDEA

WHAT'S IN IT FOR YOU?

• **Increase your effectiveness by using your vocal qualities to your advantage**

VOCAL QUALITY

10.17 How Do <u>You</u> Say What You Feel?

The guidelines in the previous section helped you interpret other peoples' vocal qualities more accurately. When you communicate, you can increase your effectiveness if you pay attention to your vocal qualities. Professionalism takes awareness, practice, and control. You can help yourself achieve a strong image by speaking with the following vocal qualities:

- You will appear confident if, *without shouting*, you project your voice in a full, strong manner.
- Intelligent people speak clearly and distinctly, enunciating and pronouncing their words properly. "The rain in Spain falls mainly on the plain."
- Enthusiasm is one of the greatest assets a salesperson can possess. It's part of what you sell. Convey your enthusiasm by increasing your pitch and rhythm, *when appropriate*. There's nothing worse than inappropriate, hollow enthusiasm.
- Place emphasis and punctuation in your sentences by changing your vocal qualities. Stress importance by slowing down. Pause to let an important point sink in. Raise your volume slightly for enthusiasm and lower your volume to convey importance, confidentiality, or concern.
- Be an interesting speaker. Avoid — like the plague (and sales slumps) — monotonous speech. If you speak monotonously, do something to change. Hire a speech coach, take an acting class, or drink a strong cup of coffee.
- You will gain trust only when you speak with your natural vocal qualities. If you look like you are acting, you will quickly undermine your credibility. The key is to relax and be yourself, while keeping your "techniques" at hand to use if appropriate.
- As you do on the telephone, try to match the pace of your customer. If your customer is slow, low-keyed, and quiet, be the same.

- An important part of being effective is matching your vocal style to the personal style of your customer. Even though you want to use vocal qualities to enhance your words, be careful to choose qualities that will be well received by the listener. Thinkers and Directors are less comfortable with enthusiasm than Relaters and Socializers. At all times, remember to adapt your style to your customer.

If you doubt the importance of being aware of your vocal qualities, consider the differences in meanings in the following sentences when the emphasis is moved around:

"*I* didn't say she took the money."

"I didn't *say* she took the money."

"I didn't say *she* took the money."

"I didn't say she *took* the money."

"I didn't say she took the *money*.

SECTION ELEVEN

EXPLORING

WHAT'S IN IT FOR YOU?

- Qualify leads so you spend time only on prospects with potential.
- Learn how to gather information painlessly and effectively.
- Build an arsenal of questions that uncovers needs and promotes rapport.

The exploring stage gives you a chance to get deeply involved with the prospect to determine exactly how your product or service will help. It's where the partnering process really begins.

Exploring refers to the research you do before you contact the prospect as well as the information gathering you do with the prospect. In this section, you'll develop the questioning skills you need to identify prospect needs and to develop useful solutions.

I D E A

• Discover what questions can do for you

IDENTIFY LUCRATIVE PROSPECTS

11.1 What Questions Reveal

Sales professionals ask questions because they

- Elicit information that facilitates a sale
  What color do you prefer?

- Stimulate the conversation required to build a relationship
  What kind of a writer are you?

- Help you discover someone else's views
  What do you think about the new computer system?

- Confirm whether you understand each other
  Do you mean ... ?

- Help build rapport with a prospect
  Tell me about your goals for this department.

- Uncover facts
  How did the Model LX 772 hold up under your production deadline?

- Reveal a prospect's feelings
  Are you happy about the project?

- Draw out your prospect and generate hidden information
  Can you tell me more about that situation?

- Point the conversation toward a particular goal.
  Can we make our decision by Wednesday?

I D E A

- **Learn to qualify your leads so that you only spend your time on prospects with potential**

IDENTIFY LUCRATIVE PROSPECTS

11.2 Qualifying Questions

Not every lead turns into a prospect, unless you don't mind wasting your time and money. There are a myriad of leads in your target market, so you must pare them down to a manageable number that hold the greatest promise. Of course, not every prospect can be an "A" account. To determine if a lead is worth upgrading to prospect status, ask yourself the following questions:

1. Does this company need the products/services I am selling?
2. Does this company perceive a need that I may fill?
3. Does this company have a sincere desire to solve this problem or fill this need?
4. Can this company's desire to solve its problem be converted into a belief that my product/service is the answer?
5. Does this company have the necessary financial resources?
6. Will this prospect's order be significant enough to be profitable, given the amount of time needed to make the sale?
7. Is the competition so well entrenched with this firm that it will take an inordinate amount of time to get an order, thus making it unprofitable at this time?
8. If the answer to 7 was yes, does this company have the potential to be a significant account in the future and, therefore, should I invest time now to plant seeds?
9. Are this company's decision makers accessible to me?

I D E A

• Discover the information you will need to gather about your prospect

IDENTIFY LUCRATIVE PROSPECTS

11.3 Know What To Wonder About

Until you know the facts about a potential buyer and the way he or she makes buying decisions, it's difficult to truly serve your customer. Here are some questions you'll need to answer:

- How will the customer use your product or service?
- Who else is bidding for the customer's business?
- When will the decision be made?
- What other needs does the customer have?
- How could the customer benefit from having more than one of your products or services?
- How long is the payment cycle?
- Why is this particular item so important to the customer?
- Where does the decision maker get his or her information?
- If there is more than one decision maker, in what sequence are decisions like this made?
- How are major decisions made in this firm?
- Who reports to whom? (To know in advance, check with an assistant to determine titles and reporting sequence.)
- Is there a break-off point where this person's decision-making authority ends? For example, does he or she need to consult a supervisor for decisions above $5,000?
- Does someone else screen purchases before the buying decision is made?
- In the case of a committee, who will present your ideas to the group? And who has the most authority in that committee?
- Who besides the decision maker influences the choices that are made?
- What does the buyer really want and need?

I D E A

• **Understand the basic types of questions**

COMMUNICATE BETTER AND SELL MORE

11.4 The Nuances of Asking Questions

TYPES OF QUESTIONS

Open-ended questions begin with who, what, where, why, when, and how. They:

- let the other person speak in narrative form
- increase the other person's involvement in conversation
- encourage people to discover things on their own
- create an unstructured dialogue in which the person's behavioral style can be revealed.

"Tell me more about your business."

"How are you going to define and measure increased productivity?"

"What benefits are you seeking to derive from a service such as ours?"

Developmental questions start with a narrow focus and lead to more specific questions. "Tell me about your customer service training."

Clarifying questions seek feedback, an explanation, or more details. "What exactly do you mean by 'close tolerance'?"

Third-party questions make a statement about other people's feelings or experience and ask for feedback. "*Consumer Reports* rated our laptop as the best value in its price range. Is this the price you had in mind?"

Close-ended questions seek a yes, no, or brief answer. They:

- Serve as a form of feedback or seek agreement
- Direct the conversation

"How many employees do you have?"

"Do you know anything about Local Area Networks or compilers?"

"Have you ever worked with a voice-mail system before?"

I D E A

COMMUNICATE BETTER AND SELL MORE

11.5 Ten Tips for More Effective Questioning

1. **Ask permission.** In some situations, it is understood that you are there to gather information. In other situations, it is appropriate to show respect by asking permission to ask questions. "May I ask you some questions about your business?" may be a rhetorical question, but it is worth asking anyway.

2. **Start broad, then get specific.** Broad, open-ended questions are a good way to start gathering information. They put your prospect at ease because they allow any type of response. "Could you tell me about your business?" is a nonthreatening way to begin. Listen to what your prospect *says* and what she *omits*. Both will suggest areas to explore in greater depth, such as, "Could you tell me more about how absenteeism impacts your bottom line?"

3. **Build on previous responses.** Any good interviewer knows that the most logical source of questions comes from the interviewee's responses. Dovetail your questions with the responses by listening for key words. For example:

   "I own six flower shops that specialize in large event decorating."

   "You specialize in large events. Why did you choose that niche?"

   "Lower overhead. I can work out of a warehouse rather than a storefront. I don't have to maintain perishable stock; I order in large quantities only when needed, which keeps my prices down."

   "What do you mean by large events? How would you define that? What are the minimum orders?"

4. **Use the prospect's industry jargon, if appropriate.** If you are talking to an expert, show your expertise by sounding as if you've spent your whole life in his industry. If you are talking to a neophyte, don't embarrass him with your technical jargon. This is especially true in retail sales in which customers look to salespeople for guidance, not confusion.

5. **Keep questions simple.** If you want useful answers, ask useful questions. Convoluted or two-part questions should be avoided. Ask straightforward questions that cover one topic at a time.

6. **Use a logical sequence for your questions.** Prospects like to know where your questions are headed. If they can't tell, they may suspect you are manipulating them. By following key words and asking questions in a logical order, you will keep your intent clear and build trust.

7. **Keep questions nonthreatening.** Start off safe, general, and nonthreatening. That means asking open-ended questions that do not touch on sensitive subjects. Later, after you have built up trust—and when it is appropriate—you can ask about financial ability, business stability, credit rating … anything relevant.

8. **If a question is sensitive, explain its relevance.** It makes sense to justify a sensitive question to your prospect. After all, she has a right to know why you are asking.

9. **Focus on desired benefits.** Not all prospects are experts in their field. Many need to be educated, especially about your product's features and benefits. So ask what they hope to achieve, not necessarily how they hope to achieve it. That will put you in the position of being able to show how your product or service will fulfill those needs.

10. **Maintain a consultative attitude.** Ask questions in a way that will yield the most information with the least strain. Be prepared. Ask questions in a relaxed manner and patiently wait for responses. Investing a little time now will save a lot of time later.

I D E A

WHAT'S IN IT FOR YOU?

• **Build an arsenal of questions that uncover needs and promote rapport**

IDENTIFY CUSTOMER NEEDS

11.6 How to Ask the Right Questions

A direct, tactful approach to questioning prospects will help you uncover needs, build rapport, and customize your presentation. Use open-ended questions to stimulate discussion. Use other questioning tactics to draw out your prospects before moving on to the next subject. The order of the following questions is unimportant.

To determine: Sales potential and buying cycle.
Ask: "How much and how often do you buy?"

To determine: Buyer's needs
Ask: "What problems have you been having with _____?"

To determine: Current supplier
Ask: "What company is now supplying you with _____?"

To determine: Long-term potential
Ask: "What are your company's long-term goals? Paint a picture for your company for me as you see it three to five years from now."

To determine: When the sale may be confirmed
Ask: "Would you walk me through your decision-making process for a purchase such as this?" "How is a decision like this typically made?"

To determine: New prospects or markets
Ask: "Who is the end-user? Where and how will this product/service be used?"

To determine: The ultimate decision maker
Ask: "Besides yourself, who else will be involved in the decision-making process?"

To determine: Your prospect's buying authority
Ask: "What is your role or responsibility for this purchase?"

To determine: The quality of service provided by present supplier
Ask: "Typically, how long does it take to get a quote/delivery/service from your present vendor?"

To determine: Other problems with present supplier
Ask: "How do you think they could improve? What have you been striving for, but unable to attain?"

To determine: Knowledge of your product/service (This provides an opportunity to talk about benefits.)
Ask: "What do you know about my company's product/service?"

To determine: Expectations of quality and price
Ask: "What kind of quality do you need? How important is price versus value? What is your price range or budget for this?"

To determine: Referrals
Ask: "Who do you know here or elsewhere who might have a similar need for my product/service?"

To determine: Other needs or expectations
Ask: "What else do you look for in a top-notch supplier?"

IDEA

IDENTIFY CUSTOMER NEEDS

11.7 And Yet More Questions

These questions will help you learn more about your prospects' needs and customize your presentation to address them.

What are your short-term goals? Long-term goals?

What does this purchase mean to you? What does it mean to your company?

What do you perceive as your greatest strength? Weakness?

How do you perceive my company? Its strengths? Its weaknesses?

How is the potential of new products or services evaluated?

Who has your business now? How did they get it? How can I get it?

What are your buying criteria and success criteria?

Where would you put the emphasis regarding price, quality, and service?

What level of service are you willing to pay for?

What do you like best about your present supplier? What don't you like?

What do you look for in the companies you do business with?

What might cause you to change suppliers?

What do you like best about your current system? What would you like to see changed?

What do you perceive your needs to be? How important are they?

If you were me, how would you proceed?

Which trade associations do you belong to?

What will it take for us to do business?

How soon can we begin?

Can you tell me why you decided against us?

What is my best shot for getting back the account?

What did we do in the last sale that impressed you most?

What do you look for in your relationship with a supplier?

Who was the best salesperson who ever called on you?

When would be the best time for me to call you back?

What else can I do for you?

I D E A

- **Ensure that you elicit all the information you need**
- **Ask questions in a way that builds trust and rapport**

IDENTIFY CUSTOMER NEEDS

11.8 Your Questioning Plan

To ask questions effectively, you need to develop a questioning plan.

Think of a funnel: broad at the top, narrow at the bottom. Start off with broad, non-threatening questions. Questions that ask for general information about your buyer and his or her business. Make these broad questions relevant to why you are calling on this person. As you continue, gradually become more specific. If you build up slowly, the buyer will be more receptive to answering specific questions because you have taken the time to build trust and cooperation.

Use this list to develop your questioning plan:

1. Plan your questions in advance so you are sure to obtain the answers you need. Begin by listing information you need and then develop questions that will uncover that information.
2. Begin with broad questions and progress to more specific ones.
3. Build on the buyer's previous responses when formulating your next questions.
4. Eliminate the use of jargon or technical terms that might confuse the buyer.
5. Ask questions that focus on one idea at a time.
6. Keep the questions short and simple.
7. Make the questions nonthreatening.
8. Give a reason for needing to know before you ask sensitive questions.
9. Ask questions that uncover desired benefits rather than focusing on features.
10. Uncover the ideal solutions. (If the world were perfect, what would you like this product to do for you?)

SECTION TWELVE

STUDY THE SITUATION

WHAT'S IN IT FOR YOU?

- Increase your understanding of the "need gap."
- Determine the information required to uncover your prospects' needs.
- Understand and appreciate the value of the needs summary and success criteria.

Knowing your prospect or customer is only half the equation. You also must know the situation you are dealing with because *you* are your customers' problem solver. The only way you can fill this role is to know your customers' problems and needs. The following pages will give you tips on how to determine a prospect's needs and how to match your company's product benefits to those needs.

IDEA

- **Understand the importance of the need gap**
- **Determine which to discuss first — the prospect's current situation or future goals**

IDENTIFYING CUSTOMER NEEDS

12.1 The "Need Gap"

A need gap is simply a discrepancy between what a person or company wants and what they have at present. It's the difference between the ideal situation and the actual situation. Studying needs is a process of gathering information by asking questions, doing research, and making observations. It culminates in an understanding of your prospect's business that lets you identify need gaps that you may be able to close.

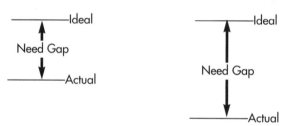

CURRENT SITUATION VERSUS GOALS

Your prospect's current situation and future goals are the two primary areas you should investigate. Which should you study first? Believe it or not, the order is important. Goals are abstract ideas that pertain to the future. The current situation is a concrete topic. Some people prefer to talk about one over the other. Using your knowledge of relationship strategies, you should gear your conversations accordingly.

As you learned in Section 9, Socializers and Directors are dreamers who focus on goals and future objectives. Relaters and Thinkers, on the other hand, are more grounded and focused on the present. To more quickly establish a rapport, discuss goals first with Socializers and Directors. Discuss the here and now of the current situation first with Relaters and Thinkers.

Many salespeople think they can create a need in their prospect's mind for the product or service being sold. That is not how ethical, nonmanipulative sales are conducted. You cannot create needs. They either exist, or they don't. An ethical, consultative salesperson gathers information to determine if there is a need gap. If there is and it can be filled with your product or service, that's great. If there is no need gap or it requires a different solution, then the ethical salesperson admits this and does not try to force the sale. Instead, the salesperson would contact the prospect again in six months to see if his or her situation has changed.

W O R K S H E E T

WHAT'S IN IT FOR YOU?

- Determine the information and the documents you will request from prospects
- Formulate specific questions to ask prospects

IDENTIFYING CUSTOMER NEEDS

12.2 How to Uncover the Need Gap

Begin researching your prospect's need gap by determining the information you will need and planning questions that will help you thoroughly probe the gap.

1. What information do you need to determine your prospect's need gap?

    a. _____

    b. _____

    c. _____

2. What are six specific questions you can ask to uncover the above information?

    Three open-ended questions:

    a. _____

    b. _____

    c. _____

    Three closed-ended questions:

    a. _____

    b. _____

    c. _____

3. Documents/data to ask for:

    a. _____

    b. _____

    c. _____

4. Other sources of information (e.g., publications/people/company records)

    a. _____

    b. _____

    c. _____

I D E A

IDENTIFYING CUSTOMER NEEDS

12.3 Topics to Study

The process of studying needs depends on many factors, including the nature of your product or service, the behavioral style of your prospect, your relationship with your prospect, and the typical sales cycle in your industry. Your information gathering could be highly structured—with you asking a lot of questions and taking copious notes—or more informal: you might simply get to know your prospect and develop trust and rapport.

When you choose the structured approach, you need to know what to study. The more complicated the sale, the more important the following areas will become to you:

1. **Current situation versus goals = need gap.** What they need now versus what they are getting. What they hope for versus where they are now.

2. **Psychological factors.** Try to discover if your prospect is buying for prestige, love, imitation, fear, variety, or purely practical reasons.

3. **Prospect's point of view.** How does your prospect feel about this purchase? Is she afraid to spend the money? Is her reputation on the line? What are the personal risks and rewards associated with this sale?

4. **Key decision makers.** You've got to know the cast of characters and their input into the decision-making process. Otherwise you may spend too much time with the wrong person.

5. **Buying urgency.** Is your prospect shopping around leisurely or getting bids, or is he in a hurry to make a deal?

6. **Buying criteria.** What characteristics of your product or service are most important to your prospect? Is she buying quality, price, service, or the ability to customize?

7. **Political influences.** You may be bidding against your prospect's brother-in-law. Knowing this will help you form your strategy and determine the amount of time you devote to this account.

8. **Bad experiences.** It is not uncommon for a salesperson to find accounts who have bad experiences with his or her company. The ideal solution, if possible, is to resolve the problem, change the prospect's attitude to a positive one, and move on.

9. **Product service demands.** If you are penetrating a new industry, you must find out as soon as possible whether your product or service will have to meet some standard of quality, performance, or certification.

10. **Monetary constraints.** Part of qualifying a prospect is determining buying power, but that changes over time. Keep your understanding of buying ability current by asking questions. If the situation sours, don't lose hope. Sometimes prospects can borrow or take money from other departments to pay for your product or service. It's your job to show how borrowing that money will be a wise move.

I D E A

• **Organize the results of your needs survey into a logical, compelling presentation of your analysis**

IDENTIFYING CUSTOMER NEEDS

12.4 The Needs Summary

When you have finished studying your prospect's needs, it is time to present a needs summary. This is a formal summary of your prospect's needs presented in their order of importance. This presentation—like any—should be well organized, well documented, and professionally delivered. Keep in mind these tips:

1. **Seek agreement and feedback.** If you have been communicating well with your prospect and asking the right questions, your assessment of his business situation should be accurate. However, you should always confirm your findings by asking for feedback and agreement. That way you can fine-tune your summary and eliminate any potentially embarrassing mistakes.

2. **Categorize problems and opportunities.** Organize your summary by categorizing your findings into six categories:
   a. Problems for which you have the solution
   b. Opportunities that should be pursued immediately, with which you can help
   c. Problems that are unimportant to your prospect and can be ignored
   d. Opportunities that are worth considering, but belong on the back burner
   e. Problems that need to be fixed for which you have no solutions, but hopefully can provide suggestions or referrals
   f. Opportunities that should be pursued, but that you have no way of helping him capitalize on. Again, give suggestions or referrals.

3. **Conduct situational triage.** When you uncover many need gaps, never attempt to solve them all at once, unless they are *all* related to the benefits that your product or service can provide. Conduct a situational triage to determine which problems or opportunities should be tackled first and which can wait. As a salesperson and consultant, you will gain credibility.

4. **Don't oversell.** If you try to solve all the prospect's problems with one huge solution, you run the risk of overselling. Overselling often scares prospects away. It is better to break problems down into manageable increments and solve them slowly, comfortably, and affordably over time. Make it clear to your prospect that you see the big picture and plan to solve the balance of the problems in a timely manner.

5. **Propose solutions.** By now you know who to meet with, what materials you will need, what specific needs you will address, and how your prospect regards you and your company. The next logical step is to move on to proposing solutions. Set an appointment for a presentation, if appropriate.

I D E A

WHAT'S IN IT FOR YOU?

- **Find out how your product/service will be evaluated after the sale**
- **Use the evaluation criteria to add credibility to your presentation**

IDENTIFYING CUSTOMER NEEDS

12.5 Establish Success Criteria

The only way to determine if your product or service will truly be the solution to your prospect's needs is to discuss success criteria when you are studying needs. There are several ways to approach this. You could ask, "What are you going to measure to determine if this worked for you?" Or, "Imagine you are looking back on this purchase six months from now. What criteria will you use to judge the success of my product/service?"

Establishing success criteria early in the sales process serves many purposes. The most obvious is that you will have a *concrete, measurable* basis with which to track performance and judge success or failure after the sale.

As a presentation tool, success criteria will help you customize your solution and directly address your prospect's needs. In addition, they will allow you to put features, benefits, and price in the proper perspective. It's valuable to be able to say, "For the level of performance you demand, you will need the Model XYZ. If you were willing to settle for a lower level of performance, you could spend less and get Model ABC, but I wouldnt recommend it, based on what you've told me."

Discussing success criteria during the studying phase of the sale will show you how realistic your prospect is and whether his or her expectations can be met by your company. It may be appropriate for you to size up the prospect's situation and try to lower his or her performance expectations. Sometimes propsects want more than they really need or are willing to pay for. Part of your job is to paint a more realistic picture.

When discussing success criteria, take notes. Later, after you have confirmed the sale, again bring up the subject of success criteria. This time, put everything in writing and give your customer a copy. As a part of the follow-up process, help your customer track your product/service's performance. This process will help you keep in touch, strengthen your relationship, and show both of you how good (or bad) your product or service is.

WORKSHEET

WHAT'S IN IT FOR YOU?

• Get your client to identify priorities to enable you to better meet his/her needs

IDENTIFYING CUSTOMER NEEDS

12.6 Getting Agreement on Cost, Quality, and Time

Ask your client the following questions to help define cost, quality, and time.
- What does quality mean to you?
- How would you define quality?
- How do you define time? Is it a delivery date, responsiveness, or something else?
- What specifics do you include when you think about cost?
- In what context do you think about cost? Is it in terms of product price? terms? alternatives?

Show your client the diagram below. Ask, "Where would you place the dot to indicate your priorities for this purchase?"

Indicates price buyer

Indicates quality and time top priorities —
willing to pay for quality and time

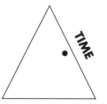

A buyer who will pay for
responsiveness

A buyer who is willing to wait
for the right quality and price

Note: Adapted from *Beyond Selling: How to Maximize Your Personal Influence* by Bagley and Reese.

I D E A

• **Understand the many factors that enter into a buying decision**

HOW DECISIONS ARE MADE

12.7 Buying Influences

The notion that selling is a one-on-one interaction between a corporate buyer and a salesperson is a bit too simple. The bigger the company, the more influences come to bear on a buying decision. Understanding these influences is important. Take them into account when planning your sales approach.

THE ENVIRONMENT

The environment is everything outside the company that has an impact on market conditions or the company itself such as economic, political, legal, technological, and competitive factors.

THE ORGANIZATION

You might call this the internal environment. Every company has a unique culture that affects the structure and functioning of the buying process. The bigger the purchase, the more the organization's "personality" influences the buying process.

THE GROUP

The personalities and positions of the decision makers play a big role in shaping the buying process. Other influences include their decision criteria, the risks involved in the purchase, and the unwritten rules of behavior within the group.

THE INDIVIDUAL

Your contact's agenda and behavioral style are major influences. If you are involved in selling to a prospect's team, the individual dynamics become even more complex and deserving of attention.

IDEA

WHAT'S IN IT FOR YOU?

• **Learn the most effective way to reach decision makers**

HOW DECISIONS ARE MADE

12.8 How Decision Makers Obtain Information

People in different target markets gather information differently. By knowing the various media that are effective in reaching decision makers, you will be able to better promote your product/services and yourself.

Use the following worksheet to comment on the effectiveness of each promotional strategy as a way to reach decision makers in each market segment. Fill in as you see fit, and make additional copies if necessary.

Information Source	Target Market Segment		
	1.	2.	3.
1. Catalogs Comments:			
2. Price Lists Comments:			
3. Newspaper Ads Comments:			
4. Radio Advertising Comments:			
5. Direct Mail Promo Comments:			

Information Source	Target Market Segment		
	1.	2.	3.
6. Inside Salespeople Comments:			
7. Outside Salespeople Comments:			
8. Published Reports or Stories Comments:			
9. Comments:			
10. Comments:			

I D E A

- **Know the people who play a major role in the decision-making and purchase processes**

THE DECISION-MAKING PROCESS

12.9 Understand the Cast of Characters

Many people in your prospect's organization may play a role in making a purchase. To make a sale, you have to distinguish the major characters from the minor, and make sure you meet everyone who will influence the decision.

Role	Description
Users	As the name implies, these are the people who will use the product. Users' influence may range anywhere from inconsequential to extremely important on the purchase decision. In some cases, the users initiate the purchase by requesting the product. They may even develop the product specifications.
Gatekeepers	Gatekeepers control information to be reviewed by other members of the buying center. They may control the dissemination of printed information or advertisements, or determine which salesperson will speak to which individuals in the buying center. For example, the purchasing agent might perform this screening role by opening the gate to the buying center for some sales personnel and closing it to others.
Influencers	Although Influencers are not Users, Deciders, or Buyers, and can only say no (but not yes), they have important relationships with Deciders or Buyers because they filter information in a way that exerts significant impact on the decision-making process and the sale.
Deciders	Deciders actually make the buying decision, whether or not they have the formal authority to do so. The identity of the Decider is the most difficult role to determine; buyers may have formal authority to buy, but the president of the firm may actually make the decision. A decider could be a design engineer who develops a set of specifications that only one vendor can meet.
Buyers	The buyer has formal authority for selecting the supplier and implementing all procedures connected with securing the product. The power of the buyer is often usurped by more powerful members of the organization. Often the buyer's role is assumed by the purchasing agent, who executes the clerical functions associated with a purchase order.

I D E A

THE DECISION-MAKING PROCESS

12.10 Understand the Interactions of Key Players

For a relatively simple purchase, the purchasing agent will function as gatekeeper, influencer, and, quite often, the decision maker.

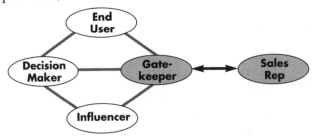

For purchases that involve a great deal of financial, personal, and organizational risk, the buyer–seller relationships might be paired off as follows:

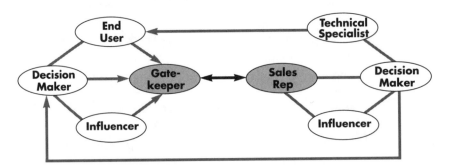

I D E A

THE DECISION-MAKING PROCESS

12.11 Selling Through Others

When you meet a potential buyer, it's important to determine whether you are talking with the person who actually makes the buying decision. Find out by asking, "Who usually makes these buying decisions for your company?" If the reply is, "I screen the products and recommend the top two or three to the supervisor for a final decision," then you know you will have to make two sales: one to the contact, and one to the supervisor.

The contact will become your sales representative when the decision maker gets involved, so it's imperative to prepare your contact to represent you and your product or service. If you don't take the time to prepare your contact, you reduce your chances of a recommendation.

1. Outline the key points and summarize the main reasons why that company should buy from you.
2. Include enough copies of your sales material so that each person who might be in on the discussion has his or her own copy.
3. Highlight key points that make your product or service different from the competition and put those points in writing.

Here are some important questions to answer before you attempt to sell through others.

1. Where does the decision maker get his or her information?
2. If there is more than one decision maker, in what sequence are decisions like this made?
3. Who reports to whom?
4. In the case of a committee, who will present your ideas to the group? And who has the most authority in that committee?
5. If you were contacted by the prospect, did the prospect initiate the contact or was he or she asked to contact you by somebody else?
6. Who besides the decision maker influences the choices that are made?
7. What does the buyer really want and need?

From *Relationship Selling: The Key to Getting and Keeping Customers* by Jim Cathcart, Perigee Books, 1990.

SECTION THIRTEEN

COLLABORATING AND PROPOSING SOLUTIONS

WHAT'S IN IT FOR YOU?

• Increase your understanding of the theory and practice of giving presentations.

• Learn to speak in terms of benefits rather than features.

• Learn how to plan effective presentations.

• Discover how to modify your presentations to complement the behavioral styles of your prospects.

L ots of people can find problems. It's the one who proposes the right solution who gets the sale. Often, this is a matter of how you make your presentation. This section focuses on how you can present your products' benefits in ways that will enable you to make the sale.

I D E A

• **Understand the basic components that go into a good presentation**

PRESENTATIONS THAT SELL

13.1 The Structure of Presentations

Although many salespeople like to wing it rather than prepare a structured presentation, the majority of professionals rely on an outline. Whether you speak well extemporaneously or depend on copious notes, you still must give a logical flow to your ideas. In your presentation, cover five general areas.

The Claim You are making a presentation because you offer the promise of some benefit. That benefit may be increased sales, fewer sick days, less paperwork, fewer mechanical breakdowns . . . it doesn't matter. Whatever the claim, it must be related to your prospect's need gap.

The Need Gap Over half of your work as a salesperson is uncovering and diagnosing a prospect's need gap. During a presentation, you must keep him or her aware of that gap and continually relate your product's benefits to that need.

The Solution Your product or service must genuinely be able to solve your prospect's problem. You must be able to present a clear, concise statement of how your product will do so. Your proposal may include specific, measurable criteria by which the success of the solution will be judged. This may be a point of negotiation and will ultimately reflect the guarantee that comes with your product/service.

Documentation How can you prove your claims? Document successes. Offer testimonial letters with lots of specifics. Give an impressive demonstration. Break out the slides and show pictures, graphs, data, and other proof.

A Call to Action You've got to ask for the sale. Too many salespeople fail to do this. It's a natural thing to ask for feedback on your presentation and your product/service and then to ask for your prospect's business.

IDEA

PRESENTATIONS THAT SELL

13.2 Toward More Effective Presentations

During a presentation, you not only sell your product or service, you sell yourself and the presentation process. You cannot hope to make a sale with an excellent product, a good rapport with your prospect, and an inept presentation.

Entertain Your Prospect Capture your prospect's attention 100 percent of the time. That means *be interesting*. Vary the pace of your speech, involve your prospect with questions, use visual aids, and present data in ways that are understood.

Remember Murphy's Law Precisely those things that you cannot prepare for, you must prepare for. Anything can happen: interruptions, equipment failures, unexpected time constraints, and other snafus. During your presentation, recover from an interruption by summarizing what has recently transpired and moving on unflustered.

Play Off of Needs Keep your prospect aware of his or her need gap and continually relate your proposal to the closing of the gap.

Keep it Relevant Customize your presentation. Follow a structure. If you have a canned presentation, be sure to tailor it to the prospect. If your product has 42 features, *only* discuss the ones most important to your prospect. Failing to customize shows that you have failed to get to know your prospect and her needs.

Be Ethical Avoid the temptation to exaggerate. Tell the truth. If you do not know the answer to a question, be honest and tell the person you will find out.

Build Perceived Value Again, customize by putting your product or service's price, quality, performance, delivery, service, and other factors into the perspective that your prospect will appreciate. By the time you propose a solution, you should know your prospect's buying criteria and success criteria. Be sure you address both, especially when they are different, which they should *not* be.

Differentiate Yourself From the Competition Nothing is worse than trying to sell a commodity. If you are, you can only compete on price, which is a neverending, no-win battle. You must find ways to make yourself, your company, and your product/service different — those differences play a large part in your presentation.

Be Confident Rehearse your presentation until you have lost the fear that you may forget what to say. Relax, control your pace, make eye contact, stay tuned in to your prospect.

Share Your Enthusiasm Enthusiasm is a big part of what you are selling. It shows confidence in your product/service.

Stay Sensitive To Your Prospect's Needs Although most salespeople would rather reschedule an appointment than condense their presentation, you may not have a choice. Some prospects are difficult to catch, so make the most of the time you're given. When you are forced to condense your presentation, pare away the extras and concentrate on the relevant benefits. Being sensitive also means giving your prospect the floor when she seems to have a question or some resistance. Look for signs that something is on her mind.

Create Descriptive, Carefully Worded Phrases Describe your product or service quickly and clearly with phrases that have impact. By repeating these phrases throughout your presentation, you will reinforce your message. Slow down after presenting an important point. Slowing down creates an emphasis and allows the idea to sink in.

Present Simple Concepts First, Complex Later The simple ideas will help prospects understand the complex ideas. Avoid concepts that are too detailed for prospects to understand. It's better to hand out supplemental material to be read later than to make prospects feel ignorant.

Customize Your Presentation to the Prospect's Behavioral Style Vary the amount of statistics, figures, graphs, computer readouts, spreadsheets, and other numbers you present depending on your prospect's behavioral style. Thinkers want lots of numbers. Directors just want bottom-line figures. Socializers and Relaters want fewer numbers still. Shape your presentation according to the guidelines given in 8.13 "Collaborating on Solutions by Style."

Ask for Feedback Make sure everything you say is understood. Leave no room for confusion or misunderstanding. There are practical and legal implications to this piece of advice.

Involve Your Prospect Use questions and hands-on participation (if appropriate). The earlier in a presentation a prospect asks questions, the less chance there will be for unanswered questions to become objections later.

Believe In Yourself and Your Product/Service It will show and be contagious.

I D E A

• **Deliver sales presentations to groups with confidence**

PRESENTATIONS THAT SELL

13.3 Speaking Persuasively

The following points can help you succeed whenever you give a sales presentation to a group.

1. Know your subject.
2. Know your audience.
3. Know why you are giving the presentation.
4. Know what you want the audience to know or do and how you want them to feel.
5. Focus on the big idea.
6. Develop a basic outline that takes you through the three basic parts of your presentation:

    Introduction. Start your presentation with power. Grab attention with a meaningful quote or statistics. Write out your introduction word for word to get yourself off to a good start and help calm your nerves.

    Main body. Be as short and interesting as possible. Keep attention focused by tossing in a story, illustration, or exercise every 5 to 10 minutes. Involve the audience with visual aids, questions, and discussion. Use examples, statistics, comparisons, and testimonials to get your point across more and to make it more believable. Be sure to state your main ideas more than once. And avoid delivering your presentation in a monotone. Vary your tone of voice.

    Conclusion. To ensure a strong wrap up, review the main points. Be succinct and persuasive. Remind them of why it is important to know this.

7. Rehearse your presentation aloud several times. Time your presentation and practice your visual aids so everything will be perfect.
8. To boost confidence, visualize your presentation several times before you deliver it. Mentally go through the whole thing from introductory applause to final words. Repeat this several times to increase your confidence and sense of preparation.

W O R K S H E E T

WHAT'S IN IT FOR YOU?

• **An organized and cogent way to compare your company with your competitors**

PRESENTATIONS THAT SELL

13.4 Comparisons with the Competition

Selling's first rule of thumb is: *Don't knock the competition*. It's terribly amateurish and potentially unethical. A better approach is to know your competition well and compare yourself with them fairly, but only after your prospect has asked you to do so. The worksheet below can be filled out in advance or you can work on it with your prospect. In either case, it is a valuable selling tool.

Comparing Your Company and Its Products and Services with Your Competitors				
Product or Service	**Yours**	**Competitor A**	**Competitor B**	**Competitor C**
Specifications				
_____	_____	_____	_____	_____
_____	_____	_____	_____	_____
_____	_____	_____	_____	_____
Features				
_____	_____	_____	_____	_____
_____	_____	_____	_____	_____
Benefits				
_____	_____	_____	_____	_____
_____	_____	_____	_____	_____
Service	_____	_____	_____	_____
Delivery	_____	_____	_____	_____
Price	_____	_____	_____	_____
Terms	_____	_____	_____	_____
Other				
_____	_____	_____	_____	_____
_____	_____	_____	_____	_____

I D E A

WHAT'S IN IT FOR YOU?

- **Learn to tie your presentations to the important benefits that your prospect hopes to derive from your product or service.**

PRESENTATIONS THAT SELL

13.5 Speak the Language of Benefits

New salespeople are often confused by the difference between features and benefits and the role each plays in a presentation. A *feature* is an aspect of the product or service that exists regardless of the customer's need for it. A *benefit* is the use or advantage a customer derives from a feature. For example, a customer who is shopping for a truck may not care about four-wheel drive. It is a feature, but an irrelevant one to some people. However, when an off-road enthusiast walks up to the truck, that feature suddenly becomes a benefit.

A benefit, then, is a feature in action. Most customers, especially end-users on the retail level, think in terms of benefits. They don't care what features make something work. They are only concerned with the end result — the benefits they can derive from the purchase.

During a presentation, you must know what kind of person you are dealing with. If you are selling to an engineer, you must discuss features as well as benefits. Most of the time, however, you will not need to cover features in such detail. In fact, most final decision makers only care about the bottom line, which is how they will benefit from the purchase.

Concentrate on speaking the language of benefits. This means addressing your prospect's problems or needs one at a time and showing how your product/service will solve each *specific* problem. Get your prospect involved by using the Feature-Feedback-Benefit (FFB) method. Present a feature and ask for feedback.

Salesperson:
   "This computer has a 1000 gigabyte hard disk. How important is that to you?"

Customer:
   "I don't know. Is that enough to store at least 200,000 names for a mailing list?"

The customer has done two things: 1) revealed a lack of knowledge and need for consultative help; and 2) described an important benefit that must be provided by the

product. Later in your presentation, you would come back to this benefit and make a point of showing how it will be provided.

Keep in mind that a feature can provide more than one benefit. Similarly, a described benefit can be accomplished with more than one feature. For example, a fireplace can provide more than heat. The benefit of recreation can be derived from a swimming pool, a big backyard, a finished basement, or proximity to a park.

During your presentation, be sure to point out all the possibilities, especially if flexibility and diversity are desired benefits. In addition, use the following questions — or similar ones — to uncover other desired benefits.

"How do you see this fitting into your current or future situation?"

"Have I missed any advantages that this may provide you? What might they be?"

"This is how my product/service can be used in (Situation A); can you see ways that it will help you with (Situation B)?"

"How do you see this addressing the problem/opportunity we discussed earlier?" (Be specific.)

"Does this look like it will meet your needs?"

If the answer is no, say, "I'm sorry, I must have missed something. What are you looking to accomplish that I have overlooked?"

W O R K S H E E T

WHAT'S IN IT FOR YOU?

• **Increase your knowledge of your products' or services' features and benefits**

PRESENTATIONS THAT SELL

13.6 Features/Benefits Identification

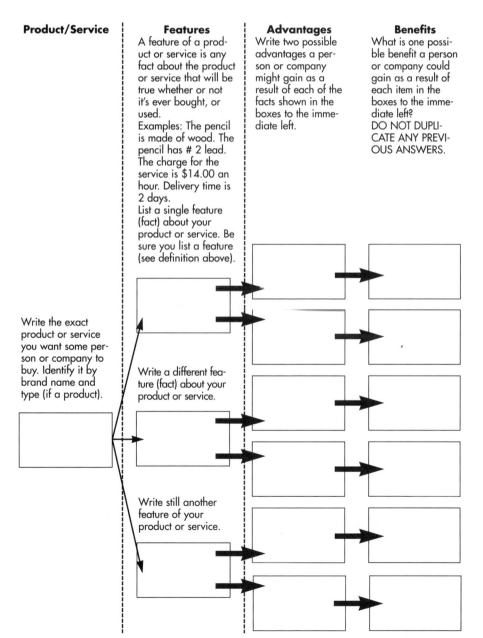

Product/Service

Write the exact product or service you want some person or company to buy. Identify it by brand name and type (if a product).

Features
A feature of a product or service is any fact about the product or service that will be true whether or not it's ever bought, or used.
Examples: The pencil is made of wood. The pencil has # 2 lead. The charge for the service is $14.00 an hour. Delivery time is 2 days.
List a single feature (fact) about your product or service. Be sure you list a feature (see definition above).

Write a different feature (fact) about your product or service.

Write still another feature of your product or service.

Advantages
Write two possible advantages a person or company might gain as a result of each of the facts shown in the boxes to the immediate left.

Benefits
What is one possible benefit a person or company could gain as a result of each item in the boxes to the immediate left?
DO NOT DUPLICATE ANY PREVIOUS ANSWERS.

I D E A

- **Organize ahead of time, so you are completely prepared before each presentation**

PRESENTATIONS THAT SELL

13.7 Presentation Planning Guide

Prepare the following worksheet in advance to help you with your presentations.

Company: _____ Buyer's name: _____

Industry: _____ Phone: _____

Address: _____ Appointment date: _____

Prospect's behavioral style: _____

Call objectives: _____

_____

1. Introduction to use: _____

2. Initial questions to ask: _____

3. Initial summary or statement to make: _____

4. Questions to ask to further explore need gap: _____

5. Needs to address: _____

6. Features and benefits to emphasize: _____

7. Benefits to seek agreement on: _____

8. Plan for presentation: _____

9. A/V aids to use and equipment needed: _____

10. Testimonial letters to bring: _____

11. How to get prospect involved: _____

12. Feedback questions to ask:_____

13. Possible resistance and how to handle it:_____

14. Key points in summary of presentation: _____

15. How to ask for the sale: _____

16. Outcome of presentation: _____

17. Suggestions for improvements:_____

I D E A

WHAT'S IN IT FOR YOU?

• Effectively use demonstrations to help prospects visualize your product/service's success.

PRESENTATIONS THAT SELL

13.8 Fine Points for Presentations

We all know that a picture is worth a thousand words and that a demonstration is worth 1,000 pictures, models, descriptions, and testimonials. A well-done demonstration will catch your prospect's attention, emphasize your main points, help prospects understand complex concepts, combine seeing and hearing to aid memory, stimulate your own enthusiasm, reduce the amount of resistance that arises, and help you achieve the purpose of the proposal!

The key is to have your prospect visualize the success of your product/service for himself. To achieve this, remember these fine points when preparing or presenting your demonstration.

1. Keep visuals simple. Use words, graphics, or both to reinforce or explain your main points.
2. Limit text to 40 characters. Most people can grasp this much at a glance. Never put your entire presentation on slides and read it to a prospect.
3. Slides with text should be written in phrases, not complete sentences. You will fill in the details and clarify any unclear phrases.
4. Use upper- and lower-case letters. All caps are difficult to read.
5. Give the text room to breathe on the slide or page and situate it in a similar location from page to page or slide to slide.
6. Keep it short and simple (KISS). Graphs or charts should present only one idea at a time to increase comprehension.
7. Line charts are best used to show how one or more variables changed over time.
8. Bar graphs are best used to show the relationship between two or more variables.
9. Pie charts show the relationship between parts within a whole.

10. Tables and charts with complex data would only be used with groups that will understand them, and only when the group plans to study the graphics closely. In the average sales proposal, complex concepts should be simplified and explained.

11. Spend the money to make slides colorful, but not gaudy. Red should be used very sparingly. Bright colors are OK for main points, while shading, arrows, and highlighting add interesting dimensions to the slide.

12. Always have a duplicate videotape, audiotape, slide set, computer disk, or whatever A/V medium you are using.

13. Learn to be your own repair person. If possible, carry along a kit that includes critical items you need most often:

projector bulbs	electrical tape	head cleaner	back up disc
duct tape	pressurized air	pliers, knife	
3-prong adapter plugs	flashlight	projector trays	

Call ahead to ensure that critical items are available. And, be sure to bring along the phone number of a local expert to help you.

14. Use a room that is larger than necessary rather than one that is just right or too small. People don't like feeling crowded.

15. Arrange the chairs so aisles are on the sides rather than down the middle. That way, late comers will not walk in front of the projector.

16. Always rehearse your demonstration, including the slides, overhead, video, computer, or other aids you plan to use.

IDEA

WHAT'S IN IT FOR YOU?

• **Know how to control the setting for maximum impact**

PRESENTATIONS THAT SELL

13.9 Seating for Sales

How a room is arranged is a key factor in the success of your sales presentation, whether it is to a group or an individual. Keep these key points in mind before you assign seating or choose a seat of your own.

- All humans need their personal space. We rely on the air space around us and the way we touch to define and defend our personal space. Whether you are selling to an individual or a group, respect your customer's personal space. Try to keep 2 to 4 feet between you and your prospect and avoid inappropriate touching. Move closer only as you build trust. Accidentally (or intentionally) infringing on someone's personal space increases tension and decreases trust. Plus, it can so infuriate your prospect that he or she may not listen to a word you say!

- Side-by-side seating arrangements make it awkward to track facial expressions and may force uncomfortably close proximity — but they are useful for getting down to business. Sitting next to your prospect conveys that you intend to cooperate and work together on the project or problem at hand.

- Corner-to-corner seating allows unlimited eye contact and maximum use of body language, facial gestures, and other nonverbal signals.

- Across-the-table seating stresses the competitive aspect of a presentation, and makes conflict more likely. On the other hand, it enables both parties to watch closely for nonverbal cues.

- Don't stand or lean over people when you present. It's intimidating and uncomfortable for the person underneath you.

- When you sell to a group, try to determine how buying decisions typically are made within that group. Watch carefully to see who defers to whom in making even small decisions. The way they handle the little decisions may very well be the way they handle the large ones. Tailor your presentation to reach the key people.

I D E A

WHAT'S IN IT FOR YOU?

• **Ask the right questions and let your customer do the selling**

PRESENTATIONS THAT SELL

13.10 Let the Customer Sell Himself

Many years ago, professional sales trainer Fred Herman had the opportunity to appear on the Mike Douglas Show. Before the show, he was screened by one of the show's producers; the following exchange took place:

> Producer: *"So, Mr. Herman, you're a sales expert. If you're so good at selling, sell me something."*
>
> Fred Herman: *"What would you like me to sell you?"*
>
> Producer: *"Sell me that ashtray."*
>
> Fred Herman: *"Why would you want that ashtray?"*
>
> Producer: *"Well, it's a needed item in this office, and it helps keep the office clean."*
>
> Fred Herman: *"And what other reasons would you have for wanting that ashtray?"*
>
> Producer: *"The colors fit in; it's about the right size."*
>
> Fred Herman: *"What do you think that ashtray is worth?"*
>
> Producer: *"Oh, about twenty dollars."*
>
> Fred Herman: *"Well, I guess I'll let you buy it."*

By asking the appropriate questions, Fred was able to lead the producer through an evaluation of the product in light of his own needs. When the producer saw how the product met his needs and agreed on a reasonable price for it, there was no selling to be done. The customer had literally sold himself.

On your next sales contact, try letting your customer sell him- or herself by asking the right questions.

SECTION FOURTEEN

HANDLING CUSTOMER RESISTANCE

WHAT'S IN IT FOR YOU?

- Gain insight into why customers resist.
- Learn to handle resistance more effectively.
- Understand the traditional and nontraditional forms of customer resistance.
- Learn how to handle the common excuse, "It's too expensive."

Most parents will tell you that the first word their children learned to say was "No." It makes sense—it's a short word, easy to say, and it ends all further need for discussion or decision making—at least as far as the speaker is concerned.

This principle is true for adults, including customers. "It's too expensive." "It's too big." "It's too small." "It's too complicated." "It's not complicated enough." All of these—and a lot more—are the kinds of resistance you face every day. Some of these objections point to real customer concerns and needs, and you will need to address them in an appropriate manner. But some of these objections are part of other agendas, and you need to be able to determine the source of these kinds of resistance to overcome them. This section gives you tips on how to do that.

I D E A

UNCOVERING RESISTANCE

14.1 Resistance is Feedback

Inexperienced salespeople see customer resistance as potholes or stop signs on the road to a sale. Experienced salespeople realize that customer resistance is a normal, natural, and necessary part of the sales process. Resistance is not a stop sign; rather, it is an arrow pointing in the right direction. When a customer brings up some resistance, it does not mean, "I'm not going to buy;" it just means, "I'm not sold yet." Big difference.

Let's face it — very few sales proceed from start to finish with the customer agreeing 100 percent on every point. If that happened, you would be in shock. Similarly, few customers disagree with 100 percent of what you say. So most sales fall in between these two extremes. Part of the give-and-take of the sales process is getting feedback from your prospect.

You will have a much healthier attitude if you expect and welcome resistance rather than fear it. Fearing resistance may make you resent your prospect for making your job more difficult. Welcoming resistance as a form of feedback puts you in a helpful and understanding frame of mind.

Inexperienced salespeople fear customer resistance because they find themselves at a loss for answers. Only experience (which includes role-playing) and study will calm your nerves and prepare you for your most common objections. The ideas that follow will show you how to get a handle on one of the most common stumbling blocks in sales.

W O R K S H E E T

WHAT'S IN IT FOR YOU?

- Become aware of the ways you typically handle resistance now (the first step in making changes)
- Evaluate yourself on several abilities related to handling customer resistance.

UNCOVERING RESISTANCE

14.2 What You Do Now

1. Recall a recent unsuccessful sale in which you handled a prospect's resistance poorly.

   a. What was your customer's concern? _____

   b. What was your response? _____

   c. How could you have answered more effectively? _____

   _____

2. When a prospect tells you that your price is too high, how do you respond?

   _____

3. When a prospect has doubts about the quality of your product or your company's reputation, what do you say? _____

   _____

4. On a scale of one to 10, rate yourself on the qualities needed when dealing with customer resistance:

   a. Confidence _____

   b. Confidence in your company/product_____

   c. Product knowledge _____

   d. Industry knowledge_____

   e. Knowledge of human nature _____

   f. Patience _____

   g. Ability to avoid argument _____

   h. Calmness under stress _____

   i. Ability to be diplomatic _____

I D E A

UNCOVERING RESISTANCE

14.3 Why Customers Resist

Resistance can take many forms, but there is a finite number of reasons why customers resist. It is your job to tactfully, patiently, and emphatically find out the reason(s). The reasons fall into five broad categories: need, relationship, ability, product, service, and price.

Need. Sometimes a prospect's need decreases after you contact him or her. Markets change, sometimes overnight. The problem also may be perceived need. You may have failed to show your prospect the extent of his or her need and exactly how your product or service will be the solution. It's time to do more information gathering, research, and custom-tailoring of your presentation.

Relationship. People do business with people they like. Your customer may be resisting because something went wrong with your relationship. There may be a lack of trust, confidence, or comfort with you personally. If that is the case, either work to improve the relationship or turn over the account to someone else.

Ability. Your prospect may not be the final decision maker. You should have found this out earlier, during your information gathering. An inability to buy also may be due to high interest rates, a lack of space, or seasonal fluctuations in business.

Product. The worst reason for a prospect to resist a sale is that your product is inferior or your company has a bad reputation. If true, these issues are difficult to overcome. The best way to deal with them is to present concrete evidence that things are improving. Assure your customers that the past will not adversely affect their future satisfaction.

Price. Not everyone can afford to buy what they want or truly need. An important part of prospecting and information gathering is qualifying your prospects. However, not all salespeople do a thorough job of this. It is conceivable that you would ask for the sale from someone who truly cannot afford what you are selling.

It is also conceivable that the issue of price is a cover-up. It is easy to use "It costs too much" as an excuse for some other problem. It is your job to not only build perceived value (so you can justify your prices), but also to find out the real reasons your customer is resisting.

I D E A

- **Expand your knowledge of types of resistance**

UNCOVERING RESISTANCE

14.4 Types of Resistance

Resistance is valid when the questions or statements have a logical basis. Invalid resistance is an insincere excuse used to stall or hide a valid issue.

Valid resistance is always legitimate. It does not mean the sale is doomed, and should always be addressed directly. Some resistance sounds as if it would stop the sale instantly, but further probing reveals that is usually not the case. An example of valid resistance that would stop a sale is the inability to deliver on time. Your prospect may need the product in 90 days, but you cannot deliver in less than 180 days. There's no way out of that bind.

Most resistance really hides a desire for more details. By finding fault with something, your customer may actually be looking for assurance regarding quality, guarantees, or warranties. "That metal looks awfully thin" can be interpreted as "What assurances can you give me that it will stand up to my intended use?"

> **"I don't need any more at this time"** could mean **"I haven't had the time to think about this"** or **"Show me how your product is different from what I'm now carrying."**

> **"My boss isn't going to go for this"** can mean **"You should give me some collateral material to help me sell this to my boss."** It could also mean, **"I'm afraid to make this decision on my own."**

When that happens, either make the decision making easier, or try to meet with the boss.

Invalid resistance sometimes masquerades as valid resistance. That is why you have to be able to recognize the difference. Invalid resistance presents a stall or put-off — a way for your customer to say, "I don't want to think about this now because I'd be forced into making a decision." Invalid resistance has many sounds to it:

> **"I have to leave in fifteen minutes."**
> **"I'll be out of town next week."**
> **"Leave your material with me and I'll look it over when I get a chance."**
> **"I have to discuss this with my partner/wife/boss."**

All of these excuses seem valid, so it may require careful judgment to determine if they are genuine or not. Through observation and knowledge of your customer you will know whether you are hearing the truth or a stall.

Invalid objections pose a challenge to your attitude. Your positive attitude must be conveyed as you handle the resistance. For example, you could say.

> **"I understand that you are busy; may I see you this afternoon or tomorrow morning?" "I don't mind leaving some materials with you, but I get the impression that you are still unclear on some aspect of what we have just discussed. Is there some point I could explain better?" "I don't blame you for wanting to involve your partner/wife/boss in this decision. Let's ask her to join us now for a few minutes and we'll bring her up to speed."**

With other types of invalid resistance, the prospect's statements don't even make sense. The change in attitude may be sudden and without cause. When this happens, you have to find out what the invalid resistance is hiding. Beneath the surface, a problem exists with the prospect's need, your relationship, the customer's ability to make a decision, your product or service, or its price.

To find out the real reason behind an invalid resistance, use the four-step process in Idea 14.5, which follows.

IDEA

WHAT'S IN IT FOR YOU?

- **Learn the four basic steps for handling resistance**

UNCOVERING RESISTANCE

14.5 A Four-Step Plan for Handling Resistance

Every prospect and sales situation is different, but handling resistance can follow some general rules. Keep these in mind:

1. **Listen carefully.** Never interrupt someone. You may have heard all the common resistances, but your customer has the right (and the need) to speak his mind. Take the time to note your customer's body language, vocal inflections, and other buying signals.

2. **Check your understanding with feedback.** You can get feedback in the form of a question or a statement. Either way, you should put the prospect's concerns in your own words and turn it into an issue you can address. Never argue with a customer. Don't try to win a battle of logic. Simply turn their issue into a question you can answer.

3. **Address the issue effectively.** This means using a direct and convincing method. Sometimes prospects cannot see their own business dilemmas. It is your job to clarify issues and help them overcome their fear of spending money, making decisions, change, or whatever it is bogging them down. Worksheet 14.7 covers valuable methods for addressing resistance. Study and practice them.

4. **Confirm acceptance.** If you handled the resistance well, it should no longer be an issue. How will you know? You have to ask point-blank, "Are you completely satisfied with the answer?" or "Have I put your concerns to rest regarding this matter?" Be sure to consider the person's behavioral style when asking this question. Try to use the word *think* with Directors and Thinkers and *feel* with Relaters and Socializers.

Once you have dealt with the resistance, you may be in a position to ask for the sale. The closer you are to the end of your presentation, the more appropriate it will be to ask for the sale or at least test the waters, depending on the buying signals you pick up.

W O R K S H E E T

UNCOVERING RESISTANCE

14.6 When to Respond to Resistance

When should you respond to a customer's resistance? There are only three good choices: before the issue comes up; immediately; and later, after postponing.

Before the Issue Comes Up. Every product and service has its strengths and weaknesses. Knowing a weakness and building an answer into your presentation is a smart practice. It handles the resistance before it ever comes up. Doing this also allows you to discuss the weakness, put it into perspective, and possibly lessen its severity. In addition, honesty builds credibility and trust.

List three common issues that customers bring up about your product or service. What could you say about them in advance to eliminate these sources of resistance?

1._____

2._____

3._____

Immediately. Customers do not like to be ignored, so the safest bet is to answer questions when they are asked. Unless you have a logical reason to postpone your answer, handle the resistance immediately. Immediate responses convey respect, empathy, and good communication skills.

List three common objections that you must answer immediately.

1._____

2._____

3._____

Later, after postponing. Some issues are better off postponed. Perhaps you plan to cover an issue later and your prospect has jumped the gun. The most common question that comes up prematurely is price. (For ways to handle the price issue, see Idea 15.7, "Timing and Perceived Value.") Prospects always want to know how much something is going to cost before they know what it is and how it will solve their problem. This is natural, so be prepared for it. The way to handle the price issue is to postpone it:

"That's an important question, but one I'd like to cover in a few minutes, if you don't mind. I want to put my product into perspective so the price will have some meaning to you. Is that OK?"

This postponing method acknowledges the value of the question, gives an honest reason for delaying, and shows respect by asking (twice) for the prospect's permission to postpone the answer.

Think of three common resistances that you can postpone answering and what you will say to do so.

1._____

2._____

3._____

I D E A

WHAT'S IN IT FOR YOU?

• **Learn seven of the most tried-and-true techniques for handling customer resistance**

STRUCTURED RESPONSES AND STRATEGIES

14.7 Methods of Handling Resistance

After you have listened to your prospect's resistance and clarified it with feedback, you must respond in a way that makes sense. Only you can determine the best method for the situation, but having some options will enable you to remain calm.

Feel, Felt, Found. This method conveys understanding, assures your prospect that he is not alone, and reassures him that this common misgiving becomes unimportant when additional information is considered. This ties into a person's need to be appreciated, accepted, informed, and in control.

You're probably familiar with this method. You say, "I can understand how you *feel* about … I have had other customers who have *felt* the same way until they found out that …"

Use the Balancing Act. There are times when a product or service has a definite weakness but is a good buy for a prospect anyway. When someone points out a valid disadvantage, the only thing you can honestly do is admit it. Then show her all the reasons your product is still a good buy. Point out all the ways that the benefits compensate for a minor weakness.

> **"I understand that this computer system will require more room than you anticipated, but based on the needs we've discussed and your projected expansion, it is a system you will soon grow into."**

If appropriate, use testimonial letters, case histories, or statistics to help your case.

The Ben Franklin Balance Sheet. The Ben Franklin Balance Sheet is an exercise in logic. Here's how to do it *right*: Vertically divide a sheet of paper in two. On one side, list the reasons to buy; on the other side, list the reasons not to buy. Some salespeople only help with the positives. Nonmanipulative salespeople are fair; they help with both sides. Since no two reasons are equal, it is important to give weight to each. For both columns, have your prospect prioritize the entries by dividing 100 points among them. So one reason may deserve 25 points, another may only deserve ten points, and so on. Then add up the points and divide by the number of reasons. This will give you a weighted average—a more accurate picture of which way to go.

Get Clarification. Often resistance is vague or generalized. A statement such as "Your service won't work for us" is impossible to respond to unless you ask for clarification. Ask simple, open-ended questions to uncover the root of the problem.

> Salesperson: "Can you tell me what you mean when you say it won't work?"
>
> Customer: "The response time is too slow."
>
> Salesperson: "I can easily upgrade the system to double or triple the response time. Which of those would be fast enough for you?"
>
> Customer: "Triple will work fine. Can I give you my order now?"

Deny and Correct. Sometimes a prospect is misinformed. He may have received inaccurate information or he might have misunderstood something you said. In either case, you have to gently set him straight. The way to do this is to say something like, "It may be my fault, but it seems you have gotten the wrong impression. Please, let me set the record straight. Of course there are other things you could say. Whatever you say, it has to 1) sound real, not canned; 2) be diplomatic; and 3) set the stage for a correction.

Compare Apples with Apples. To win an argument you must be fairly well versed in the rules of logic. Along the same lines, logic dictates that, when you make a comparison, you compare apples with apples. Resistant prospects do not always follow a logical train of thought. It's up to you to keep the logic train on track.

> Customer: "This laser printer won't print 15 pages per minute."
>
> Salesperson: "When we first talked, you said your higher priority was high-resolution print quality. Is that still your first priority? If not, let's rank your priorities so I will know what to recommend."

Put the Ball Back in the Court. This is also called the Boomerang method. There are times when a customer's reason for not buying is the precise reason why he should buy. This is the perfect example of a customer not being able to see the forest for the trees.

> Customer: "I can't afford an 800 number."
>
> Salesperson: "You can't afford not to have an 800 number! The business that a toll-free number will generate will more than pay for the service."

To make your argument completely sound, back it up with hard evidence. Use charts, graphs, statistics, case studies, and testimonials to show how much time or money will be saved or earned with your product or service. The Boomerang method works well when your customer lacks some information or fails to see the big picture.

I D E A

WHAT'S IN IT FOR YOU?

- **Learn to increase your credibility with effective proof of your claims**
- **Identify people and companies that can support you in your sales effort**
- **Determine ways to improve your company's warranty**

STRUCTURED RESPONSES AND STRATEGIES

14.8 What Evidence Does Your Customer Trust?

No matter what method you use to deal with resistance, you must produce evidence to prove what you are saying. That's part of your job. Simply knowing what to say to change a prospect's perspective is not enough. The proof you offer can take many forms.

Make a Comparison. Different customers have different buying criteria. If your prospect is mentally comparing your product/service with another, it is essential to help with that process. You can use a system such as the Ben Franklin Balance Sheet (or Worksheet 13.4, "Comparisons with the Competition") to list advantages and disadvantages of yours versus theirs. The method of comparison that you use will depend on what you are selling. The higher the cost, the longer the sales cycle, and, the more high-tech your industry, the more you will have to use sophisticated comparison techniques. These may include computer data analysis, slide shows, tours of manufacturing plants or other locations, presentations by engineers, and so on.

List three ways you can make a convincing comparison between your product/service and a competitor's.

1. _____

2. _____

3. _____

Present Testimonials or Case Histories. One of the most convincing forms of proof is to present a company in a similar situation and show how your product/service solved the problem.

This can be done with testimonial letters or the presentation of a case history, which can take the form of a slide show. The combination of the two is very powerful.

List three companies that can serve as case histories to bolster your presentation.

1._____

2._____

3._____

List three people from whom you can get testimonial letters.

1._____ Company _____

2._____ Company _____

3._____ Company _____

Demonstrate. This was covered in detail in Idea 13.8.

Present Warranties and Guarantees. Unconditional guarantees are a very powerful way to make the buying decision safe and easy for your customer. Even conditional guarantees can be very effective. What they say about the product/service and company is: "We believe in the quality of what we are selling and have the integrity to stand behind it." Of course, a strong reputation and long history in the business help as well.

How effective is your company's warranty or guarantee? List three ways it could be improved.

1._____

2._____

3._____

Calculate the Cost of Waiting. Customers often agree that a purchase is in their best interest, but then want to wait a while before making a final decision. If you can honestly show how delaying will cost them money, prospects will be motivated to decide now. In your calculations, include rising interest rates, price increases, changes in the market, potential decreases in the customer's market share, and so on. Your knowledge of the industry plus an understanding of the economic, political, technical, and other factors affecting it will add to your credibility.

What are some of the factors that might increase your customer's cost if he or she delays action?

1._____

2._____

3._____

W O R K S H E E T

WHAT'S IN IT FOR YOU?

- **Specify ways that you will apply what you have learned in this section to future customer resistance.**

STRUCTURED RESPONSES AND STRATEGIES

14.9 Handling Future Resistance

To improve the way you handle resistance, list the most common resistance you encounter at different phases of the sale, what type it is, and how you will deal with it in the future:

1. Resistance upon contact (What do they say?):
   Type (What do they mean?): _____
   Your new response: _____

2. Resistance when setting up an appointment:
   Type: _____
   Your new response: _____

3. Resistance when gathering information:
   Type: _____
   Your new response: _____

4. Resistance at the beginning of your presentation:
   Type: _____
   Your new response: _____

5. Resistance during your presentation:
   Type: _____
   Your new response: _____

6. Resistance upon asking for the sale:
   Type: _____
   Your new response: _____

W O R K S H E E T

WHAT'S IN IT FOR YOU?

• **Learn a better way to respond to resistance.**

STRUCTURED RESPONSES AND STRATEGIES

14.10 "It's Too Expensive"

How do you handle this objection? "It's too expensive" can mean several things. It can mean:

1. "Your product costs more than I have in my budget. My budget is $5,000; your product is $7,500."

2. "I don't think your product is worth the price. I have $7,500, but I wouldn't spend it on your product."

3. "Your product is worth what you're asking and I have that amount, but I don't need to spend that much — it's more than my needs require."

The key is to find out which of the three meanings apply to the objection, "It's too expensive." Think of three questions you could ask to uncover the real meaning.

1. _____

2. _____

3. _____

Customer: "I like your product, but it's too expensive."

Your First Response: _____

Another Response: _____

A Third Response: _____

OUR SOLUTIONS

Once you have clarified your prospect's meaning, you have several options. If your prospect does not have the money in the budget, work with him to 1) see if funds can be shifted from other sources; 2) try to work out financing; 3) sell someone higher in the company so that additional funds can be allocated.

If your prospect does not think your product or service is worth the asking price, you need to increase the *perceived value*. To do so, you can 1) add value with additional services or add-on products; 2)compare every facet of your product to your competitors—show how your product is better in terms of quality, service, reputation, warranty, etc; 3) negotiate a lower price, if your company routinely does this.

If your prospect tells you that you are trying to sell him more than he needs, sell him less. If your product line does not include something with fewer features that is less expensive, then refer him to another company.

Point out the differences between buying criteria and success criteria. Your customer is basing his buying decision on price, but later will evaluate the success of your product/service on different criteria. The key is to show your prospect that his buying decision should be based on the same criteria that he'll later use to judge success. This is how you build perceived value.

YOUR SOLUTIONS

What are some things you can say to address the three meanings of "It's too expensive"?

1. _____

2. _____

3. _____

IDEA

• **Recognize what makes negotiation succeed or fail**

STRUCTURED RESPONSES AND STRATEGIES

14.11 Ten Factors That Affect Power in Negotiations

Negotiation is one of the oldest skills used to gain desired results. It's also a skill that many people misunderstand and find intimidating. But negotiation is simply the way in which we interact with others to compare offers and relative value and to analyze our decisions.

Power, information, and time are three of the factors that affect negotiation. According to negotiating expert Herb Cohen, the person with the most power has an edge in the negotiation. The person with the most information has an edge, and the person with the most flexibility of time has an edge.

The following ten factors affect power in a negotiation and are from *Negotiating Your Success* by our colleague, James F. Hennig Ph.D.

1. **Alternative power.** Have or develop alternatives. Know the opposition's alternatives.

2. **Legitimacy power.** What credibility do you have?
   • Track record power — What has been your past performance?
   • Referral power — What are others saying about you?
   • Title power—Office or position, academic degree or license, award or honor

3. **Risk power.** Can you afford to have the negotiation fail?

4. **Commitment power.** What is the demonstrated commitment behind the position? More commitment = more power. What you don't know *can* hurt you.

5. **Knowledge power.** The more knowledge, the more power.
   • Topic knowledge — knowledge of what you are negotiating.
   • Negotiations knowledge — of the negotiation process itself.
   • Opposition knowledge — of the other party.

6. **Expert power.** When you lack knowledge, use an expert.

7. **Reward or punishment power.** The ability to reward or punish provides power in negotiation.

8. **Time or deadline power.** Try not to have a deadline. Know the opposition's deadline.

9. **Perception power.** It's not who has the power, but who is perceived to have the power.

10. **Relationship power.** When the relationship is good, details rarely get in the way.

Reprinted with permission of James F. Hennig, Ph.D.

SECTION FIFTEEN

CONFIRMING THE SALE

WHAT'S IN IT FOR YOU?

- Understand the difference between manipulative and nonmanipulative confirmation.
- Learn to recognize confirming opportunities and the importance of the benefit summary.
- Learn to review some traditional confirmation techniques — with a unique twist.

Manipulative people study closing techniques as a way of building up their arsenal of weapons for the sales battle. Nonmanipulative salespeople see the sales effort as a cooperative effort. They study closing techniques to give themselves various options to use with different types of people in different situations. Part of maintaining a smooth working relationship is selling to someone the way they want to be sold; in other words, making the buying process easy for the customer.

Confirmations come in many shapes and sizes. Your customer's behavioral style, the length of your relationship, their interest level, and other factors will dictate the best way to ask for the sale. Only you can determine which confirmation is best in a given situation. Keep the following options in mind.

I D E A

CONFIRMING THE SALE

15.1 Confirming Versus Closing the Sale

Traditional salespeople think of "the close" as a series of techniques used at the end of a presentation. These techniques are designed to get the prospect to say yes and give an order, even if he doesn't want what is being sold.

Today, consultative salespeople take a more enlightened view of confirming the sale. To nonmanipulative salespeople, confirming the sale is a natural process — the logical outcome of involving the customer in every step of the sales process. There are two ways to involve a prospect: the manipulative way and the nonmanipulative way. Traditional salespeople often ask questions that give the prospect frequent opportunities to say either yes or no. Some people believe that a prospect is more likely to say yes to the sale if she has gotten into the habit of answering yes to all the previous questions. It's a twisted game in which the salesperson wins agreement throughout, hoping that the final answer will also be yes. The problem is that the prospect answers yes to simple, superficial questions that don't build an argument in favor of the sale.

Other salespeople think prospects have a need to say no. By giving them the opportunity to say no to a lot of questions, the thinking goes, the prospect will have the no's out of his system and be ready to say yes when the salesperson asks for the sale.

Both tactics are silly. The real way to involve a prospect is to make sure the two of you are on the same wavelength at all times. The ideal sales process is a mutual journey of uncovering a need, working on a solution, and confirming a sale. When the journey is mutual, confirming the sale is a matter of *when*, not *if*. When the journey is not mutual, salespeople spend their time trying to convince prospects that they need what's being sold. The sales process can become the type of unethical, arm-twisting, manipulative hustle that everyone loathes.

For the nonmanipulative salesperson, the sale *begins* when the customer says yes. It's the start of an ongoing business relationship. An analogy can be drawn between the confirming process and asking someone to marry you. If you were worried about the answer, you wouldn't ask. Obviously, the question would be premature. The decision to marry is the outcome of a mutually developed relationship. Usually the issue has been discussed before the question is formally asked. When it is asked, it is a rhetorical question that simply serves to crystallize already understood feelings.

I D E A

WHAT'S IN IT FOR YOU?

• **Understand the emotional elements of making a purchase**

CONFIRMING THE SALE

15.2 Lead With Your Heart, Guide With Your Head

People love to buy. They love it because the buying experience gives them a sense of satisfaction. They buy to gain that feeling of satisfaction rather than only to satisfy a logical need.

A person making a buying decision justifies the buying decision with his or her head. A buyer uses logic to analyze, examine, and research the buying decision to make sure it's a wise decision that will be of lasting value. But when it comes time to make the commitment to buy, the decision is made on an emotional level.

The best way to deal with this dichotomy is to lead with the heart, but guide with the head. Use emotional elements to help your buyer decide to make the purchase. Appeal to your buyer's wants and their needs, show that you care, and that you're doing something good. Then, when your buyer steps back to examine the purchase, appeal to his or her logic. Show how your purchase enhances his or her life and prevents possible problems.

In your next sales presentation, remind yourself to first talk about *why*, and then focus on *how* only to the extent that it satisfies the concerns and interests of the client. Your logic won't persuade the buyer, but it will help your buyer persuade himself. It's the emotion that causes the person to take the action to buy now.

I D E A

CONFIRMING THE SALE

15.3 The Benefit Summary

Traditionally the benefit summary has been regarded as an integral part of most confirmation techniques. The enlightened salesperson, however, sees the benefit summary as part of every sales process. No presentation—no matter how abbreviated—is complete without a benefit summary.

In the benefit summary, the points to which your prospect has responded positively are summarized. Be sure to go over benefits, not features. There is a big difference. This is especially important if your prospect takes the information back to another decision maker. When this is the case, your prospect becomes the salesperson, so you must prepare him well to present you and your company. Leave as little to his memory as possible, which means putting everything in writing and providing collateral materials.

You will know which benefits to emphasize by 1) your prospect's reactions during your presentation and 2) the data you gathered during your information gathering.

One way to involve your prospect in your presentation is to have him create his own list of benefits. Get him to imagine how he would use your product/service and then ask him to come up with his own list of benefits. As he does this, he will sell himself.

You can accomplish this by asking how your product/service will help him with a specific problem. After he tells you the benefit, ask, "What other problems could this solve for you?"

The benefit summary capsulizes your presentation highlights. It is an opportunity to ask for feedback and a way to help your prospect retain the most important points. When you present your benefit summary, list the most important items first and last. They are the ones that stick the most.

At the end of your summary, give your prospect the opportunity to agree, disagree, or ask questions. Once agreement has been expressed, the buying signals should turn green.

The language of a benefit summary is simple: "Mr. Rush, we've talked about many things in the last hour. Let me summarize what I see as the key benefits for you. You're looking for a car that will bring you prestige. You're looking for something that will travel smoothly at higher speeds. You mentioned that you want something small for easy parking. It is also important for you to be the first person on your block to have one. Based on all those things, I would strongly recommend the XYZ as the perfect car for you."

Follow up with an open question with direction, such as, "Mr. Rush, how would you like to proceed?" or "Where would you like to go from here?"

I D E A

• **Learn to recognize and capitalize on positive, negative, and neutral buying signals**

CONFIRMING THE SALE

15.4 Confirming Opportunities

The key to recognizing confirming opportunities is to know your prospect. By the time you get to the proposal and confirmation stages, you should be familiar with the person's behavioral style and other personality traits. This knowledge will help you understand the signals he or she is sending.

Always be sensitive to your prospect's needs. If you are in the middle of a presentation and you get cues that it is time to ask for the sale, do so. Make sure, however, that you have created sufficient perceived value in your prospect's mind. Condense your presentation, but do not end it abruptly. Give a benefit summary and ask for the sale. Find out what is needed and provide it.

It helps to be able to recognize a prospect's verbal and nonverbal buying signals. Buying signals come in three shades: red (Negative or stop), green (positive or go), and yellow (neutral or caution).

Listen to questions your prospect asks. They are good indicators of his or her mind-set. Interpret questions and comments within the context of your proposal and relative to your prospect's other characteristics (behavioral style, body language, etc.). Some typical questions are:

1. Could I try this one more time? (+)
2. Is it possible to install this on a trial basis? (+)
3. What kind of warranty/service contract is available? (+)
4. What sort of credit terms do you offer? (+)
5. How soon can you deliver? (+)
6. Is this system more reliable than mine? (0)
7. This is interesting. What else can you tell me? (0)
8. Can you leave some catalog sheets with me so I can go over them with my colleagues? (0)
9. I can't consider this with interest rates so high. (−)
10. Will these prices still be good in six months? (−)
11. I'm overstocked now. Where am I going to put more merchandise? (−)

Yellow (neutral) buying signals indicate that the person is still undecided. Perhaps you haven't presented enough information or the right kind of information; or perhaps the person is a slow decision maker. If that is the case, try helping with the Ben Franklin Balance Sheet.(See Idea 14.7, "Methods of Handling Resistance.")

When the buying signals are red, it is time to back up a step or two. Give a benefit summary (always your best transition) and politely ask an open-ended question with direction such as, "Where do we go from here?" "What's our next step?" or "How do we proceed?"

Above and beyond these specific suggestions, remember to always stay tuned to what is happening in your prospect's mind. Remember the body language cues discussed in Ideas 10.4 and 10.5.

1. A prospect who sits with open arms is receptive; one who sits with arms crossed tightly is defensive. For the latter, find out what's wrong. Work on the relationship.

2. Interest is conveyed by leaning forward, listening carefully, and nodding in agreement.

3. A prospect who is supporting his head with one hand and gazing off has lost interest.

4. People relax when they decide to buy. A tense posture is a sign that all is not well. Find out why.

5. Happy, animated facial expressions show that a prospect is relating well to you.

I D E A

TYPES OF CONFIRMATION

15.5 The Tentative Confirmation

The tentative confirmation is a useful option when a prospect is interested but hesitant to make a commitment. It offers the flexibility of a "way out" and, at the same time, puts an end to shopping. There are several scenarios in which the tentative confirmation works.

Airlines, hotels, and car rental agencies use the tentative confirmation all the time. Imagine a car rental clerk giving a travel agent some information about a car. It is available on a specific date, but the travel agent has to check with her client before confirming. The reservationist usually says, "It is not uncommon for all of our cars to be out on the weekends. I'd hate for you to call back and find this car unavailable. Why don't we go ahead and reserve the car for you? If your client says OK, then your work is done. If your client changes his mind, just call back and we'll cancel."

The tentative close begins the commitment process. It's ideal for customers who need a little push before they will commit themselves. Some personal styles will sit on the fence forever until they are pushed gently one way or another. What little commitment is gained is not very strong—but in these cases, a small commitment is sometimes better than none.

Most people do not have the time or inclination to exhaustively comparison shop to find the best deal possible. That's why the tentative confirmation also puts an end to or slows down the shopping process. The customer's mindset usually changes from "I'm still uncertain" to "I've made a decision."

The tentative confirmation is not a trick or manipulative technique, but an option that may work for some customers. It is appropriate for the person who wants what you are selling, not the customer who is uninterested. It is commonly used in sales in which the customer needs to arrange financing or other details. Imagine these situations:

> **"It's going to be six weeks before your order is delivered anyway. In that time, if you decide you don't want it, just call me and I'll allocate the shipment to another customer."**

"For our publication, the deadline for camera-ready art is the tenth of the month. Occasionally we run house ads. Why don't I reserve a space for your ad? If you decide by the ninth that you don't want to run it, we'll just insert a house ad."

With the tentative confirmation, you are saying, in effect, "To make it easy for you, I'm willing to let you have your cake and eat it too." This type of confirmation creates a commitment that is not legally binding, but has a powerful psychological effect.

I D E A

TYPES OF CONFIRMATION

15.6 The Pilot

The Pilot—often known as the puppy dog close—is a valuable service that is often misused. It works when used to ensure customer satisfaction as an adjunct to a commitment. It fails when used to confirm a sale.

Some people misuse the pilot by trying to gain commitment when no commitment is present. The salesperson says, "Look, I can see you're undecided. Why don't you take six gross and see how you like them. If you like them, we'll do business. If you don't like them, I'll take them back." The problem is, without a genuine commitment, your customer is going to take the product, look for all the things that are wrong with it and find reasons *not* to buy. The lack of commitment combined with having the product forced on her will create a negative selective perception. It's human nature.

The right way to use the pilot confirmation is to assure customer satisfaction when a commitment exists. When a customer says to you, in essence, "If everything you said is true, then I want to buy," offering a trial run or sample can help you back up your claims. It's an easy way to help a customer become comfortable with the commitment she has already made. In this situation, selective perception will be positive and your customer will look for things that are right. This is why the pilot is a powerful tool for assuring customer satisfaction, not for confirming the sale.

I D E A

WHAT'S IN IT FOR YOU?

- **Learn ways to postpone discussing price until after you've created value in your prospect's mind**

TYPES OF CONFIRMATION

15.7 Timing and Perceived Value

Salespeople often ask, "If I'm in the middle of my presentation and my prospect gives strong buying signals, should I stop and ask for the sale?" The answer is yes, but no.

Yes, you don't want to continue to the end of your presentation and risk boring your customer. But no, you can't drop everything and ask for the sale. Why? You have to create a perceived value in your prospect's mind by furnishing relative features and benefits that put everything in the proper perspective. They key is to speed up your presentation and cut out any unnecessary parts. Get to the most relevant points quickly, and then ask for the sale.

When should prices be revealed? Ideally, only after the perceived value of the product or service is high. If, in the middle of your presentation, you are asked, "How much is it?," you should tactfully avoid giving the price. To give the price at that point would risk presenting a lopsided view of the product (and, therefore, an unreasonable price). Finish your presentation and then give the price. That way it will have more meaning and a higher probability of being accepted.

There are many ways to avoid giving prices. The most honest way is to say, "With all due respect, a price without a context is meaningless and unfair to both of us. If you don't mind, I'd like to tell you more about my product before getting to the price." You can also say, "there are a number of different plans possible. I'd like to give you a better feel for our product/service and then see which plan suits you best. At that point, I will tell you exactly what the price is for *your* plan." If you sense that this is acceptable to your prospect, you could continue by asking more information-gathering questions.

If your prospect asks again, offer a range of prices. If you're asked a third time, give one price. It's better to risk a misunderstanding than to risk making your prospect angry.

Giving a price before creating a sense of value in the customer's mind is a disservice to the salesperson and the customer. In a sense, the customer is misled because he does not know what he is getting for the price, which makes the price meaningless. He is more apt to reject the product or service based on inadequate information. At the same time, the salesperson is hindered from accurately presenting his product or service and loses sales from customers' lack of understanding. Both should be avoided.

I D E A

TYPES OF CONFIRMATION

15.8 Assumptive Confirmations

Assumptive confirmations are generally abused by traditional, manipulative salespeople. They are taught to use this "closing technique" as a way to force the sale. The basic premise is, if you don't give your prospect the choice of saying no, you will make the sale.

Nonmanipulative salespeople use these confirmations differently. They use them as *trial confirmations*—questions that determine whether a prospect is ready to make a commitment. The assumption is not that you are going to force the sale, but that you and your prospect have been and continue to be on the same wavelength. The sale, therefore, is a given. Even so, assumptive confirmations must be used respectfully.

The Alternate-Choice Confirmation This is a common traditional confirmation in which the prospect is given the choice between two positive alternatives. The manipulative use of this option seeks to replace the yes or no choice that most prospects want with a pressured "yes or yes" choice.

The alternate-choice confirmation is used by nonmanipulative salespeople when the prospect's buying signals are green. The customer is saying, verbally and nonverbally, "Yes, I'm buying." It would be unnecessary to ask for the sale. In this situation, it is perfectly acceptable to give your customer the choice of two positives.

> **"Do you want delivery made to your New York warehouse or your New Jersey distribution center?"**
>
> **"Do you want special terms or is our standard 2 percent 30 days good enough for you?"**
>
> **"Do you want the standard service contract or would you like more comprehensive coverage?"**

Another nonmanipulative way to use the alternate-choice confirmation is to test the waters. If a prospect's buying signals are unclear, you could ask, "Would you want the modular office system or the custom-designed layout?" Notice that the nonmanipulative way of asking is to state the question hypothetically, saying "Would you...?" rather than "Do you...?"

The Minor Point Another assumptive closing technique used by the manipulative school of selling is the minor point. It seeks to get the prospect to answer a question about some minor detail of the product or service. If the question is answered, the assumption is that the sale is made. It is not a very safe assumption, unless the buying signals are clearly positive.

Nonmanipulative salespeople can use minor points as steppingstones to confirming the sale, but with a slight twist. The questions are asked, not with assumption of the sale being made, but as a way to get the prospect to visualize and mentally own the product/service. This is part of information-gathering and is an effective way to get someone involved in the sales process. Again, the questions are asked hypothetically, with the premise being, "If you were to buy … " or "Imagine yourself using this product/service … " Some examples:

> **"Would you use your cellular phone in just one car or would you want a portable that can be moved?"**
>
> **"Do you want to train your entire staff simultaneously or one at a time?"**
>
> **"Do you want your VIPs picked up at the airport in a limousine or a shuttle bus?"**

We all know that a picture is worth a thousand words. When you get your prospect to visualize your product/service, you smooth the way for his or her acceptance of it.

Physical Action or Order-Blank Confirmation Here again, the assumption for a traditional salesperson is, "If I just act as though the sale were made, my prospect may not object." To accomplish this, the salesperson begins filling out an order form without asking for the sale. As we discussed previously, the nonmanipulative salesperson would only use an assumptive confirmation like this if the prospect's buying signals were clearly green. It is rude, insensitive, and absurd to ignore yellow or red buying signals by acting as if all is well.

IDEA

TYPES OF CONFIRMATION

15.9 The Direct Confirmation

There is nothing wrong with being straightforward and confidently asking for the sale. It is a natural thing to do after you have studied the prospect's needs, proposed a solution, and covered the relevant benefits. Yet the majority of salespeople fail to ask for an order. Every year corporate surveys are conducted to determine the shortcomings of salespeople. Without fail, corporate buyers report that salespeople flop by being poor listeners and failing to ask for the sale.

Fear of rejection is the only reason why someone would fail to ask for an order. If you have conducted the sales process in a consultative, nonmanipulative way, you have nothing to fear. The lines of communication are open. You have sought your prospect's agreement every step of the way. Now that it is time to ask for the sale, it's an easy step, especially if you have been observing buying signals.

Many buyers appreciate a no-nonsense approach to confirming the sale. There's nothing wrong with asking, "May I have your business?" It is direct and polite. But be careful who you use it with. While Directors and Socializers may appreciate it, Relaters and Thinkers may be put off.

Whatever you do, avoid asking for the sale in a negative way, such as, "Why don't we write up an order?" That is an invitation to rejection, and it sounds terribly wishy-washy. Exude confidence in yourself and your product/service. Try:

> **"Let's set up your account next week so you can start using the service as soon as possible."**

> **"I have a truck coming into town this Thursday, and I'd love to put your order on it."**

> **"I know you're going to be happy with this system. Can I turn in your order today?"**

Automobile salespeople use the direct approach all the time. They ask their prospects, "What will it take to get you to buy today?" If they get a decent answer, they'll know what is important to the customer and what aspects of the sale need to be emphasized (price, monthly payments, trade-in, etc.).

I D E A

- **Understand when to motivate a prospect with a promotional special or an impending price increase**

TYPES OF CONFIRMATION

15.10 The "Act Now" Confirmation

Nonmanipulative salespeople don't rush or pressure their prospects into making commitments. Nevertheless, sometimes a price or quantity will only be honored for a limited time. Telling your prospect about price increases or promotional specials can motivate an undecided buyer by creating a sense of urgency.

> **"My company has announced that prices will go up by 5 percent next month due to supplier increases. If I can write up your order now, you can stock up before the increase takes effect."**

The "act now" confirmation must only be used when it is factual. It should never be used deceptively. There is no denying that some people—primarily Thinkers and Relaters—are slow decision makers. Sometimes they need to be motivated to get off the fence. When you are selling something a prospect truly needs, there is nothing wrong with urging him or her to act now to save time or money or avoid inconvenience.

The "act now" confirmation can create wonders for your reputation. You will be a hero any time you prevent a customer from running short of inventory or paying higher prices.

SECTION SIXTEEN

ASSURING CUSTOMER SATISFACTION

WHAT'S IN IT FOR YOU?

- Retain more customers.
- Increase your awareness of the importance of customers.
- Learn the three R's of customer service.
- Learn how to protect your current customers from competitors.
- Increase your understanding of the role that company-wide service has on sales.
- Enhance your reputation as a caring, conscientious sales consultant.
- Discover the best way to handle customer complaints.
- Learn the many ways to follow up after the sale to ensure customer satisfaction.
- Discover effective, creative ways to improve service and, therefore, sales, in your company.

WORKSHEET

UNDERSTAND THE VALUE OF YOUR CUSTOMERS

16.1 Customer Asset Management

Customers aren't just people who buy products — they are assets! That's because one of the primary assets of any sales career is the relationships one builds with customers. Your customer relationships are directly related to the sales you are likely to generate in the future, and the ease (or difficulty) with which they will be generated. Any improvement you make in the number of customers or the quality of your relationships translates immediately into an improvement or increase in future sales.

Regard your customer database as an asset and design your programs to manage those assets as well as possible. Manage your contacts with each customer. Take a look at how often you're in touch with each one and what you talk about during your meetings. Are you making a new sale, reviewing the status of their account, checking on their level of satisfaction with your product or service, or identifying referrals or further business opportunities? Each contact should have its own specific goal and blend into an overall pattern that strengthens your relationship with that customer for many years to come.

When you think of each customer as an asset, you will greatly increase your ability to quantify your goals and the number of contacts and other steps it will take to achieve them.

I D E A

• **Understand the importance of balancing profits and customer satisfaction**

UNDERSTAND THE VALUE OF YOUR CUSTOMERS

16.2 pH Balanced

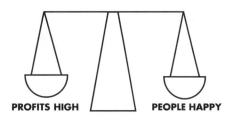

PROFITS HIGH   **PEOPLE HAPPY**

In any business situation, two elements must be attended to: the generation of profits and the satisfaction of the people involved. It's your job to see that both elements stay in balance throughout the sales relationship.

If profits are high but people are not happy, the sale is not likely to last, and there will be no follow-up purchases. People are happy when they feel understood and when they feel that you are taking care of their needs. The more they can rely on you, the more they can focus on receiving the benefits that you have promised them.

How did profitability and personal satisfaction compare in your most recent sales? Use a scale of 1 to 10 to answer. (High profit and high satisfaction earn 10s; low profit and low satisfaction earn 1s.) What do the numbers tell you? What steps are indicated for your next contact with these clients?

WORKSHEET

WHAT'S IN IT FOR YOU?

• **Increase your awareness of the dimensions on which you are judged as a professional salesperson**
• **Determine professional areas in which you need improvement**

HOW DO YOUR CUSTOMERS DEFINE SERVICE?

16.3 The Personal/Performance Model

When you meet with someone for business, you are judged on two levels of service: personal and performance. Your customer's judgment process is unconscious, but it has a profound effect nonetheless.

The *performance level of service* includes all the things you do to give customers what they want: your product and industry knowledge, effective presentations and demonstrations, reliable follow up on your promises, accurate orders, on time delivery, and much more. You could think of performance level as the tasks in your job description, and then some.

The *personal level of service* is your communication skills: how well you listen, ask questions, give feedback, show empathy, build trust, create rapport, adapt to other people's behavioral styles, and so on.

Both levels are important and affect customers' opinions of you, your company, and your product/service. The performance and personal levels of professionalism do not always contribute equally to a buyer's decision-making process. The ratio varies from industry to industry. A life insurance agent is more likely to be judged on a personal level than on a performance level. Conversely, the performance level probably plays a larger role for people who sell high-tech products or services.

1. Are you judged more on your personal or performance level in most selling situations in your industry? Use this chart to determine the percentage that each contributes.

Performance

100%	75%	50%	25%	0%

0%	25%	50%	75%	100%

Personal

2. Now that you are aware of the personal/performance model, identify those areas that need improvement.

W O R K S H E E T

WHAT'S IN IT FOR YOU?

- Control the three elements that influence how customers see you and your company

HOW DO YOUR CUSTOMERS DEFINE SERVICE?

16.4 People, Processes, and Products

When customers look at you and your company, they see three elements:

- the products or services they receive from you
- the processes they have to go through
- the people they deal with

All three elements are within your control. You can certainly determine which products or services to discuss and how to focus on those products or services. You can look for ways to streamline your processes so customers find it easy to deal with you to get what they want. Finally, it's important to continually enhance the relationship between your customers and *everyone* in your organization.

Look over your past 5 sales and determine which of these areas need attention in order to improve the sales relationship with that customer.

Customer	Area That Needs Attention
1. _____	_____
2. _____	_____
3. _____	_____
4. _____	_____
5. _____	_____

W O R K S H E E T

WHAT'S IN IT FOR YOU?

- **Define your service standards**
- **Brainstorm ways to improve your service and your company's level of service**

HOW DO YOU DEFINE SERVICE?

16.5 What Are Your Service Standards?

1. Have you defined a level of service that you strive to deliver? If not, develop standards for:
   - how quickly you return phone calls
   - How closely you monitor the timely delivery of products or services
   - How often you keep in touch with customers and prospects
   - How frequently you solicit customer feedback on your products and service quality

What other aspects of service can you add to this list?

2. List three ways to make it easier for customers to do business with your company.
   a. _____
   b. _____
   c. _____

3. List three ways to streamline the problem-solving process for customers.
   a. _____
   b. _____
   c. _____

4. List three ways to reduce or eliminate any recurring problems your customers experience with your products or services.
   a. _____
   b. _____
   c. _____

5. What opportunities are presented by the recurring problems that you listed in question 4? How can you turn unhappy customers into loyal customers?

_____

W O R K S H E E T

WHAT'S IN IT FOR YOU?

- Take a close look at your company's performance on 11 measures of customer service to determine how you and your company can create greater customer satisfaction
- Identify customer expectations you create and influence (that is, things you can control)
- Identify problems you can anticipate and respond to (things you can control)
- Identify key customer concerns that you can use to "sell" people internally in your organization to give you and your customers better service

HOW DO YOU DEFINE SERVICE?

16.6 How Does Your Company Rate?

On a scale of 1 to 10, rate your company on the following measures of service quality:

Responsiveness. Do your customers get cookie cutter service or does your company treat people as individuals?

1 _____ 2 _____ 3 _____ 4 _____ 5 _____ 6 _____ 7 _____ 8 _____ 9 _____ 10 _____

Competence. Does your company have an image of expertise in which customers can place their trust?

1 _____ 2 _____ 3 _____ 4 _____ 5 _____ 6 _____ 7 _____ 8 _____ 9 _____ 10 _____

Reliability. How dependable is your product or service? How well does your company follow through on promises?

1 _____ 2 _____ 3 _____ 4 _____ 5 _____ 6 _____ 7 _____ 8 _____ 9 _____ 10 _____

Relationship. How well does your company show customers that they care and want long-term relationships?

1 _____ 2 _____ 3 _____ 4 _____ 5 _____ 6 _____ 7 _____ 8 _____ 9 _____ 10 _____

Accuracy. How well does your company avoid mistakes, especially expensive or time-consuming mistakes?

1 _____ 2 _____ 3 _____ 4 _____ 5 _____ 6 _____ 7 _____ 8 _____ 9 _____ 10 _____

Personal Service. How well do service representatives, receptionists, and other front-line people show customers that they are special?

1 _____ 2 _____ 3 _____ 4 _____ 5 _____ 6 _____ 7 _____ 8 _____ 9 _____ 10 _____

Courtesy. Does *everyone* in your company treat customers with this most basic ingredient of human interaction and service?

1___ 2 ____ 3 ____ 4 ____ 5 ____ 6 ____ 7 ____ 8 ____ 9____ 10_____

Active Listening. Are people in your company good listeners, especially when it comes to customer problems?

1___ 2 ____ 3 ____ 4 ____ 5 ____ 6 ____ 7 ____ 8 ____ 9____ 10_____

Perceived Value. Does your company give customers good value and make them aware of that value before *and* after the sale?

1___ 2 ____ 3 ____ 4 ____ 5 ____ 6 ____ 7 ____ 8 ____ 9____ 10_____

Professional Appearance. Is your company aware of the importance of making a good impression with a clean, safe, well-maintained place of business?

1___ 2 ____ 3 ____ 4 ____ 5 ____ 6 ____ 7 ____ 8 ____ 9____ 10_____

Keeping in touch. Does your company make an effort to stay close to its customers and solicit their opinions?

1___ 2 ____ 3 ____ 4 ____ 5 ____ 6 ____ 7 ____ 8 ____ 9____ 10_____

W O R K S H E E T

WHAT'S IN IT FOR YOU?

- **Become aware of the ways that your service is better than, the same as, or worse than your competitors'**
- **Explore ways to provide extra service and gain a competitive edge**

HOW DO YOU DEFINE SERVICE?

16.7 Anticipate Service Opportunities

Describe each of your products/services in the following terms. Spend the most time on the third category — the one that differentiates you and your company from the competition. Try to come up with additional ways to set your company apart.

1. **Tangible product/service.** These are the features of what you sell. Tangibles are usually the same for you and your competition.
2. **Expected services.** The second level of services includes delivery, installation, warranty, financing, and other things that customers normally expect. *How* you provide these services is as important as what you provide.
3. **Extra services.** These services are ones you provide when you see an opportunity to exceed customers' expectations. For example, customizing a product/service, babysitting a delivery, arranging particularly creative financing, and so on.

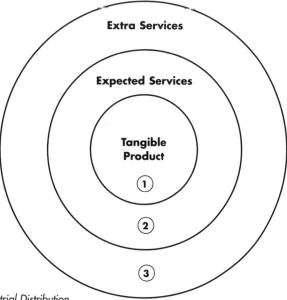

Source: B. Merrifield. *The Dynamics of Industrial Distribution.*

WORKSHEET

WHAT'S IN IT FOR YOU?

- **Increase your understanding of how expectations are created**
- **Learn new ways to raise and meet customers' expectations**

INCREASING YOUR CUSTOMER AWARENESS

16.8 Creating Realistic Expectations

One important way to make your customers happy is to manage their expectations. You cannot promise a delivery on Tuesday, have it show up on Friday, and expect your customer to be happy. The key is to understand and overdeliver. Make your promises realistic—perhaps even slightly understated—and then exceed expectations.

Think about how you and your company affect customer expectations and you can do a better job of it.

1. In your company's advertising, is the primary emphasis placed on product features or service quality?

   _____

2. Does your advertising adequately differentiate your company from the competition?

   _____

3. What expectations are created by the content of your company's advertising?

   _____

4. What image of your company is created by the choice of media used to advertise?

   _____

5. List some better ways to create positive expectations in your company's promotions.

   _____

6. When giving a presentation to a prospect, what expectations do you intentionally create? Do you concentrate only on selling the sizzle and risk misleading people about the steak, or do you present and accurate representation of your product/service?

   _____

7. Are the expectations you create centered around the features of your product/service and your company and its reputation, or your qualities as a salesperson and service provider?

_____

8. What are some ways you can sell yourself better? what can you say or do that will show prospects the benefits of doing business with *you*?

_____

9. Do you make it clear what customers can expect after the sale in terms of product performance and service quality?

_____

10. Do you and your prospects set up specific success criteria to be monitored after the sale?

_____

11. Do you conceal bad news about your product, service, or industry when you become aware of it? Are you straightforward about bad news, or do you let customers find out on their own?

_____

12. Do you or your company have a system for measuring customer expectations, satisfaction, or retention rates?

_____

13. Does anyone seem to care?

_____

I D E A

INCREASING YOUR CUSTOMER AWARENESS

16.9 The Three R's of Customer Service

What do customers expect from you and your company? We have distilled service down to its basic elements and found that every interaction with a customer entails three basic components — the three R's of service.

RELIABILITY

There are several facets to reliability: fulfilling promises, creating realistic expectations, delivering quality products, and dependability.

Organizational reliability Product or service quality; efficient, dependable operational systems; policies and procedures that consistently serve the customer; quality employee training; creating realistic expectations with accurate customer education and communication.

Personal reliability Timely follow-up on all matters; product knowledge; integrity; and overall professionalism.

RESPONSIVENESS

Responsiveness includes the willingness to incorporate flexibility in the decision-making process; giving a higher priority to customers' needs than to company operational guidelines; and timeliness.

Organizational responsiveness Structuring company policies and operational procedures so that employees can respond to and serve customers in a timely manner. This requires management to empower employees with the authority to give customers what they want, within reasonable parameters. The decision-making process must be moved as close to the customer as possible.

Personal responsiveness The willingness and ability to work the system on behalf of the customer. Salespeople and employees must be willing to take the responsibility for customers' problems and, if necessary, sell their solutions upstream.

RELATIONSHIP

Building positive, loyal, long-term business relationships is important.

Organizational relationship Focusing on building long-term relationships rather than one-time sales; market research and customer perception research that determine what is important to your target markets; determining and administering guarantees and warranty policies.

Personal relationship In a nutshell, treating people well. This includes courtesy, recognition, caring, empathy, sincerity, ethical selling, building rapport, establishing trust, and communicating effectively.

W O R K S H E E T

WHAT'S IN IT FOR YOU?

• Increase your ability to see business from your customer's point of view

INCREASING YOUR CUSTOMER AWARENESS

16.10 The Three R's in Your Business

Refer back to the previous worksheet on the three R's of Customer Service. Then give two examples each of specific aspects of reliability, responsiveness, and relationship that are important to your customers.

Reliability

1. _____

2. _____

Responsiveness

1. _____

2. _____

Relationship

1. _____

2. _____

I D E A

WHAT'S IN IT FOR YOU?

- **Increase your awareness of people's needs**
- **As a way to improve your relationships, find ways to meet your customers' personal needs in the course of doing business**

INCREASING YOUR CUSTOMER AWARENESS

16.11 Human Needs

We all have needs — some of them basic, others sublime. Think of ways to meet some of the following customer needs:

- The need for recognition
- The need for physical comfort
- The need to be competent
- The need for timely service
- The need to avoid stress
- The need to be understood
- The need for self-esteem
- The need to be remembered
- The need to be respected
- The need to be wanted
- The need to make one's own decisions
- The need for information
- The need for camaraderie
- The need to trust
- The need to be trusted
- The need for emotional support
- The need for laughter
- The need for intellectual stimulation
- The need for meaningful work
- The need for accomplishment
- The need for recreation
- The need for self-disclosure.

W O R K S H E E T

WHAT'S IN IT FOR YOU?

• **Brainstorm ways to increase customer loyalty**

INCREASING YOUR CUSTOMER AWARENESS

16.12 Strategies to Protect Current Accounts

You cannot make a decent living or sleep well at night if you are constantly seeking new prospects to replace customers you have lost. Sales and career growth come from maintaining existing customers while generating new ones.

In the exercise below, develop three goals that will help you keep your customers happy. Write out specific activities that will help you achieve your goals.

Sample Goal: Keep in close contact with customers after the sale.

Sample Activity: Call or stop by on the 7th, 21st, and 60th day after the sale.

1. Goal: _____

   Activities: _____

2. Goal: _____

   Activities: _____

3. Goal: _____

   Activities: _____

I D E A

WHAT'S IN IT FOR YOU?

• **Learn subtle ways to put customers at ease**

INCREASING YOUR CUSTOMER AWARENESS

16.13 How to Make Customers Feel Comfortable

- Use good eye contact
- Smile
- Touch (use only in a professional manner and with appropriate behavioral styles; note it is influential only with Relaters and Socializers)
- Ask questions (people hear questions better than they hear statements)
- Encourage participation in the sales process
- Listen! Make customers feel understood
- Give feedback
- Focus on your customer, and block out all distractions
- Show empathy and be sensitive to customers' needs
- Adopt a sense of urgency about everything you do for customers
- Never try to place blame—it's irrelevant when solving a problem

I D E A

INCREASING YOUR CUSTOMER AWARENESS

16.14 How Important Are Customers?

How important are customers? You be the judge. Did you know that...

- five out of six customers who come to you with complaints will continue to do business with your company even if you do not fix the problem — *if they perceive the person who took the complaint as friendly, caring, enthusiastic, and committed to the relationship?*
- unhappy customers will tell an average of eight to 20 people about their bad experiences? Happy customers tell an average of five friends.
- it costs five to ten times more to acquire a new customer than to maintain a current customer?
- people are willing to pay for better service? A *Wall Street Journal*/NBC News poll asked over 1,500 consumers, "How often do you purchase from a business that has excellent service but higher prices?" Their answers:

All the time	7%
Most of the time	28%
Sometimes	40%
Only rarely	17%
Never	6%
Not sure	2%

I D E A

FOLLOWING UP AND STAYING IN TOUCH AFTER THE SALE

16.15 Assuring Customer Satisfaction

Whether you are a salesperson or a front-line customer service representative, you need to understand some of the things that can go wrong after the sale. Customers become disgruntled for a number of reasons, most of which turn out to be minor — once they are handled tactfully. Your patience and understanding of human nature will help you remain calm when panic-stricken customers call and demand service.

Selective perception is a common mindset that customers often adopt after a purchase. They tend to focus on one or two annoying details, despite the overall positive picture. For example, a new copying machine may work perfectly except for the sound of the motor. The customer might call and complain about the motor and portray it as an intolerable nuisance. He may be stuck in selective perception, focusing only on what is wrong rather than what is right.

People expect their purchases to be perfect and, in general, the more they spend, the greater their expectations of perfection. In fact, the more someone spends, the more they are entitled to perfection. The world is made up, however, of a lot of imperfect but useful products and services.

How should you deal with selective perception? When someone lodges a complaint, check it out to see if it is a valid, correctable problem. The motor of the copying machine may be defective. If the customer's complaint is exaggerated, however, you have to do some selling. Put the negative detail in perspective by pointing out the positives, namely the benefits. You can also compare your problem to your competitors' and show your customer that nothing would be gained by switching companies. In addition, you can suggest creative ways of solving the problem. A copy machine may be moved or soundproofed.

User error is another common source of frustration for customers. If you have ever bought a computer, you can easily relate to this concept. Computer users usually go through hours of anxiety while they are learning to use the system. This is why a computer installation in an office should be accompanied by a formal training program for everyone who will use it.

Part of a salesperson's job when confirming the sale of a technical product or service is to try to avoid user error. To do so, you must evaluate your customer's technical ability and recommend training if necessary. You must also make your customer aware of the learning period required, during which the full benefit of the product/service may not be realized. This is equally important if your customer will be keeping track of results that prove or disprove your performance claims. The true test of your product/service will come only after everyone is using it correctly.

Buyer's remorse is a catch-all phrase that encompasses all the reasons why a customer might regret having made a purchase. It doesn't matter if the reason is selective perception, user error, or simply the fear of having made the wrong decision. The bottom line is that the customer has not yet realized the benefits of the purchase. It is your job to assure him or her that you have provided the solution and that the benefits will become apparent soon enough. The more specific you can be, the better. This is a perfect time to remind your customer of your service guarantee, if you have one.

IDEA

FOLLOWING UP AND STAYING IN TOUCH AFTER THE SALE

16.16 Warning Signs of Dissatisfaction

One of the most difficult things for salespeople to do is juggle the pursuit of new customers with servicing current accounts. This takes some organization, but with the right scheduling, you should be able to find time for each activity.

It costs five to ten times as much to acquire a new customer as it does to maintain a current customer, and that estimate doesn't take your time into consideration. That's why it's important to remain sensitive to your customer's needs after the sale. Pay attention. Look for these warning signs of dissatisfaction.

Decrease in Purchase Volume Because external factors may affect your industry, decreased sales may not be a reflection of dissatisfaction with your product — but you'll never know if you don't check it out. If external factors are not the reason, you may have a situation in which a complaint has gone unresolved. It is not uncommon for customers to fail to express their complaints. Your job is to pull those complaints out so that they can be corrected.

An Increase in Complaints This is obvious. If the number or frequency of complaints increases, you have to quickly and effectively resolve the situation. In addition, you must go one step further. If there is an operational flaw in your company, work to get it corrected. Chances are good that more than one customer is having problems. How many are quietly taking their business elsewhere?

Repeated Comments about the Merits of the Competition Whether you hear it directly from a customer or through the grapevine, this is a sure sign that someone is ready to defect. If the competition's grass is greener, you have to get out there and resell your company. Increase the perceived value. Build trust again. Bend over backwards if the account is worth it.

A Decline in the Business Relationship If you find a customer is less cordial during your sales calls or less receptive on the phone, find out the reason. Either you are making a pest of yourself, or he has become less enamored of you or your company's product/service.

New Management This may not be a sign of dissatisfaction, but when new management is hired, you need to pay close attention. Your task may be as simple as introducing yourself with a phone call or letter and assuring them that their satisfaction is your highest priority, or you may be required to start from scratch — build trust, identify needs, and so on to sell them all over again.

Change in Ownership Whenever your customer's company is sold or absorbed by a larger firm, you need to establish a working relationship with the new people. Sometimes, companies start over by soliciting bids on various products or services. That puts you back at square one. They are now a new prospect, so you'll have to do some homework. One advantage, however, is that your product or service was in place before the change, which is a selling point for you if your track record was good.

If you are lucky, the change in ownership will not affect your relationship with the company. In this case, you simply have to get in touch and assure them that service will continue as smoothly as before the change.

WORKSHEET

WHAT'S IN IT FOR YOU?

• **Organization** — the ability to compile valuable information to (1) help you evaluate an account's profitability and (2) present an informed overview to your customer during an annual review meeting

FOLLOWING UP AND STAYING IN TOUCH AFTER THE SALE

16.17 Semiannual Account Review Profile

Every six months, you should review your accounts. How has the big picture changed? Do some accounts need to be recategorized? What opportunities lie ahead? Use the following worksheet for this analysis.

ACCOUNT PROFILE

Company name:_____

Street address: _____

City/State/Zip:_____

Telephone: _____

Background

Buyers (in order of importance): _____

Products/services purchased:_____

Growth rate: _____

Buying Characteristics

When does customer buy?_____

How often? _____ Average order/call: _____

Gross sales volume (yearly):_____

Past sales (last 4 years): _____

Company Goals

Short-term (as perceived by?): _____

Long-term (as perceived by?): _____

Competitors (for this account): _____

Current competitors: _____

Potential competitors: _____

Your Company

Your company/product strengths: _____

_____

Your company/product weaknesses: _____

_____

Your goals for account _____ as of (date) _____

New potential services: _____

Specific account needs: _____

_____Pricing _____Delivery _____Service

_____Credit _____Reliability _____Other

_____

Profitability Analysis

Profit Margin _____ Margin percentage (GMP) _____

Number of calls necessary/year: _____

Average time per call: _____

Travel time per call: _____

Planning time per call: _____

Your cost per hour (CPH): _____

Your cost per call hour (CPCH): _____

Break-even volume: _____

Break-even volume/call: _____

Return of time invested: _____

Account classification: _____

CPH = Direct Cost (DC) ÷ Working hour (WH)

   CPCH = DC ÷ CH (Call Hours)

   BEV = DC ÷ GMP

   BEV PER CALL = CPCH ÷ GMP

   ROTI = GM ÷ DC

W O R K S H E E T

WHAT'S IN IT FOR YOU?

• **Gain the ability to act as a marketing consultant by presenting the big picture to your customers on a yearly basis**

FOLLOWING UP AND STAYING IN TOUCH AFTER THE SALE

16.18 Effective Annual Review Meetings

Once or twice a year you will evaluate your accounts to determine their A, B, C status, among other things. (See Section 5 for other ways to evaluate your accounts.) Once or twice a year, you should also meet with your customers—or at least your best customers—to review where things stand. This is a way to evaluate the account's activities, the industry in general, the economic climate, and what to anticipate, competitor's strengths and weaknesses, and so on. This is identical to the research you did when they were still prospects, but now you meet with your customers to get their input. This annual or semiannual meeting is an opportunity to 1) keep the relationship strong; 2) ask for feedback; 3) introduce new products/services; and 4) shape the direction of future business.

Every review meeting is different, but take the general guidelines below and use as many of them as you can.

1. If possible, arrange a breakfast or lunch meeting. Eating tends to relax people and gives the meeting a more informal tone.
2. Select a place that is conducive to a meeting. It should be well-lit with a large table in a place that won't rush you out after the meal.
3. Invite every significant participant in the account. If there are two buyers, make sure both can attend the meeting.
4. Bring all the spreadsheets necessary to discuss the previous year's business. In addition, bring all the documentation you may need to substantiate your claims regarding industry trends, product reports, etc.
5. Allow an adequate amount of time for the meeting. An hour might be rushing it.
6. Organize your presentation. Use your time logically. Ask questions about performance, quality, satisfaction, and so on. Ask about their business and their future. Introduce something new.

7. Give your customers plenty of time to talk. Ask open-ended questions to draw them out and encourage them to say whatever is on their minds. Take notes or record (with permission) the meeting. Send a copy of your notes to your customer as a follow-up.

8. Convey by actions and words your commitment to service and your desire for a long, mutually beneficial relationship.

9. After your review and other discussions, introduce a new product, service, or marketing idea. You can also offer a special discount or promotional package, which are nice ways to thank them for their time and business.

10. Look for opportunities and needs beyond the obvious. Focus on the big picture as well as the small details.

11. If appropriate, ask for referrals and/or testimonial letters. Your present customer base is one of the best sources of new business.

IDEA

WHAT'S IN IT FOR YOU?

- **Learn the many ways to maintain or increase your relationships with customers**

FOLLOWING UP AND STAYING IN TOUCH AFTER THE SALE

16.19 15 Ways to Stay Close to Your Customers

1. **Show them that you think of them.** Send or fax helpful newspaper clippings, relevant cartoons, and Christmas and birthday cards. Here's a new one—send a card on the anniversary of the day they became your customers!

2. **Drop by to show them what's new.** Always make an appointment or call first—and do it when you're in the neighborhood—for a brief visit to show a new product or leave a brochure is a good way to stay in touch and increase sales and get referrals.

3. **Follow up a sales with a free gift to enhance the purchase.** You should also make an appointment to see how your product/service is being utilized and to suggest other ways to derive more benefits. Customers often do not use their purchases correctly.

4. **Offer "valued customer" discounts.** These can take the form of coupons, letters, or other sales promotions. This not only garners more orders, it also makes your customers happy to be getting such good deals.

5. **Let customers know that they should contact you when they hire employees** so you can train the new people *for free*!

6. **Compensate customers for lost time or money,** if they were caused by problems with your product/service. Have a well-thought-out recovery program and stick to it. Better to err on the side of generosity than lose an account out of stinginess.

7. **Be personal.** Keep notes in your customer files on every little detail you know — everything from spouses' names to hobbies and especially their behavioral style.

8. **Always be honest.** Nothing undermines your credibility more severely than dishonesty. Lies have a way of coming back to haunt you. Why lie?

9. **Accept returns unconditionally.** The few dollars you may lose in the short run is far less than what you gain from acquiring a new customer. For example, ADI, Inc., calculates that it costs them an average of $25 to correct a customer's problem. Their average customer spends $15,000 per year with them. They tell their employees, "Don't quibble."

10. **Honor your customer's privacy.** If you have been a truly consultative salesperson, then you may possess some knowledge that should be kept confidential. Your ethical standards demand that you keep it that way.

11. **Keep your promises.** Never, ever promise something that you cannot deliver. This principle applies to little things such as returning phone calls as well as big things like delivery dates. If you must, babysit deliveries and promised service. See that they get done. Your reputation (and your commissions) are on the line.

12. **Give feedback on referrals.** This is the right way to show your appreciation for the referral. Tell your customer the outcome. This is also a good way to get more referrals without asking for them directly.

13. **Make your customers famous ... for 15 minutes.** If your company has a newsletter, ask your customer for permission to write about their success with your product/service. Then send a copy to your customer. The same can be done for industry publications.

14. **Arrange periodic performance reviews.** As a consultant, you should meet annually with your customers to review their competitive posture in their industry, their satisfaction with your company, and any other concerns that may affect business.

15. **Keep communication lines open.** As in any relationship, assure your customers that you are open to all calls about everything and anything — ideas, grievances, advice, praise, questions, and so on. This is one way to maintain that all-important rapport.

Remember, people do business with people they like!

I D E A

WHAT'S IN IT FOR YOU?

- **Learn five effective methods for getting referrals or increasing sales from current customers**

FOLLOWING UP AND STAYING IN TOUCH AFTER THE SALE

16.20 Referrals: If You Don't Ask, You Don't Get

When prospecting, many salespeople completely forget about their current customers. Current customers are an excellent source for new business, but are perhaps too obvious. If you have a strong relationship with your customers, you should not feel uncomfortable asking them for favors. Here are some ways to develop new business from current customers.

1. **Ask for referrals within their company.** Sure you've asked for referrals before, but were you specific about it? Probably not. If you direct a customer's thinking internally, you may come up with more prospects. For example, some companies (banks, real estate companies) have more than one branch. Ask if a new branch is opening. Expansions take place all the time and represent new opportunities. People are hired and fired. Fires and floods create changes. People get married and divorced. Births and deaths create opportunities. If you don't ask, you won't get.

2. **Ask for referrals outside their company.** People in business tend to know people in similar businesses. Funny how that works, but if you're specializing in a certain industry, you can take advantage of this small world. When you solve a problem for one customer, he or she may know someone who has a similar record. The key is not to only ask for the sale, but to follow up periodically and ask again . . . and again.

3. **Sell more of the same.** Many companies, especially small- to medium-sized retailers, tend to order conservatively until a product proves its salability. They then have a hard time breaking out of the habit of small orders. If you see a company that has the capacity to sell more of your product, encourage them to increase their orders and show them how they will benefit. If necessary, offer them flexible financing to ease them into the bigger investment. You may also need to consult with them about how they can sell more of your products to current or new target markets.

4. **Cross-sell your customers.** Again, if and only if you see the need or the ability to sell other products, present them to your customers. You have already proven that you are trustworthy, so they will listen when you suggest they carry something else. The same principle applies to services. Once you've solved a problem with one service, perhaps you can tackle another need with another service. Cable television companies do this constantly. Every month they use statement stuffers to try to entice subscribers to sign up for additional services such as HBO.

5. **Upsell your customers.** This is easy to relate to in the computer industry. You've sold a system to a customer and they are doing well with it. By keeping in touch and conducting periodic reviews of their business, you will learn how rapidly they are growing. Rapid growth means their computer needs are becoming greater. Time for an upgrade to a more powerful, more expensive system. This is natural. The key is to see their increased need before your competitor does, but, of course, that is why you stay in touch.

6. **Upserve your customers.** *Upselling* means increasing the size of a transaction. *Upserving* means increasing the size of the satisfaction by looking for ways to increase the benefits the customer receives and increase the value that the customer perceives. When you focus on upserving, customers feel better served by you. They trust you more, and are more likely to be receptive when you try to find new sales. Give upserving a try. You'll find it's easy to think of new ways to serve your customers at no significant cost—and they will make a big difference.

IDEA

WHAT'S IN IT FOR YOU?

• **Prepare a file of testimonial letters that strengthen your credentials and claims**

FOLLOWING UP AND STAYING IN TOUCH AFTER THE SALE

16.21 Testimonial Letters

Testimonial letters are a powerful form of referral that you can use again and again. When a customer writes you a recommendation or letter of praise and permits you to share it with others, you can benefit from your customer's credibility and testimonial many times over—without having to contact your customer each time you need a referral.

To prepare a file of testimonials, plan ahead. After each successful sale, ask your customer if he or she would be willing to write a short letter summarizing the benefits gained from doing business with you or from using your product or service.

A testimonial letter should add strength to your credentials, your claims, and the value of your products in the marketplace. A common mistake is securing letters that simply speak well of the salesperson, but don't relate to the value of the product. For the greatest effectiveness, a testimonial letter should support the claims that you make to your prospects. It should specifically state the benefit received by the customer, and describe the need addressed when you made the sale.

If you haven't been using testimonial letters, get some. Start now by asking each customer to provide a testimonial.

I D E A

FOLLOWING UP AND STAYING IN TOUCH AFTER THE SALE

16.22 Measuring Customer Retention

How do you know if your customers are satisfied? You can ask, but good surveys are difficult to construct and administer. The most simple and accurate measure of satisfaction is *customer retention*.

THE SATISFACTION BAROMETER

Customer retention is a valuable measure of a company's product or service quality. On average, most companies lose 10 to 15 percent of their customers each year. With the cost of acquiring new customers estimated to be six times the cost of maintaining current customers, companies cannot afford to be cavalier about this. Retaining customers must be given as high a priority as acquiring new ones. Consider the fact that in many industries, increasing customer retention by 5 percent raises the average value of the customer's long-term business by 85 percent. Other reasons to fight to keep current customers:

- Long-term customers generally expand their annual order.
- Serving long-term customers is easier because both sides know what to expect; the kinks have been worked out.
- Long-term customers are often willing to pay a premium for consistent, valued service.
- Long-term customers are the best source for referrals.

W O R K S H E E T

WHAT'S IN IT FOR YOU?

• Become aware of how you typically handle customer problems

HANDLING CUSTOMER PROBLEMS

16.23 How You Resolve Customer Problems

Describe two situations in which you dealt successfully with a customer problem. Then describe two situations in which your handling of a problem was unsuccessful.

Successful Resolution 1: _____

What you said or did: _____

Outcome: _____

What you could have said or done better: _____

Successful Resolution 2: _____

What you said or did: _____

Outcome: _____

What you could have said or done better: _____

Unsuccessful Resolution 1: _____

What you said or did: _____

Outcome: _____

What you could have said or done better: _____

Unsuccessful Resolution 2: _____

What you said or did: _____

Outcome: _____

What you could have said or done better: _____

W O R K S H E E T

WHAT'S IN IT FOR YOU?

• **Brainstorm new, creative ways to effectively solve problems**

HANDLING CUSTOMER PROBLEMS

16.24 How to Evaluate Responses to Problems

Your responses to common customer problems should meet four criteria if they are going to make good business sense. They should:

1. create customer satisfaction and a sense of loyalty.

2. have a reasonable chance of success.

3. be cost-effective.

4. be within your control to provide.

1. List a typical problem that your customers experience with your products or services.

_____

2. Think of three or more *creative, new* ways to respond to and solve that problem. Those solutions must satisfy all four requirements listed above.

a. _____

b. _____

c. _____

I D E A

• **Learn the seven basic steps in resolving customer complaints**

HANDLING CUSTOMER PROBLEMS

16.25 Resolving Customer Problems

When a customer has a problem with you or your company, follow these seven steps to achieve a mutually satisfactory solution.

1. **Handle the person first, then the problem.** Let angry people vent their frustrations. This alone will go a long way toward resolving the problem. Problems seem less severe after a person has gotten rid of the anger.

2. **Apologize.** This is often left out, but it is a crucial gesture. Offer a sincere, *personal* apology, not one on behalf of the company. Show that you are committed to the relationship.

3. **Show empathy.** Assure your customer that he has every right to be angry and disappointed and that you would feel the same way if it happened to you.

4. **Find a solution.** Resolve the problem *with* your customer, not *for* her. Ask questions that will get her involved in the process. Some possible questions include:
   How would you like to see this problem resolved?
   What would be an acceptable resolution to this problem?
   If you were in my position, how might you resolve this kind of problem for your customer?
   Would a refund be acceptable to you?

5. **Jump through hoops.** Immediately take over and make the recovery process easy for your customer. If there are phone calls to make or forms to fill out, you assume responsibility and do the work. If the resolution of the problem is going to be complicated, explain the system to your customer. People feel much better when they are informed than when they are kept in the dark.

6. **Offer compensation.** If the service breakdown was severe enough ("severe enough" is an individual judgment call, but should also be a standard set by your company), you need to say "I'm sorry" with a concrete gesture. Compensation should have these characteristics:
   It should be immediate. Giving a gift long after the fact makes it lose its meaning and appear insincere. Give the gift immediately. For this reason, you must be clear about the parameters for compensating customers.

Make it meaningful. A meaningful gift is something that has a high *perceived value* to your customer. It should also differentiate you from your competition. Be creative—customize the gift to your customer's personality. Don't send flowers or a box of candy—everyone does that. Know your customer well enough to determine whether a pair of tickets to a baseball game or a hot air balloon ride would be appropriate.

The gift should be consumable. If you send a calendar or a clock to say, "I'm sorry," your customer will be reminded of the incident every time she looks at it. Save those gifts for positive occasions. Your customer should be able to eat or use your recovery gift relatively soon. That way the gift is appreciated, but soon out of sight and mind.

It should be inexpensive. The combination of high perceived value and low cost to the company is ideal, especially if you are compensating customers regularly. (If you are, correct the situation that is causing these repeated service failures!) Giving away more of your company's products or services may be appropriate (and inexpensive), but only if they won't cause more problems. The worst thing you can do is offer your customers more of something that has already caused them grief.

7. **Follow up.** After resolving a problem, with or without a gift, you must follow up. As with any follow-up, you will not only make sure things are OK, you will also look for additional needs that represent selling opportunities. Follow-up is essential because there is nothing worse than a fouled-up recovery. A *recovery* snafu is a guaranteed way to lose a customer forever.

WORKSHEET

WHAT'S IN IT FOR YOU?

- **Increase your knowledge of *levels* of customer dissatisfaction**

HANDLING CUSTOMER PROBLEMS

16.26 Determining Customer Dissatisfaction

Before you do anything to help a disgruntled customer, it is important to determine how upset he or she is. The more upset, the greater and faster your efforts will have to be to correct the situation. To determine the customer's degree of dissatisfaction, you must do three things:

1. **Listen actively.** Use your communication skills to read your customer accurately. Observe body language. Read between the lines of what is said. Tune in to your customer.

2. **Ask questions.** Avoid misunderstanding. Ask for clarification. Find out how your customer was inconvenienced and how he or she would like the problem resolved.

3. **Empathize.** Put yourself in your customer's place and imagine the frustration you would feel.

Your customer's frustration level will fall into one of three levels. After reading the definitions below, write out two examples of typical problems in your company that cause customers to experience these levels of emotion.

LEVELS OF CUSTOMER DISSATISFACTION

Bothered. Customers are bothered when service falls below their expectations, disappoints them slightly, or surprises them (negatively), but does not cause inconvenience.

Examples from your experience: _____

Irritated. Customers become irritated when they are annoyed by poor service, are mildly inconvenienced, or have lost time but not money.

Examples from your experience: _____

Abused. Customers feel abused by you or your company when they are grossly inconvenienced, have lost a lot of time or even a little money, are personally insulted, unfairly treated, or made angry or upset.

Examples from your experience: _____

I D E A

- See at a glance the steps you need to take when a customer has been bothered, irritated, or abused

HANDLING CUSTOMER PROBLEMS

16.27 Customer Problem/Solution Grid

	When Your Customer Is ...		
	Bothered	**Irritated**	**Abused**
You Need To: Express concern and apologize	✓	✓	✓
Immediately make things right	✓	✓	✓
Acknowledge the problem and show empathy		✓	✓
Make a gesture of compensation		**Optional**	✓
Follow-up			✓

WORKSHEET

WHAT'S IN IT FOR YOU?

• **Prepare yourself for handling customer dissatisfaction**

HANDLING CUSTOMER PROBLEMS

16.28 Responding Correctly to Typical Problems

Take one typical customer problem from each level of dissatisfaction in Worksheet 16.27 and write out what you would say and do in those situations.

IDEA

HANDLING CUSTOMER PROBLEMS

16.29 Courteous Phone Skills

You may or may not answer your phone. If someone else does, that person should be trained to give customers the best possible impression. If you answer the phone, you need to take the time to do it properly. There are no excuses for rude or unprofessional behavior. Either use common courtesy, or don't answer the phone at all. Rude phone habits can quickly burn leads.

The five basic messages a caller should receive are:

1. I will not waste your time.

2. I care about you and your business.

3. I am competent and well organized.

4. I can be trusted to help you get through to your party.

5. I am proud of my company and enjoy working here.

There are some *shoulds* that everyone needs to know:

- **Answer calls in no more than four rings.** If your phone traffic is too heavy to allow this, hire an additional receptionist. Remember, a good receptionist is not measured by how quickly he or she handles calls, but by the positive outcome of each call.

- **Be prepared.** It looks silly when you have to search for a pen and notepad. Similarly, if prices or other information are commonly requested over the phone, that information should be readily available.

- **Identify yourself or your company.** The caller should know immediately who has taken the call. It not only gives information, but adds a personal, friendly, professional touch.

- **Screen calls tactfully.** It is better to make a request or ask a question than sound demanding. "What is this about?" is a rude way to ask, "Will she know what this call is in reference to?" By the same token, "May I tell her who is calling?" is more polite than "Who is calling?" Anything can be said nicely if you try.

- **Don't make customers repeat their stories.** It's happened to you. You call up and tell someone why you're calling. They transfer your call. You tell the next person why you're calling. You get transferred again, and so on. The right way to handle this situation is for the first person to find the proper person to handle the call and tell that person the customer's story. Making a customer repeat themselves is making them jump through hoops to get service. That's what happens when front-line people get lazy—they make the customers do *their* jobs. Customers shouldn't have to do the jumping.

- **Maximum hold time is 15 seconds.** If you have to keep someone on hold longer, arrange to call him or her back. Keep closely in touch with people who are on hold.

- **Train, test, coach.** Good telephone skills are common sense, but many entry-level employees lack them. Train them well—tell them exactly what you expect. Don't assume they know how to answer the phone. Test them by having a friend call to see how she is treated on the phone. Use this insight to coach your people to further improve their skills.

IDEA

HANDLING CUSTOMER PROBLEMS

16.30 When to Fire a Customer

Most people are willing to do business with anyone who is willing to buy, and for the most part, that's as it should be. We all want to build a large customer base.

Unfortunately, too many salespeople fail to sift the "chaff" customers from the "wheat" customers. Wheat customers are profitable and reasonably easy to do business with. Chaff customers gobble up our time, energy, and emotional capital and often leave us with little or nothing to show for it — not even acceptable compensation for the effort expended.

Another way to think of this is establishing win–win relationships. The key is keeping the relationship balanced. You are there to serve your customers as long as it is rewarding to do so.

Let's consider two examples:

The bigger the discount, the bigger the aggravation. It's common practice to deeply discount price or terms to gain a prospect's business. Too often the resulting aggravation will be in direct proportion to the amount of the discount. It's as if some customers "devalue" your goods or service if you discount too deeply. Many expect similar — and more — allowances for all future business. Remember: you can choose not to do business with an account if the payoff doesn't outweigh the expenditure. Be careful not to discount for the sake of discounting, or simply because the prospect asks. Focus on selling *solutions* and *value*.

Does the client do business the way you do? If candor, honesty, and integrity are important to you — as they should be — and your client suggests cheating his company, your company, or a third party, you're headed for major challenges down the road. Choosing not to do business with such people is your best defense. It may be your *only* defense.

These are only two of many possibilities. Where are your boundaries? What makes a customer or prospect more trouble than they are worth?

Are you willing to fire a customer?

SECTION SEVENTEEN

BE YOUR OWN SALES MANAGER

WHAT'S IN IT FOR YOU?

- Measure your sales results to pinpoint areas for improvement.
- Become aware of how you spend (and waste) your time.
- Learn time management skills that make you more efficient.
- Delegate routine tasks.
- Discover secrets that help you win sales contests.
- Tap the power of electronic sales support.

As a sales professional, you have two major responsibilities: to get yourself to make sales and to develop yourself as a salesperson. In other words, as you grow in your knowledge of selling, you have to grow in your ability to manage yourself as a sales performer.

These are separate jobs, but they are permanently intertwined. The less effective you are in managing yourself, the more dependent you will be on others to keep you at the top of your form. The less effective you are in selling, the more energy you will waste, making far too many calls and producing far too few sales. Keep these two in balance throughout your sales career. Think of yourself as the owner of your own company, and then ask yourself, "How can I increase my value to the marketplace?"

I D E A

• **Identify some of the basic keys to successful sales and sales management**

SELLING BY THE NUMBERS

17.1 Doing the Basics Right

It is amazing how many times success can be assured by attending the basics of the job. For example, a study of 257 Fortune 500 companies found that only:

- 17 percent do not determine an approximate duration for each sales call.
- 23 percent do not use a computer to assist in time and territory management.
- 28 percent do not set profit objectives for their accounts.
- 37 percent do not use prescribed routing patterns in covering their territories.
- 46 percent do not look at their use of time in an organized way.
- 49 percent do not determine the *economical* number of calls for each account.
- 49 percent do not use prepared sales presentations.
- 70 percent do not use call schedules.
- 75 percent do not have a system for classifying customers according to sales potential.
- 76 percent do not set sales objectives for their accounts.
- 81 percent do not use a call report system.

How can you assure your future success by eliminating these oversights?

I D E A

WHAT'S IN IT FOR YOU?

• **Increase your understanding of the value of record keeping**

SELLING BY THE NUMBERS

17.2 Numbers Can't Lie

The flip side of setting goals is measuring performance. Measurement helps you determine what you are doing right and wrong. If you don't keep records, you won't have a clue as to how to improve your performance and reach your goals.

There are many ways to measure and evaluate performance. Only you can determine which methods make the most sense for you, given your industry and the nature of your sales process. The methods you choose should complement—if not be identical to—the ones used by your sales manager. The five areas to measure are sales calls, expenses, nonselling activities, market opportunities, and results.

To interpret your records, look for two things: changes from last year and poor current ratios. Current ratios are excellent indicators of areas that need work. For example, a life insurance salesperson whose appointments-per-call ratio is low may need to work on her phone script. A low sales-per-appointment ratio may indicate a need to improve presentation skills. If the number of calls she makers per day is low, she is simply not picking up the phone.

Sales is a numbers game. Keeping records will show how these numbers apply to you. For example, knowing that you have to contact 25 prospects to average ten appointments to make five presentations to make one sale is valuable information.

W O R K S H E E T

WHAT'S IN IT FOR YOU?

• **Understand the many ways to measure sales calls and determine which are appropriate for your business**

SELLING BY THE NUMBERS

17.3 Measuring Sales Calls

Measuring the number of sales calls and the number of customer prospect contacts is a key method of measuring performance. Most salespeople don't like to spend their time on measuring. They'd rather be selling. But top performers consistently measure what they do, so they leverage what's working and develop what isn't working.

Sales Calls:

- Number made on current customers
- Number made on potential new accounts
- Average time spent per call
- Number of sales presentations
- Selling time versus nonselling time
- Call frequency ratio per customer type
- Calls per day
- Calls-per-day ratio $= \dfrac{\text{Number of calls}}{\text{Number of days worked}}$

- Calls-per-account ratio $= \dfrac{\text{Number of calls}}{\text{Number of accounts}}$

- Planned call ratio $= \dfrac{\text{Number of planned calls}}{\text{Total number of calls}}$

- Orders-per-call (hit ratio) $= \dfrac{\text{Number of orders}}{\text{Total number of calls}}$

I D E A

- **Understand the many ways to measure sales expenses and determine which are appropriate for you**

SELLING BY THE NUMBERS

17.4 Measuring Sales Expenses

Cost control is a watchword in business today. Here is a simple approach.

Sales Expenses:

- Average per sales call
- Expenses as a percentage of sales quota
- By customer type
- By product category
- Direct selling expense ratios
- Indirect selling expense ratios
- Sales expenses ratio $= \dfrac{\text{Expenses}}{\text{Sales}}$

- Cost-per-call ratio $= \dfrac{\text{Total Costs}}{\text{Number of calls}}$

I D E A

- **Understand the many ways to measure results and determine which are appropriate for you**

SELLING BY THE NUMBERS

17.5 Measuring Results

Results come in many shapes and sizes. Consider these measures for determining your results from each sale.

- Total dollar contribution
- Average contribution margin
- Current versus past sales
- Current sales per call
- Account penetration ratio $= \dfrac{\text{Account sold}}{\text{Total accounts available}}$

- New account conversion ratio $= \dfrac{\text{Number of new accounts sold}}{\text{Total number of potential new accounts}}$

- Lost account ratio $= \dfrac{\text{Prior accounts not sold}}{\text{Total number of accounts}}$

- Sales-per-account ratio $= \dfrac{\text{Sales dollar volume}}{\text{Total number of accounts}}$

- Average order size ratio $= \dfrac{\text{Sales dollar volume}}{\text{Total number of orders}}$

- Order cancellation ratio $= \dfrac{\text{Number of canceled orders}}{\text{Total number of orders}}$

WORKSHEET

WHAT'S IN IT FOR YOU?

• **Become aware of how you spend (not waste) your time**

CONTROL YOUR TIME/BOOST YOUR PRODUCTIVITY

17.6 The Time Log

Directions: Make 10 copies of this log and fill out one a day for the next 10 days. Once each hour, try to stop what you are doing and record your activities. It's really not difficult or time consuming.

___

TIME LOG

Time Log For _____

Date_____ Day _____ Analysis _____

Hour	Time Frame	Actual Time	Description of Activities	Comments for Better Time Use
7	0-30			
	30-60			
8	0-30			
	30-60			
9	0-30			
	30-60			
10	0-30			
	30-60			
11	0-30			
	30-60			
12	0-30			
	30-60			
1	0-30			
	30-60			
2	0-30			
	30-60			
3	0-30			
	30-60			
4	0-30			
	30-60			
5	0-30			
	30-60			
6	0-30			
	30-60			
7	0-30			
	30-60			

W O R K S H E E T

WHAT'S IN IT FOR YOU?

- **Analyze your daily activities**
- **Determine productive and unproductive activities**

CONTROL YOUR TIME/BOOST YOUR PRODUCTIVITY

17.7 Daily Time Analysis Questions

Directions: Make 10 copies of this worksheet. For the next 10 days, answer questions at the end of each workday. Be as detailed as possible. Try to state specifically how you will make the next day better.

1. What went right today? Why?

2. What went wrong today? Why?

3. What time did I start on my top priority task? Why? Could I have started earlier?

4. What patterns do I see in my time logs?

5. What part of the day was most productive? Least productive?

6. What were my three biggest time wasters today?

7. Which activities need more time? Which need less time?

8. Beginning tomorrow, what will I do to make better use of my time?

WORKSHEET

WHAT'S IN IT FOR YOU?

• Determine which activities are most and least productive for you

CONTROL YOUR TIME/BOOST YOUR PRODUCTIVITY

17.8 Identify Good and Bad Habits

It's impossible to develop good time management habits unless you understand which activities deserve more time and which should be downplayed or pruned out altogether.

At the end of the 10 days, look back over the daily time logs and questions. Determine the six most productive and least productive activities you engaged in during that period. Compute the total amount of time spent on these activities.

My Six Most Productive Activities   **Between (Dates)** _____

1. _____   Total Time: _____

2. _____   Total Time: _____

3. _____   Total Time: _____

4. _____   Total Time: _____

5. _____   Total Time: _____

6. _____   Total Time: _____

My Six Least Productive Activities   **Between (Dates)** _____

1. _____   Total Time: _____

2. _____   Total Time: _____

3. _____   Total Time: _____

4. _____   Total Time: _____

5. _____   Total Time: _____

6. _____   Total Time: _____

W O R K S H E E T

WHAT'S IN IT FOR YOU?

• **Identify more ways you may be wasting your time**

CONTROL YOUR TIME/BOOST YOUR PRODUCTIVITY

17.9 Identify Time Wasters

Some unproductive activities are all too common. In addition to the time wasters you identified in the last two exercises, see which of the following apply to you.

	Never	Sometimes	Always
1. Overpreparing for sales calls.	_____	_____	_____
2. Scheduling less important work before more important work.	_____	_____	_____
3. Starting a job before thinking it through.	_____	_____	_____
4. Leaving jobs before they are completed.	_____	_____	_____
5. Doing things that can be delegated to another person (across or down; not upward).	_____	_____	_____
6. Doing things that can be delegated to modern equipment.	_____	_____	_____
7. Doing things that aren't actually part of your real job.	_____	_____	_____
8. Keeping too many complicated or overlapping records.	_____	_____	_____
9. Pursuing prospects you probably can't sell.	_____	_____	_____
10. Paying too much attention to low-yield prospects.	_____	_____	_____
11. Handling too wide a variety of duties.	_____	_____	_____
12. Failing to build barriers against interruptions.	_____	_____	_____
13. Allowing conferences and discussions to wander.	_____	_____	_____
14. Conducting unnecessary meetings, visits, and/or phone calls.	_____	_____	_____
15. Chasing trivial data after the main facts are known.	_____	_____	_____
16. Socializing at great length between tasks.	_____	_____	_____

WORKSHEET

WHAT'S IN IT FOR YOU?

• Identify and eliminate your three biggest time wasters

CONTROL YOUR TIME/BOOST YOUR PRODUCTIVITY

17.10 Steps to Eliminate Time Wasters

1. Time Waster: _____

Strategies for eliminating:

2. Time Waster: _____

Strategies for eliminating:

3. Time Waster: _____

Strategies for eliminating:

W O R K S H E E T

WHAT'S IN IT FOR YOU?

• **Understand which activities provide the greatest payoff for you**

CONTROL YOUR TIME/BOOST YOUR PRODUCTIVITY

17.11 Setting Priorities

There are two famous laws that govern the use of time (or so it seems):

Parkinson's Law: "Work expands to fill the time allotted for its completion."

Pareto's Principle: "Twenty percent of your time generates 80 percent of your results."

The secret to using time effectively lies in setting priorities. That means knowing which activities generate the most results. List the five highest payoff activities in your job from the points of view of your manager, your prospects and customers, and yourself. Use these three lists to determine the activities that will benefit you most overall.

In the eyes of my sales manager:

1.

2.

3.

4.

5.

In the eyes of my customers and prospects:

1.

2.

3.

4.

5.

In my own eyes:

1.

2.

3.

4.

5.

My overall high-priority activities:

1.

2.

3.

4.

5.

W O R K S H E E T

WHAT'S IN IT FOR YOU?

• Plan your workweek to accomplish your objectives

CONTROL YOUR TIME/BOOST YOUR PRODUCTIVITY

17.12 The Weekly Planning Guide

Effective time management is a discipline that must be practiced every day. You must learn to organize your days *and* weeks around activities that pay off for you.

If you spend Sunday evening planning the week ahead of you, you'll hit the ground running Monday morning. This worksheet will help.

Use your high priority worksheet to determine five objectives you can realistically achieve in one week. Write them down in the large spaces below. Then jot down the activities required to achieve those objectives. Make a new plan every week.

OBJECTIVES (what I hope to have accomplished by the end of the week)

Activities required to accomplish objectives	Priority	Time needed	Which day

W O R K S H E E T

WHAT'S IN IT FOR YOU?

- Identify some important time management areas to improve
- Understand the value of marketing these improvements
- Set specific goals for change

CONTROL YOUR TIME/BOOST YOUR PRODUCTIVITY

17.13 Time Management Action Plan

Choose the areas in which to improve your control of time. Prioritize them and choose the most important to work on first. Fill out the action plan that follows and experience some success with one change before implementing the other two. Photocopy this action plan and use it for other goals as well.

What is a major time management practice I would like to implement?

What are the potential obstacles for doing so?

What are the benefits to implementing this practice?

How will I specifically implement this practice?

What is my target date for implementing this?

How and when will I measure my success?

What will I have to give up to make this behavioral change?

How will I reward myself and when?

WORKSHEET

WHAT'S IN IT FOR YOU?

• Organize your days around your high-priority activities

CONTROL YOUR TIME/BOOST YOUR PRODUCTIVITY

17.14 The To-Do List

Your organization and productivity will increase if you organize your days around your high-priority activities. One of the best ways to do this is to use your organizer or calendar, whether it's paper or electronic.

If not, get organized by photocopying the "To-Do" list on the following page and filling it out every evening for the next day's work. List activities by priority, starting with the most important. Define specific amounts of time to be spent on each activity, as well as the desired outcomes.

Use this as a "road map" for your day. Consult it regularly to make sure you are working to meet your daily objectives. At the end of the day, file your "To-Do" list for future reference.

Things To Do Today

Item	Priority	Time Needed	Done

Notes

Date

Scheduled Events	
8:00	
8:15	
8:30	
8:45	
9:00	
9:15	
9:30	
9:45	
10:00	
10:15	
10:30	
10:45	
11:00	
11:15	
11:30	
11:45	
12:00	
12:15	
12:30	
12:45	
1:00	
1:15	
1:30	
1:45	
2:00	
2:15	
2:30	
2:45	
3:00	
3:15	
3:30	
3:45	
4:00	
4:15	
4:30	
4:45	
5:00	
5:15	
5:30	
5:45	
6:00	
Evening	

IDEA

CONTROL YOUR TIME/BOOST YOUR PRODUCTIVITY

17.15 The Paperwork Shuffle

Many people, in and out of sales, have desks that look like paper mountains. These strategies for handling mail and paperwork more effectively will free you to attend more important tasks.

1. Delegate as much as possible. What cannot be delegated must be streamlined.
2. If possible, have an assistant open your mail. Mail should be prioritized. Junk mail goes on the bottom; bills and information in the middle; and letters requiring immediate action on top.
3. If you open your own mail, set a time to do it and keep that time the same every day.
4. Answer correspondence immediately. Write on the backs of letters, or dictate your responses and have an assistant type them up.
5. Read magazines and clip articles of interest to review during downtime, travel, lunch, etc.
6. Paperwork — other than mail — ideally should be handled only once. Pick it up, act on it, and be done with it—or at least move it along to the next step toward completion.

I D E A

• **Learn to keep control of your time by handling interruptions**

CONTROL YOUR TIME/BOOST YOUR PRODUCTIVITY

17.16 Handling Interruptions

Do you ever get the feeling that, if it weren't for all the interruptions, you could get your work done? Interruptions, like time, need to be controlled. Here are some ways to prevent or skillfully handle them.

1. If you answer your own phone, you need to develop a tactful, but direct way of scheduling calls. Try, "I'm extremely busy now, let me call you back," or "I'm in the middle of meeting, let me call you back." Anything will do as long as you use it.

2. The best system is one in which an assistant or receptionist screens your calls. An answering machine is second-best.

3. If your calls are screened, devise a system to help determine the urgency of a call. Create categories such as, "Direct to someone else"; "Take number, will call back"; "Interrupt me briefly"; and "Urgent, interrupt immediately."

4. When you return calls, be sure to call at the best time for your prospect or customer. These are covered in Section 7.

5. Prepare for your calls in advance. Pull files or call up a customer's data on the computer before you dial the number.

6. Keep your calls short by getting to the point. Be careful who you ask, "How are you?" You may get a long answer. Better: Say, "Hi, Janet, just returning your call. What can I do for you?"

7. When calling customers (as opposed to returning their calls), have your objectives clearly in mind. Write out key questions so you won't lose your train of thought. Respect your customers' time as you would have them respect yours.

8. Group your calls by type so you won't have to change your mindset. For example, sales calls, especially if you are cold calling, should be made together. Other types of calls include collection, appointment verification, and problem resolution.

9. Handle visitors as if you were a doctor. Appointments need to be made. If possible, don't interrupt meetings with phone calls. Set a finite amount of time for the visitor, unless it is a customer or prospect. Diplomatically end your meetings by standing up and hinting that the meeting is over.

I D E A

CONTROL YOUR TIME/BOOST YOUR PRODUCTIVITY

17.17 The Art of Delegation

The ability to delegate sets the leader apart from the followers. That's because many people find it difficult to give up control. But delegating duties and responsibilities is essential in today's downsized organizations. Salespeople have so much work that they must delegate some activities if they hope to significantly increase their sales volume.

The following key points will help you master the art of delegation.

- **Find the right person for the project.** Don't assign the project to just any warm body. That's fine if any outcome is acceptable. If you want the job done right, however, you must find the right person for the job. If none exists, find the most capable person and train him or her well.

- **Delegate authority and accountability.** The worst thing you can do is delegate a task and then tie a person's hands. If you've picked the right person or trained someone well, you must then give them authority so the job can be done without your supervision. In addition, you should make the person accountable for the quality of the work performed.

- **Make the task perfectly clear.** Carefully explain the nature of the project to the person to whom you are giving responsibility. This may be done verbally or in writing, depending on the complexity of the task. The newer and more complex the task, the more questions your assistant will have. Answer all questions promptly and thoroughly.

- **Agree on a deadline.** When your assistant fully understands your expectations, both of you are in a position to determine a mutually acceptable deadline.

- **Review and coach.** There is a learning curve associated with any new activity. During this time, you should periodically review your assistant's progress and offer additional coaching if needed.

- **Lay the groundwork for more delegation.** Once you get your feet wet, you will find more things that can be done by others to free up your time. Begin training people to assist you in more operations and you will find yourself with more time to do what you do best: selling.

W O R K S H E E T

WHAT'S IN IT FOR YOU?

- Overcome the psychological barriers that stand in the way of delegating
- Identify the activities that can and cannot be delegated

CONTROL YOUR TIME/BOOST YOUR PRODUCTIVITY

17.18 Delegation Plan

To delegate effectively, you must let go emotionally of some of your routine tasks. This worksheet will help you categorize your activities and shed light on what can be delegated.

1. Activities I've already delegated:

_____

_____

2. Activities I haven't yet, but could delegate:

_____

_____

3. Activities I'm unsure about delegating:

_____

_____

4. Activities I must do myself:

_____

_____

5. Ways to change #3 and #4 above to #2's:

_____

_____

I D E A

• **Discover the secrets of winning a sales contest**

BOOST YOUR RESULTS

17.19 How To Win A Sales Contest

Every sales contest shares identifiable phases. It starts with a bang, slows down in the middle, and winds up with a big push. Winning a contest is easier when you understand what to emphasize in each phase.

There's no question that sales contests motivate—but they have a dark side as well. All too often, a sales professional puts so much energy into the contest that he or she burns out and suffers a big sales slump when the contest ends. Many find that they are most productive during the annual contest, but fairly unproductive the rest of the year.

True professionals know how to maximize the contest and beat their own previous performance. They also know how to use a contest to crank themselves up to a higher level of sales achievement overall. To emulate them, check to see when your company's next sales contest is scheduled. If none is planned, hold your own sales contest during a period when you are usually a little less productive. Identify a time period and challenge yourself to pull out all the stops and see just how good you can be. Use these phases to plan your activities for each part of the contest.

1. **Prepare.** Before the contest begins, inventory the skills, knowledge, tools, and information you will need to be at your absolute best for the entire contest, and then gather it.

2. **Build an inventory of qualified prospects.** People who lose sales contests typically do most of their prospecting in the early part of the contest. Those who win do it beforehand. Identify all of the prospecting methods you can use to build an inventory of qualified prospects before the sales contest begins. Spend several weeks identifying potential buyers, contacting those buyers to determine whether they're qualified, and preparing them to receive a sales call during the contest period. Often, prospecting alone is enough to generate new sales that wouldn't otherwise come about.

3. **Clear your calendar.** Take a look at the obligations that are occupying your time. Which activities directly contribute to future sales? Which activities could be delegated or postponed to a later time? By eliminating these inhibitors, you can free yourself to focus only on selling.

4. **Focus on the kickoff.** Start the contest with a sales blitz by making lots of calls in a short time. Free your *entire* schedule so that the only thing you do in the opening days or week of the sales contest is think, talk, walk, and breathe selling. When you plan your schedule, fill the entire day with quality sales contacts. When you get up in the morning, meet a prospect for breakfast. When you work out, do it someplace where you can contact a prospect. Have lunch with prospects. Spend the afternoon with prospects. Have an early dinner with prospects, and then relax that evening and regroup for the next day. Gain agreement from your family to focus all your energy on selling during the contest's first week. Get them involved in the process. Urge them to contribute ideas, identify more prospects, and help you prepare for the next day's selling.

5. **Avoid the mid-contest slump.** During a long contest, there's a point where the initial energy wears off, things grow less exciting, and a sales slump looms. Careful! Prevent a mid-contest slump by planning enough activity into each day to ensure a constant flow of new contacts, follow-up calls, and other activities.

6. **Make the final push.** At the end, concentrate on writing up business. As you did in the opening days of the contest, free your time to focus on selling. Find helpers who can do the detail work and follow-up for you so that you can spend your time helping customers make the buying decision.

   If several steps are involved in completing the sale, make sure you have a team who can help accomplish those steps for you during this critical time. Be sure you eat well and get plenty of sleep each night, so that you're at the top of your form each day.

7. **Seek satisfaction through delivery and follow-up.** As you celebrate and rest, be sure to follow through on each purchase. You want everyone who bought during the contest to be happy about their purchase and satisfied with its value.

8. **Evaluate.** When it's all over, evaluate your performance. What worked, and what didn't? Use the lessons you learn about yourself to sustain a higher level of selling year round. Change some of your regular habits and routines to keep yourself at a higher level of sales productivity. That's how true professionals grow, and that's why they beat their previous performance in every sales contest.

IDEA

- **Get more done in less time**
- **Increase your awareness of the many high-tech aids that can make your job easier**

ELECTRONIC SALES SUPPORT

17.20 The Portable Electronic Office (Part I)

Just because you're on the road doesn't mean you have to live without the conveniences or necessities of your office.

CELLULAR PHONES

Once considered expensive luxuries, "call" phones are becoming more affordable as digital technology comes on-line in more and more cities. There are three types of phones on the market, but more are on the way.

Portable or **hand-held phones** are used by construction supervisors and other people who are away from a power source. These phones can be as small as a cordless phone and may be plugged into a car's cigarette lighter for recharging.

Mobile phones are permanently installed in a vehicle. They have a high power rating and use all 832 cellular channels.

Transportable phones are not unlike portables, but they are larger and have more transmitting power and features. Instead of weighing a pound or less, transportables weigh ten to fifteen pounds.

FAX MACHINES AND COPIERS

The technology involved in both of these office machines is so similar that they are frequently combined in smaller, more convenient packages. Some models can be used in cars, phone booths, hotel rooms, or out on the golf course. The smallest fax machines are paperless, seven-ounce portables.

Copy machines have also been miniaturized. Some are about the size of a college textbook and can be used on AC batteries. Of course, fax machines also double as copiers.

PAGERS AND BEEPERS

You're never far from a phone message with one of these clipped to your belt. In fact, some people use them in lieu of car phones—at a tremendous savings. Paging com-

panies vary, so shop around for the best service and price. The simplest ones beep you when you have a message, requiring you to call the office for details.

More expensive pagers actually give you information on the spot. They have LCD displays that show a phone number and/or message, depending on the model. Some features to compare are: 1) length of message; 2) how long messages are displayed; 3) the pager's ability to store message; 4) optional flash to replace tone; and 5) its ability to be read at night.

LAPTOP COMPUTERS

If you spend a lot of time on airplanes, you will love a laptop computer. Laptops are now lightweight, powerful, and inexpensive. With increased memory and bigger hard drives, some models are more powerful than desktop systems. Check the screen under different lighting conditions. Some can be difficult to read. Backlit screens are generally more legible.

I D E A

• Identify electronic systems that help you improve your sales efficiency

ELECTRONIC SALES SUPPORT

17.21 The Portable Electronic Office (Part II)

DICTATING MACHINES AND TAPE RECORDERS

If you write a lot of letters, take expensive notes after meetings, or aspire to write a book, a dictating machine is worth its weight in platinum. The tapes now come in three sizes: standard, micro, and pico. One pico is only 4 1/4" x 1 1/4" x 3/4" and weighs three ounces.

To choose among the many microcassette machines on the market, look for features such as voice-activated recording, and tape-end warning. Reputation and warranty are important as well. These machines are very fragile, so buy a well-known brand that can be serviced. Standard cassette recorders are the most durable, but their size may create limitations for some people. They are getting smaller. In fact, one weighs a mere eight ounces, and measure 4 1/2" x 3 1/4" x 1 1/4".

There are many creative uses for tape recorders. One is to use it prospecting. Drive through a new town or industrial park and record the names of the stores that look like prospects. Another use is for recording orders. You may have a busy, impatient customer who doesn't want to wait for you to fill out paperwork. Streamline the order-writing process with a tape recorder and transcribe it later. Worried about not having the customer's signature? Let's be real — customers accept orders because they want them, not because they've signed their names on a dotted line.

AUDIO/VIDEO SYSTEMS

Audio/video aids to presentations are big these days. They run the gamut from flash cards to flip charts to multi-media computerized slide shows and films. The most portable are what interest us here.

Self-contained video players/monitors combine a videotape player and TV. Starting at around five pounds, these battery-operated, two-person viewing units enable you to show a video virtually anywhere.

Video playback units are similar to VCRs, but are designed for travel. Some of them fit under a plane seat and have such handy features as remote, freeze-frame, and automatic repeat. The latter is ideal for trade show booths. These units need to be hooked up to a TV monitor.

Computer data projection panels are portable LCD screens that project a computer's screen onto an overhead projector. They vary in size, the smallest about one foot square. Used in conjunction with expandable computer graphics programs such as HyperCard, these panels can lend a very high-tech look to your presentation.

POCKET ORGANIZERS AND TRANSLATORS

These calculator-like devices offer dozens of functions, ranging from calendars and calculators to multi-year appointment planning, address and phone storage (with auto dialing), notepads, language translation, and dictionaries. Some even interface with a personal computer. The Sharp Wizard is a good example of one of these 10 1/2 ounce miracles.

Language translators are a must if you're doing business with the ECC and don't know French, German, or a half-dozen other languages. One 10-inch, 4-ounce model translates 1,400 phrases into ten different European languages for the fraction of the cost of a translator.

I D E A

ELECTRONIC SALES SUPPORT

17.22 Selecting Sales Automation Software

Many sales forces use sales automation software to build and maintain a database of their contacts and a record of their contacts and sales activities. The list below shows the benefits of sales automation software to the salesperson, the company, and the customer.

The only "fly in the ointment," is the bewildering array of software packages available. To find the software that is right for you, determine how you will use it — how it will enhance the way you sell.

Make a list of what kind of information you want and what you will do with it. Then identify tasks you would like to be able to do more easily or more quickly. Don't worry about whether the computer can do them. When your list is done, compare your "want" list with the software you are using or thinking of buying. Make sure the new software will make these functions easier for you.

BENEFITS TO SALESPERSON

- Makes it easier for salespeople to manage their pipeline, which empowers them to run their businesses more efficiently and effectively.
- Highlights weaknesses in the pipeline that can prevent sales "droughts" that often follow strong periods.
- Allows salespeople to prospect (via letters and phone calls) in ways that are virtually automatic. Companies can provide direct mail letters and phone scripts that will save time for salespeople.
- Allows salespeople to develop and implement personal activity plans (an automated series of action calls, meetings, letters, etc.) to manage their pipelines.

COMPANY BENEFITS

- Provides management with a total pipeline perspective, which furnishes a better long-term sales indicator. Also provides short-term closing projections.

- Allows management to develop prospecting strategies to help salespeople fill their pipeline while they are pursuing other business.
- Pipeline management is a natural byproduct of the system—zero selling time is needed for projections.
- Focuses everyone in the company on the strategies that relate to each phase of the sale. The team can include managers from advertising, marketing, technical support, etc. This expands management's role in the sales process and produces more customer-driven products, services, and support.
- May also offer training and sales-context sensitive help, in order to improve performance with tools, reminders, and coaching based on the phase of the sales cycle.
- Correlating selling strategies to the phases of a sale allows promotional vehicles to be used effectively.

I D E A

ELECTRONIC SALES SUPPORT

17.23 Sales Training in Your Laptop

Whether you take notes by hand or on your computer, the system you use to manage your sales activities can increase your sales performance. The way you keep records and the types of records you keep can tell you more about yourself as a salesperson.

Examine your records closely. Which ones are thorough and complete, and which ones are not? What does the degree of detail tell you about a particular client relationship or a particular sale? Where are you most effective? To learn more about yourself, build regular reviews into your system. Ask yourself daily, what did I do well today? What did I not do well? How can I learn from this? Every now and then, review the past few sales and summarize what worked and what didn't.

The sales professionals who constantly grow and improve are constantly looking to see what they're doing right and what they could do better. You can do a better job beginning today by simply noticing more about what's working and what's not working for you.

SECTION EIGHTEEN

WHAT MOTIVATES YOU

WHAT'S IN IT FOR YOU?

• **Explore your motives.**
• **Set and reach your goals.**
• **Stay on the right side of ethics.**
• **Get your finances in shape.**

What lights your fire? What turns you on? What gets your engines started? Most people aren't aware of what motivates them because they've never taken the time to study it. They also aren't aware of their ethical standards. Use this section to explore your motives and plans for becoming a self-starter and your beliefs, standards, and ethics.

Honesty is still the best rapport builder. It's just that simple. Your long-term sales success will depend on it. But honesty doesn't exist in a vacuum. It is based on your beliefs and commitments. The more honest you are with yourself, the more integrity you will have when you deal with others.

IDEA

GETTING MOTIVATED

18.1 Eight T's for Self-Empowerment

Here are eight words beginning with "T" to use as a checklist for determining how to empower or motivate yourself. Simply ask the eight questions to determine what kind of empowerment would be the most effective.

- **Target** — Are you clear on the goal you're trying to achieve?
- **Tools** — Do you have the tools or information needed to do the job?
- **Training** — Have you received enough training to use the tools well?
- **Time** — Have you had enough time for the training to take effect?
- **Truth** — Do you know how all of this fits together?
- **Tracking** — Are you getting the feedback needed to stay on track?
- **Touch** — Are you getting enough support and encouragement?
- **Trust** — Do you trust yourself appropriately for your skill and mastery level?

Reprinted with permission from *The Acorn Letter* by Jim Cathcart, © 1995.

I D E A

WHAT'S IN IT FOR YOU?

• **Understand the value and use of affirmations**

VISUALIZING YOUR GOALS

18.2 The Daily Thought Diet

Affirmations are positive sentences that you say to yourself to replace the self-defeating thoughts that habitually pop into your mind. The daily thought diet is a card or sheet of paper that you can create to remind you of who you are, what you believe, and what you want to become.

Affirmations for your thought diet should follow three simple rules:

1. This must be stated in the positive. ("I will breathe only clean air" would be used instead of "I will stop smoking.")
2. They must be stated in the present. ("I swim a half-mile a day and love it.")
3. Like goals, they should be specific, meaningful, and measurable. ("I call five new prospects every day.")

After you have finished Worksheet 18.3, you will have a daily thought diet. Read it first thing in the morning, once or twice during the day, and before going to sleep at night. If your thought diet is the last thing you read before going to sleep, your affirmation will "stick" in your mind far longer than at any other time during the day.

Your thought diet should be broken down into manageable sections. After you have achieved one of the goals on the diet, replace it with a new one.

Reprinted with permission from *The Acorn Letter* by Jim Cathcart, © 1995.

W O R K S H E E T

WHAT'S IN IT FOR YOU?

• Create a list of daily positive thoughts that will reinforce your personal growth

VISUALIZING YOUR GOALS

18.3 Your Daily Thought Diet

1. Write out the primary goal that motivates you most at this point in time. Be specific.

   _____

2. Write out a half-dozen personal qualities you are working at developing. State them *positively* in the present. Explain how they relate to your primary goal.

   _____

3. Write out as many minimum daily "to-do's" as you can. For example, "I walk for 30 minutes each day." Relate the "to-do's" to areas in your life such as work, family, spiritual fulfillment, financial gains, social needs, physical fitness, educational goals, and so on.

   _____

4. Now, compile all your affirmations. Be sure they conform to the three basic rules mentioned on the previous page. Copy them onto something you can keep with you throughout the day. Refer to your thought diet often. The more your affirmations are repeated, the faster they sink into your unconscious mind and become *you*.

   _____

WORKSHEET

WHAT'S IN IT FOR YOU?

- **Understand the value of—and develop—a storyboard to help you visualize your goals**

VISUALIZING YOUR GOALS

18.4 The Storyboard

A good way to reach your goals is to make a storyboard—a visual graphic depiction of your goals with pictures to keep your goals in front of you and your motivation high.

A storyboard can depict the steps along the way to your ultimate goals, or it can be a collage of images showing the end results. To make one, simply get a sheet of posterboard and look through magazines. Cut out pictures that literally or symbolically represent your goals. Then paste them on the posterboard randomly or in a logical order—whichever best suits the purpose of the storyboard. Put your storyboard where you can see it every day. It will serve as a constant reminder of the goals toward which you are striving.

List the goals for which you'll put items on the storyboard.

Goal: _____

Goal: _____

Goal: _____

Goal: _____

Goal: _____

I D E A

• **Learn how to keep your motivation at a high level**

GETTING MOTIVATED

18.5 Tips for Sustaining Motivation

Not everyone can remain "up," optimistic, and energetic all the time. We all wax and wane in our moods, outlook, and energy levels. That's normal. People who are "up" most of the time have many methods to their madness. Adopt some of them to keep your motivation high.

Do What You Love and the Money Will Follow. Hopefully you love sales—the interactions with people, the challenges, the rewards, and the unlimited growth potential. Make time for what you love.

Take Pride in What You Do and It Will Have Meaning. Even if you are starting at the bottom of the corporate ladder, do your job with pride and professionalism. Excellence is its own reward and *will* be recognized. Taking pride in doing the best job you can—no matter what the task—increases your self-esteem, competence and sense of control over your life and work. Not to mention your promotability.

Challenge Yourself with Continuous Self-Improvement. Set realistic goals that are attainable in short periods of time. Break larger goals into smaller increments to give yourself frequent opportunities to experience a sense of accomplishment. Success feeds on success.

Reward Yourself for Successes *and* Failures. Salespeople are subjected to more than the average amount of rejection in their work, especially if they are cold calling on the phone. Devise ways to reward yourself for your efforts, even when you are not successful. Giving yourself an "E for Effort" will keep you going so that sooner or later you'll be rewarding yourself for a success. Remember, sales can be a numbers game, so every *no* brings you closer to a *yes*.

Think in Terms of a Career Path, Not Just a Job. Commit yourself to doing the best job you can with your present company, but remember that few jobs last forever. Always keep your future destinations in mind while your eye is on the road immediately before you.

Take Absolute Responsibility for Your Life and Career. Realize that you and only you can shape your future. Again, small, positive steps lead to bigger and bigger payoffs.

I D E A

WHAT'S IN IT FOR YOU?

• **Learn the four keys to making any kind of change a permanent one**

GETTING MOTIVATED

18.6 Changes Are Always M.A.D.E.

Developing sales leadership is not something that happens to you—it is something *you* make happen. Like any type of change, it is not easy. Change is a fact of life, something we all must learn to welcome and implement more readily. The key is to control change, rather than waiting for change to control you. By staying in control, you make change an ally rather than an adversary. Changes that are M.A.D.E. by you enhance your self-esteem. Changes that are forced upon you can undermine it. Work on the former and keep the latter in perspective.

M = Mental Pictures. First, create a new mental picture of yourself. Visualize how you will look and feel as a sales master. Visualize how you will conduct yourself on calls, and how you will meet your sales goals. Picture yourself as the new you as often as you can. Add the image to your storyboard.

A = Affirmations. Add your new self-image to your daily thought diet. When you talk about yourself to others, do so in a positive way. Don't hesitate to discuss the changes you are making. By making your goals public, you increase your commitment to them.

D = Daily Successes. Success is earned in small increments. Build confidence everyday by setting up ways to experience success. That means practicing "sales master" behaviors daily, using the many ideas in this book. Be sure to reward yourself for your successes. Treat yourself to a pleasurable experience.

E = Environmental Influences. Make your environment work for you by surrounding yourself with positive influences. Avoid people and situations that make you uncomfortable. Find a support person or group. People who have support groups are far more likely to succeed than those who go it alone.

You are what you think. To change any habit, you must first change your thoughts, feelings, attitudes, values, and behaviors. The process that M.A.D.E. you what you are today can work for you to make you what you want to be tomorrow.

WORKSHEET

SETTING YOUR STANDARDS

18.7 Your Ethical Values

Answer yes or no to the following questions. Answer according to how you act, not how you think you *should* act.

1. Do you ever make disparaging remarks about the competition to help you win a customer? If so, are they ever unfair or exaggerated? ❏ yes ❏ no

   Explain _____

2. Do you see your sales activity as being separate from and independent of your company and its image? ❏ yes ❏ no

   Explain _____

3. Considering the wealth they assumed, can you condone the business practices of people such as Ivan Boesky and Michael Milken? ❏ yes ❏ no

   Explain _____

4. Do you think getting rich is worth taking high risks for, including a possible prison term? ❏ yes ❏ no

   Explain _____

5. Do you think right and wrong are more situational than absolute? ❏ yes ❏ no

   Explain _____

6. Do you feel pressured to meet your sales quotas at any cost, regardless of what it takes? ❏ yes ❏ no

   Explain _____

7. Is the unspoken rule in your company, "Profits first, details later"? ❏ yes ❏ no

   Explain _____

8. Do you take liberty with your expense account? Would you be nervous if your company performed an audit of your expense account? ❏ yes ❏ no

   Explain _____

9. Do you ever exaggerate claims about a product or service to win an account? ❏ yes ❏ no

   Explain _____

10. Do you ever load-up customers with unnecessary products or do you oversell toward the end of the year? ❑ yes ❑ no

Explain _____

11. Do you think you can afford to bend or break company ethical values because no job lasts forever? ❑ yes ❑ no

Explain _____

12. Do you compare your standards of behavior to other people's? ❑ yes ❑ no

Explain _____

13. Do you believe all is fair in love, war, and business? ❑ yes ❑ no

Explain _____

14. Would you offer kickbacks or gifts to a buyer? ❑ yes ❑ no

Explain _____

If you answered yes to any of these questions, your ethical standards are less than angelic … and may eventually get you in trouble. Discuss these views with people you respect.

W O R K S H E E T

WHAT'S IN IT FOR YOU?

• Gain new tools for dealing with ethical and legal issues at work

SETTING YOUR STANDARDS

18.8 Ethical Decision-Making

In some industries people are faced with ethical dilemmas every day. Having an immediate, internal sense of right and wrong is ideal, but, in lieu of that, it is helpful to have a set of questions that can help you make tough decisions. Keep the following questions in the back of your mind—or in the desk drawer—to refer to when gut instinct doesn't give you much direction.

1. Who will be helped by this action? To what degree?

_____

2. Who will be harmed by this action? To what degree?

_____

To help you answer the first two questions, use the scales that follow to quantify the harm or help created by the action in question.

3. Would you want to see an article about you and your actions in tomorrow's local newspaper?

_____

4. Would you want someone to do this to you?

_____

5. How would you explain your actions to someone whose esteem you value?

_____

6. What are the probable results of your actions and are they results you can be proud of?

_____

Your Customer
HARMED ◄─────────────────────────────► HELPED
1   2   3   4   5

Your Company
HARMED ◄─────────────────────────────► HELPED
1   2   3   4   5

Your Competitors
HARMED ◄─────────────────────────────► HELPED
1   2   3   4   5

Your Customer's Competitors
HARMED ◄─────────────────────────────► HELPED
1   2   3   4   5

Your Customer's Customers
HARMED ◄─────────────────────────────► HELPED
1   2   3   4   5

Yourself
HARMED ◄─────────────────────────────► HELPED
1   2   3   4   5

W O R K S H E E T

WHAT'S IN IT FOR YOU?

• Apply some specific strategies to avoid misunderstandings and stay out of legal or ethical quicksand

SETTING YOUR STANDARDS

18.9 Staying Out of Hot Water

Ethical standards are not the only standards to which salespeople must adhere. Don't forget the law. All kinds of laws govern business transactions. Because you cannot be expected to be aware of all of them, the following guidelines will serve you well.

1. Know the difference between "sales puffery" and specific statements of fact made during the sales presentation. Avoid exaggeration to make your story sound terrific. Stick to the truth, the whole truth, and nothing but the truth.

2. Thoroughly educate your customers on all aspects of your product or service before completing the sale. Leave no surprises for later. Be thorough.

3. Know everything there is to know about your product/service: technical specifications, capabilities, design characteristics, delivery/installation abilities, and so on.

4. Read carefully all promotional literature printed by your company on the products/services you are selling. If there are any inaccuracies, make them known to management. These inaccuracies are often unintentional, sometimes originating with overzealous advertising copywriters.

5. Study your company's terms of sale policies. If you overstate your authority to establish prices, your company can be legally bound.

6. Stay abreast of local and federal laws that affect your industry, especially those pertaining to warranties and guarantees.

7. Be careful how you state the capabilities of your product or service and check the accuracy of those statements you routinely make.

8. *Never* be afraid to say, "I don't know. I'll have to get back to you about that."

IDEA

• **Increase profits by focusing on net profits over gross sales**

GETTING YOUR FINANCES IN SHAPE

18.10 Think Net, Not Gross

Jim Cathcart once employed a sales representative who was an excellent seller but tended to get more excited about the gross sales volume than the net profit on his sales. In an effort to change his thinking, Jim sent him a series of items in the mail over a one-month period. First, he sent him a hairnet. About a week later, he sent a scoop net for an aquarium fish tank. Next, he sent him a fisherman's net. Finally, he sent an extremely gross picture with a post-it note attached that said "This is *gross*."

After he received each item, the salesperson asked, "Why did you send this to me?" Jim said, "Just think about it and we'll talk about it in a few weeks." After Jim sent him the last item, he went into his office. "Okay, end the mystery," the sales representative said. "What is the purpose of these things you've been sending me?" Jim asked him what he had received. "Well, you've been sending me nets and a gross-looking picture." Jim said, "What I wanted you to do is stop thinking only about gross and start thinking about net. The profit on each sale is the key to effective selling. For you to be more effective and earn a higher income, you need to produce more net profit, not just more gross revenue."

Are you aware of the net revenue you produce when you make a sale or do you focus only on the gross revenue? The more you understand about profitability, the better you can use your time, target your energies, and increase your sales commissions.

Indicate in the space below the gross amount generated by your typical sale. Next to the gross amount, note the net profit generated by that sale. Discuss these figures with your sales manager and see if you can determine the actual net profit on each sale after all costs have been paid.

Gross amount generated by typical sale:

Net profit generated by that sale:

IDEA

GETTING YOUR FINANCES IN SHAPE

18.11 Money Management

Errol Flynn once said, "My problem lies in reconciling my gross habits with my net income." There is no doubt that a great deal of satisfaction in life comes from your ability to spend money. But far too many people overspend to sustain a lifestyle that they really cannot afford. Instead of building a portfolio of assets, they build a portfolio of debts.

Financial maturity (aka self-control) means living without some things now so you can have more later. Focusing on the long term is the only way to get ahead.

Most people live in the present and are financially immature. Their attitudes are, "I work hard. I'm not going to deny myself what I want" or "I may not be around tomorrow. Why should I worry about it?" More often than not you are around tomorrow ... and tomorrow arrives much sooner than you expected.

There are three basic things you must do to get ahead financially: live within your means, pay down your debt, and save money.

Living within your means may require some adjustments. Many people create budgets for themselves, but adhere to them poorly. The past is the best predictor of the future. If you have little self-discipline now, that's probably how much you'll have tomorrow. Maybe not.

The best way to live within your means is not necessarily to go without, but to spend less on your essentials and indulgences. Do you have to live in a $2,000 apartment? Would a $1,000 apartment serve you just as well? Do you have to eat at restaurants so often? Eating at home is much less expensive. When you do eat out, why not settle for less expensive food? Do you have to buy Giorgio Armani ties or would Pierre Cardins at half the price suffice? And must you drive a car that serves your transportation *and* ego needs? You get the idea.

Paying down your debt is a step you must take before you can hope to save money. Most people have become accustomed to paying outrageous interest rates on credit card balances. The key is to learn to pay these off and learn to pay cash.

Compile a list of your debts—every one of them. Include on this list the interest rate and the minimum monthly payments of each card. Then pay off the balances, starting with the card that charges the highest interest.

Save money, but do it with a plan. Simply saying you will save X percent of your income is too vague. You have to set specific savings goals that will provide you with an incentive. For example, you should save for next year's taxes, a new car that you will eventually need, clothes, and so on. Determine when you will incur these expenses and figure out how much per month you should save to meet the goals.

Be realistic. Avoid the myth that winning the lottery or earning X amount of money will solve your problems. If you haven't got the hang of managing your money yet, a windfall will go the way of your past income. Learn to manage your money so that, when the lottery does make you rich, you will be set for life.

Expanding your income. Look for new ways to generate sales or earn money. Perhaps some of your leisure time could be converted to income-producing time.

W O R K S H E E T

WHAT'S IN IT FOR YOU?

- Set specific long- and short-term financial goals

GETTING YOUR FINANCES IN SHAPE

18.12 Financial Goals Worksheet

SHORT-TERM GOALS
(One Year)

	A, B, C Priority*	Goal	Target Date	Time to Complete	Approximate Cost	Cost per Month
SAMPLE:		Develop a cash reserve	July 1	10 months	$2,000.00	$200.00
1.						
2.						
3.						
4.						
5.						
6.						
7.					TOTAL $ _____	$ _____

LONG-TERM GOALS
(Two Years or More)

A, B, C Priority*	Goal	Target Date	Time to Complete	Approximate Cost	Cost per Month
1. _____	_____	_____	_____	_____	_____
2. _____	_____	_____	_____	_____	_____
3. _____	_____	_____	_____	_____	_____
4. _____	_____	_____	_____	_____	_____
5. _____	_____	_____	_____	_____	_____
6. _____	_____	_____	_____	_____	_____

TOTAL $ _____ $ _____

Add cost per month from Short-Term Goals $ _____

Total per month needed to reach all goals $ _____

*A = Must Do
*B = Ought to Do
*C = Nice to Do

SECTION NINETEEN

YOUR MASTER ACTION PLAN

This guide contains an entire year of sales improvement techniques—but they will only become growth tools if you convert these ideas into action. Use the following steps to do so:

1. **Isolate the action needed.** Write it down somewhere apart from its source material.

2. **Illuminate the action needed.** Think only about this item, why it matters to you, what benefits you'll get from it, and how you'll do it.

3. **Initiate.** Take the first steps. If you plan to exercise, put on your workout clothes. If you plan to talk to someone, look up the phone number.

4. **Segregate.** Keep the action item in a highly visible spot until it is done. Don't let it get filed or stacked with other materials, not even in your wallet. Keep it visible as a reminder. After you have taken the action, you can file it.

WHERE TO START

Your needs drive your actions. Skim the *Idea-a-Day Guide* and put a paper clip on each idea that needs action SOON. When you're done, count the paper clips you've placed in it. Those are your current priorities. Take the most important ones and complete a one page action plan for each.

Three Action Plan pages follow. Photocopy them if you need more.

W O R K S H E E T

WHAT'S IN IT FOR YOU?

• Commit to your goals by writing them out, assigning completion dates and determining how you will achieve and measure them

YOUR MASTER ACTION PLAN

19.1 Key Goal Action Plans

Copy this sheet and use it to answer the following questions regarding as many aspects of your life as you want. Some areas to explore are your career, family life, intellectual development, social situation, spiritual needs, physical fitness, and financial goals.

What is the goal I would like to achieve?
What are the potential obstacles that stand in my way?
What is driving my desire to achieve this goal?
What is my action plan? How will I specifically reach the goal? Who can help? What other resources do I have?
What is my target date/deadline for implementing the goal?
How and when will I measure my success?

What is the goal I would like to achieve?
What are the potential obstacles that stand in my way?
What is driving my desire to achieve this goal?
What is my action plan? How will I specifically reach the goal? Who can help? What other resources do I have?
What is my target date/deadline for implementing the goal?
How and when will I measure my success?

What is the goal I would like to achieve?
What are the potential obstacles that stand in my way?
What is driving my desire to achieve this goal?
What is my action plan? How will I specifically reach the goal? Who can help? What other resources do I have?
What is my target date/deadline for implementing the goal?
How and when will I measure my success?

SECTION TWENTY

YOUR COMPREHENSIVE SALES SELF-ASSESSMENT PROFILE

When Jim Cathcart was young, he gathered eggs from the hens on his great aunt's farm. To find out whether they were edible, he and his sister would hold each egg in front of a candle flame. Fertilized eggs showed evidence of an embryo. Edible eggs had clear yolks that let the light shine through. Years later as Jim was taking a personality profile, his sales manager commented, "Oh, I see you're getting your head 'candled.'"

The following sales profile is our way of helping you hold yourself up to the light to see what needs and potentials are inside. It permits you to identify a multitude of elements in your personality, your relationships, and your career. It can reveal exciting insights that can help you achieve increased sales, improved performance, and greater satisfaction. Some elements will appear to contradict each other, but that is what people are like. The system known as you is a complex network of interrelated elements, some of which will be contradictory.

This is not a test. You can't pass or fail. It will simply help you identify the factors that define you. Consider it a snapshot of where you are today. Use it as a tool, a reference point to help you plan your own growth for years to come. For best results, complete this profile annually to assess your progress and identify your next growth steps.

When you complete your assessment, check the results. Skim the profile and note what you observe. Give it to your sales manager, spouse, or friend, and ask what they notice. Don't be defensive: just listen to their comments and consider what they say. Then use the Master Action Plan in Section Nineteen to plot actions that will help you grow.

Most people never take the time for this kind of comprehensive self-assessment. Those who do learn things about themselves that help them grow and transcend their former levels of performance. When you complete this, you will have joined an elite group of professionals. Start now!

Comprehensive Sales Self-Assessment

SECTION ONE: THE RELATIONSHIP IS ALL THERE IS

1. How do you incorporate self-development, or self-education into your typical day (tapes, books, *Idea-a-Day*, growth group, reminders, etc.)?

2. If you work through the exercises in this book, how are you likely to improve your performance? (Try to come up with at least six ways you will benefit from this book.)

   a.

   b.

   c.

   d.

   e.

   f.

3. What are the potential rewards of improving your performance? (Come up with at least three short-term and three long-term rewards.)

   Short-term rewards   *Long-term rewards*

   a.   a.

   b.   b.

   c.   c.

4. What is the purpose of selling as you see it?

5. How would you rate your ability to keep yourself in the right frame of mind?

Poor		Below Average		Average		Above Average		Very Good	
1	2	3	4	5	6	7	8	9	10

6. How would you rate your ability to keep others in the right frame of mind?

Poor		Below Average		Average		Above Average		Very Good	
1	2	3	4	5	6	7	8	9	10

7. How does what you do make life better for people? Be specific.

8. Use these two sentences to help you write a description of the way you would like others to describe you.

   He or she is a person who ...

   The way I feel toward him or her is ...

9. How many people are in your inner circle?

10. How many relationships are missing one of the three C's for a productive relationship? Note the quantity of each "C" that is missing.

    a. Mutual commitment:

    b. Open communication:

    c. Clear expectations:

11. What kind of people do you need in your life? List the categories in which you need more supporters or companions.

    More people to _____ with

    More people to _____ with

12. Rate your current level of credibility with most prospects.

Poor		Below Average		Average		Above Average		Very Good	
1	2	3	4	5	6	7	8	9	10

Section Two

THE SALES PROCESS

13. Rank your strengths in the six steps in the sales process — targeting, contacting, exploring, collaborating, confirming, assuring.

    a.

    b.

    c.

    d.

    e.

    f.

14. Using the illustration in Idea 25, circle your areas of greatest need or greatest potential for improvement. Note them here.

Section Three

PLANNING AND PREPARATION

15. What five qualities do you need to grow in order to live your goals and bring them into reality?

 a.

 b.

 c.

 d.

 e.

16. Which is your strongest area of the marketing/sales/service mix—marketing, sales, or service?

17. What are your current sales goals for the next three months? List them by market, by customer, by product, and by dollar value.

18. Exactly how much is a customer potentially worth to you? $ _____

Section Four

PREPARING FOR THE SALES CONTACT

19. How well prepared are you for sales calls?

Poor		Below Average		Average		Above Average		Very Good	
1	2	3	4	5	6	7	8	9	10

20. How aware are you of the philosophy, strategies, and operations of your company?

Unaware		Somewhat Aware		Aware				Very Aware	
1	2	3	4	5	6	7	8	9	10

21. What is your awareness and skill level as it relates to your products? How well do you know and how capable are you of using your own products?

Low		Below Average		Average		Above Average		High	
1	2	3	4	5	6	7	8	9	10

22. Overall, what is your current level of competitive knowledge and awareness?

Poor		Below Average		Average		Above Average		Very Good	
1	2	3	4	5	6	7	8	9	10

23. To prepare yourself mentally, specifically what do you do prior to a sales call?

24. Write out your competitive advantage statement here, and date it.

Section Five

TARGETING

25. Where are your greatest marketing opportunities?

26. What are your top three sources of new prospect names?

    a.

    b.

    c.

27. What are your best immediate sources of new sales?

28. What percent of your calls are spent calling on each of the following:

    A accounts

    B accounts

    C accounts

    D accounts

    Prospects

29. How many referrals do you generate each week, and from what source? How do you generate these referrals?

referrals generated per week:

Source(s):

How generated:

Section Six

PRECONDITIONING YOUR PROSPECTS

30. How effectively do you use advertising, sales promotion, publicity, and public relations to "blow your own horn"?

31. How can you more effectively promote yourself using these methods?

32. How many direct mail letters do you send out a year?

33. What can you do to increase that number?

Section Seven

CONTACTING PROSPECTS

34. Are you more often perceived as a partner or a persuader?

Persuader						Partner			
1	2	3	4	5	6	7	8	9	10

35. How many of the sales planning guides shown in Idea 7.5 have you written out this year?

36. Rate your telephone skills.

Poor		Below Average		Average		Above Average		Very Good	
1	2	3	4	5	6	7	8	9	10

37. Rate your telephone discipline.

Poor		Below Average		Average		Above Average		Very Good	
1	2	3	4	5	6	7	8	9	10

38. Rate your letter writing skill.

Poor		Below Average		Average		Above Average		Very Good	
1	2	3	4	5	6	7	8	9	10

39. Rate your letter writing discipline.

Poor		Below Average		Average		Above Average		Very Good	
1	2	3	4	5	6	7	8	9	10

40. Describe your knowledge and use of electronic tools and on-line communication at this point in your career.

41. What technology do you need to master within the next year? How will you master it?

42. Rate your in-person sales call skills.

Poor		Below Average		Average		Above Average		Very Good	
1	2	3	4	5	6	7	8	9	10

43. Rate your new prospect call skills.

Poor		Below Average		Average		Above Average		Very Good	
1	2	3	4	5	6	7	8	9	10

Section Eight

SELLING BY THE PLATINUM RULE™

44. Rate your ability to identify behavioral style in others.

Poor		Below Average		Average		Above Average		Very Good	
1	2	3	4	5	6	7	8	9	10

45. Rate your ability and awareness in studying customers.

Poor		Below Average		Average		Above Average		Very Good	
1	2	3	4	5	6	7	8	9	10

46. What is your preferred thinking style — conceptual, strategic, or operational?

47. What is your natural velocity? High, moderate, or low?

48. From this list of seven multiple intelligences, circle the ones you enjoy using most.

Verbal	Musical
Visual	Mathematical and Logical
Physical	Introspective
Interpersonal	

49. Circle the three natural values that appeal to you most.

Sensuality	Aesthetics
Empathy	Commitment
Wealth	Knowledge
Power	

Section Nine

COMMUNICATING FOR RESULTS

50. Rate your ability to ask good questions.

Poor		Below Average		Average		Above Average		Very Good	
1	2	3	4	5	6	7	8	9	10

51. What are your three favorite sales questions? Write them down.

a.

b.

c.

52. Rate your listening ability.

Poor		Below Average		Average		Above Average		Very Good	
1	2	3	4	5	6	7	8	9	10

Section Ten

STUDY THE CUSTOMER

53. What additional information about your prospects could make it easier for you to make a sale?

54. Regarding neurolinguistic programming, NLP, what is your preferred intake mode — visual, auditory, or physical?

Section Eleven

EXPLORING

55. How do you qualify prospects? Be specific about the method.

56. What needs do you sell to most?

57. What wants do you sell to most?

Section Twelve

STUDY THE SITUATION

58. What are the most common needs you encounter with prospects and customers?

59. How often do you know how decisions are made in your client's company?
    Never   Occasionally   Usually   Always

Section Thirteen

COLLABORATING AND PROPOSING SOLUTIONS

60. Rate your ability and confidence as it relates to giving sales presentations.

Poor		Below Average		Average		Above Average		Very Good	
1	2	3	4	5	6	7	8	9	10

61. How often do you succeed when you're forced to sell through others?
    Never   Occasionally   Usually   Always

Section Fourteen

HANDLING CUSTOMER RESISTANCE

62. Rate your confidence and ability in uncovering customer resistance and dealing with difficult customers.

Poor		Below Average		Average		Above Average		Very Good	
1	2	3	4	5	6	7	8	9	10

63. What is your favorite and most-used method of responding to resistance?

Section Fifteen

CONFIRMING THE SALE

64. Rate your confidence and ability to ask for the sale.

Poor		Below Average		Average		Above Average		Very Good	
1	2	3	4	5	6	7	8	9	10

65. What is your success ratio? (for example, number of asks versus number of sales)

Section Sixteen

ASSURING CUSTOMER SATISFACTION

66. Rate your ability to install, serve, and assure satisfaction as you expand your accounts.

Poor		Below Average		Average		Above Average		Very Good	
1	2	3	4	5	6	7	8	9	10

67. Rate your confidence and ability to do account reviews.

Poor		Below Average		Average		Above Average		Very Good	
1	2	3	4	5	6	7	8	9	10

68. How many account reviews have you done lately? In what time frame? Note the names of three clients with whom you have conducted a recent account review.

a.

b.

c.

69. Rate your ability to generate testimonial letters.

Poor		Below Average		Average		Above Average		Very Good	
1	2	3	4	5	6	7	8	9	10

70. How many testimonial letters have you received recently?

71. Rate your ability to handle customer problems.

Poor		Below Average		Average		Above Average		Very Good	
1	2	3	4	5	6	7	8	9	10

72. What tactics do you rely on to resolve customer problems?

73. Rate the degree to which you follow up and stay on top of your accounts.

Poor		Below Average		Average		Above Average		Very Good	
1	2	3	4	5	6	7	8	9	10

Section Seventeen

BE YOUR OWN SALES MANAGER

74. Rate your relative ability and mastery in your two primary jobs, selling and managing yourself as a salesperson.

    Selling

Poor		Below Average		Average		Above Average		Very Good	
1	2	3	4	5	6	7	8	9	10

    Managing yourself as a person

Poor		Below Average		Average		Above Average		Very Good	
1	2	3	4	5	6	7	8	9	10

75. Use the formula in Worksheet 17.5 to measure your selling results.

76. How do you feel about the sales contests in which you participate?

Hate them								Love them	
1	2	3	4	5	6	7	8	9	10

77. Why?

Section Eighteen

WHAT MOTIVATES YOU?

78. In your own sales achievement, which of the eight "T's" for self-empowerment most need addressing now?

79. Rate your ability to motivate yourself and produce results.

Poor		Below Average		Average		Above Average		Very Good	
1	2	3	4	5	6	7	8	9	10

80. Rate your skill and results in managing your finances and achieving your financial goals.

Poor		Below Average		Average		Above Average		Very Good	
1	2	3	4	5	6	7	8	9	10

This completes the Sales Self-Assessment Profile. By completing it, you have summarized where you think you are right now in relation to the ideas covered in this book.

Keep a dated copy of this self-assessment for later reference. For now, do the following.

1. Set this book aside for a few days, and then pick it up and read your responses to this profile.
2. What do you see as your greatest current need? Who can help you right now? Who do you trust to look over these responses with you and determine the best strategies for growth?
3. Take action on the items that matter most to you. (Use the Master Action Plan pages to help you.)
4. Answer all these questions again in three to six months to note where and how you've grown and what to work on next.

AFTERTHOUGHTS

Very few people ever get this far in a comprehensive workbook like this. Do you know how rare you are?

You have invested the time and done the work to set yourself solidly apart from others in the sales profession. You have explored more aspects of selling and more aspects of yourself than most of your competitors, so you truly have an edge. Your notes plus the information you've gained from this *Idea-a-Day Guide* give you the ability to make decisions, identify strategies, select alternatives, and generate new thoughts far beyond your previous abilities.

Make this book your friend. Turn it into a journal. Date each of your entries in it so that you can see how you were thinking and how you were answering questions at a particular point in your life and career. Hang on to this *Guide* for years into the future. You might even want to get a separate *Idea-a-Day Guide* for each year to use to track your progress as you grow.

Congratulations. You are now truly a cut above the rest in the sales profession. You really are different and you deserve to feel very good about what you've done. Best wishes for your continued professional growth.

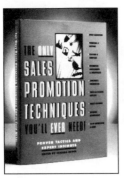
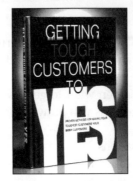

LEADING YOUR SALES TEAM

HOW TO MANAGE A WINNING SALES TEAM

By Jim Pancero

Stop being a "doing" sales manager, and start being a "managing" sales manager. Sales management expert Jim Pancero's unique "prescription for success" gives sales managers the courage to examine and improve every facet of their performance as sales managers ... so they can focus 100 percent of their efforts on building and leading motivated, winning teams.

241 pages; 6" x 9" hardcover; $31.50; Book Code: 1202

THE SALES AUTOMATION REPORT

Get ahead and stay ahead with the latest ins and outs of sales automation with *The Sales Automation Report*. Keep on top of an ever-changing area. This timely newsletter will arrive on your desk 10 times a year, offering 12 pages chock-full of advice, information, and ideas about sales automation, written in nontechnical language that is easy to understand.

Special Charter Subscriber Rate: $175; Order Code: 5017

Books may be ordered from your local bookseller or from Dartnell. Prices subject to change without notice.

☑ *YES!* Send me the book(s) and/or newsletter(s) I have indicated. I understand that if I am not completely satisfied, I may return the book(s) and/or cancel the newsletter subscription(s) within 30 days for a full refund. (Shipping and handling charges will be added to your invoice. IL residents please add 8.75% sales tax; IN residents add 5% tax; Canadian residents add 7% GST.)

_____*Solving the Sales Manager/ Sales Automation Equation*
$45; Book Code: 1252

_____*The Only Sales Promotion Techniques You'll Ever Need!*
$39.95; Book Code: 1255

_____*Getting Tough Customers to YES*
$24.95; Book Code: 1250

_____*The Greatest Direct Mail Sales Letters of All Time*
$69.95; Book Code: 1239

_____*Leading Your Sales Team*
$31.50; Book Code: 1202

_____*The Sales Automation Report*
$175; Order Code: 5017

> Prices are listed in U.S. currency.
> To order from Dartnell, call toll free
> **(800) 621-5463,**
> or fax us your order at
> **(800) 327-8635.**

Bill my: ❑ Company

Charge my: ❑ VISA ❑ MasterCard ❑ American Express ❑ Optima

Card No.: _____ Exp. Date: _____

Name: _____ Title: _____

Company: _____

Address: _____

City/State/Province/Zip: _____

Signature: _____

Phone: (   ) _____ Fax: (   ) _____

E-mail: _____

(Signature and phone number necessary to process order.)　　　　96-5511